Leader's Guide for

TALKS MY FATHER NEVER HAD WITH ME
(Helping The Young Black Male Make It To Adulthood)

Rev. Harold Davis

KJAC Publishing
P.O. Box 111
Champaign, Illinois 61824

Additional books may be ordered by writing the above address or calling **1-800-268-5861**.
Rev. Davis can be reached at: 217-352-4628

Other publications by
Rev. Harold Davis

A complete mentoring curriculum is available for the public school setting. Texts are available for boys and girls in elementary and secondary editions.

NEVER ALONE
Dating From The Biblical Perspective

A book designed to help young people order their private lives according to God's Word. "Never Alone" was prepared for young people who are in their late teens and early twenties, though the principles included therein transcend age. This book is perfect for personal study or for a youth group.

Talks My Daddy Never Had With Me
A Fatherly Perspective For Young Women

A book designed to give young ladies the perspective of a model father who loves them very much. A must-read for girls who have no father, a dysfunctional father, or a father who wants to stimulate discussion.

Talks My Mother Never Had With Me
A Mother's Wisdom For Young Women

Written by Dr. Ollie Watts Davis, this text is a must-read for young women. It provides motherly talks about many pertinent issues. This text is the companion text to Rev. Davis' book and could be used for mentoring or a Sunday school class.

**To Order Your Copy call KJAC Publishing at
1-800-268-5861 - or write
KJAC Publishing
P.O. Box 111
Champaign, IL 61824**

Cover by Carlton Bruett.
Second Edition, First Printing.
©1998 by Rev. Harold Davis
All Bible verses taken from The Living Bible (TLB) c 1971, were used with the permission of Tyndale House Publishers, Inc., Wheaton, IL 60189.

The Energies And Resources Of The Black Community During The Next Millennium Must Be Directed Toward The Restoration Of Our Families. This Can Only Be Accomplished By Preparing Today's Boys To Be Future Husbands And Fathers.

Singing has always been our friend in times of trouble. Our history as a people is chronicled by the songs that we have sung. We have a rich heritage of work songs, spirituals, jazz, blues, and gospel music that tells our history. This musical history judges those who mistreated us and finds them guilty of abuse and neglect. Unfortunately, the negative music of today's youth is telling a story that sounds a warning and should serve as a wake-up call to the people of God. This music is about violence and disrespect for women and self and is an indication of the condition of our young people. Music about women and sex is nothing new but the level of violence found in the music is unprecedented. The question that we need to answer is: "Will today's generation of men be judged for their negligence in tomorrow's music?" I believe that it is time for us to begin singing positive messages again.

As a community of people, we must in our individual ways make the salvation of young men our primary thrust. With this in mind, I have taken the battle cry of our parents and applied it to our contemporary crisis, the saving of a whole generation of young men. These contemporary words carried on that old familiar melody of "We Shall Overcome" will punctuate the need and help individuals and congregations get involved in the struggle.

I am a firm believer that one man, one woman, one church can make a considerable difference in the life of a young person. This has been pointed out to me again and again. At the time that this up-dated version of this book goes to press, I can list names of men and churches across this nation who are impacting the lives of young men. Praise the Lord! To God be the glory!

Let us begin to encourage the hearts of our brothers and direct their attention to available, tried solutions to the problems. Let us network and share our struggles, drawing strength from each other. We need to employ music once again to help make our point. Consider presenting **"We Must Save Our Boys"** to your group or congregation to sing. This will heighten their awareness and help them consider personal involvement. Consider copying the next page and singing it during the Sunday morning service or at any special youth events.

It has been our song that has carried us through the hard times and lifted our heavy hearts. As I view our current dilemma, I say, let us not abandon our song but let us sing with hope of a brighter tomorrow for all of our young people.

Sincerely
Rev. Harold Davis

We Shall Over Come
The "Talks" Mentoring Ministry Version For The New Millennium

"We Must Save Our Boys"

We shall overcome—We shall overcome
We shall overcome someday
Deep in my heart, I do believe
We shall overcome someday

We must save our boys—We must save our boys
We must save our boys today
Deep in my heart, I do believe
We must save our boys today

Christ will show us how—Christ will show us how
Christ will show us how today
Deep in my heart, I do believe
We must save our boys today

I will do my part—I will do my part
I will do my part today
Deep in my heart, I do believe
We must save our boys today

HDD 1997

TABLE OF CONTENTS

While I was speaking to a White middle school principal the other day, she stated that she had heard the African proverb: "It takes a whole village to raise a child." She then looked at me and said: "I have the children, where is the village?!"

Mentoring young Black men <u>must</u> become the thrust of American churches of African descent. It is no longer an option but is now a critical necessity!

Thesis Statement for the "Talks" Mentoring Curriculum

This curriculum is based upon Isaiah 55:11:

> *So shall my word be that goeth forth out of my mouth: it shall not return unto me void, but it shall accomplish that which I please, and it shall prosper in the thing whereto I sent it.*

Christians believe that there is power in the Word of God. Our logical goal then is to plant seeds of Scripture in the lives of young men and trust God to bring the increase. Look at how the writer of Hebrews describes God's Word:

> *For the Word that God speaks is alive and full of power—making it active, operative, energizing and effective; it is sharper than any two-edged sword, penetrating to the dividing line of the breath of life (soul) and [the immortal] spirit, and of joints and marrow [that is, of the deepest parts of our nature], exposing and sifting and analyzing and judging the very thoughts and purposes of the heart.*
> Hebrews 4:12

Please take time to read each Scripture in your lesson. This is the key to your success with this ministry. This ministry is not necessarily designed to make friends with the young men, but it is designed to help them develop a relationship with God. Share the lessons, the Word, and your experience and trust God for the results.

It is the Word that will make a difference in the lives of our young Black men. What makes this concept even more appealing is that the Word is being shared by mature Black men, which makes the whole concept more palatable to the young men. Don't forget that you will benefit personally as a result of your involvement in this ministry. Mentoring is a wonderful opportunity for personal growth, and it can help you work out problems in your own life.

Don't be afraid to try mentoring because you think you don't have the time. God will multiply the time that you invest so that the results will be more than you expected. I sincerely believe that few if any of us who share God's Word fully realize the impact that we will have on eternity. Let us keep sharing and we will understand it better by and by.

The Awakening Of The Village

The Black Church in America must awaken to the moral crisis that is consuming our community. The whole Christian community must assume some responsibility for this situation, but this curriculum focuses on what the Black Church can and must do. There was a time when the challenge confronting the Black community was imposed from outside our community (Jim Crowism, separate and unequal education, etc.), yet we possessed within us the moral fortitude to move forward. We are now facing a time when much of our challenge comes from within our community (broken homes, dysfunctional families, drugs, gangs, disrespect for self and others, violence, etc.). The Church is challenged to move from a social or civil rights emphasis to the emphasis of Christianity, morality and integrity for our young men and their families. Only the Church can stand as the moral authority and provide the needed leadership at this time of crisis in our community. The Black Church in America is the greatest asset of Black people. We must wake up to the challenge that is before us.

Here Comes The Village

My church and your church represent the village. The men of my church and your church are the only hope for our Black boys. As Frederick Douglass said in 1852, "It is vain that we talk of being men, if we do not the work of men." We must not abandon our young men, nor rest until we work out a plan of uplift for them. Mentoring is that plan. As we systematically work together with parents, principals and teachers, many young men will be saved socially, academically and spiritually.

The Power Of The Village

Men have power and influence with little boys. We are valuable to our community. Only a man can teach a boy accurately and authoritatively how to be a man.

The Investment Of The Village

Mentoring (giving of one's time, talent and finances) is the capital that the men of the Church must invest to secure the future. But when one considers what is gained, the lives of young men, the investment is well worth making. The entire Church family must be involved in the mentoring program. Financially and with much prayer, the Church must support the work of the mentors, or else suffer the consequence of having mortgaged her young men's futures.

Directions For The Village: The PRESS

Prayerfully seek God's divine intervention for good success with the program.

Recruit men of integrity and character from your Church to serve as mentors.

Enlist young men who are in need of positive interaction with mature men.

Secure the consent of parents and/or guardians for interaction with their students.

Schedule the initial meeting with mentors, students and parents.

PRESS towards the mark of the high calling of God in Christ Jesus

I want to use the word "PRESS" as an acrostic that will outline our plan of action. The Press is a strategy used in the game of basketball. It is a very effective device of the defense. It may be employed at full court, hence, full-court press; or at half court, or half-court press. Its object is to disrupt the effectiveness of the opponent's offense by causing excessive turnovers that result in quick scoring on your behalf. The Press is an urgent and useful strategy.

I chose this acrostic because our work with young men is a Press: *a move by weight or force or strength in a certain direction.* We are seeking to alter the state of their present and push them toward an empowered future. Considering this, let us PRESS forward.

Part One
A CHARGE TO KEEP WE HAVE

Charles Wesley is said to have been inspired to write the text for the hymn *A Charge to Keep I Have* while reading Matthew Henry's commentary on the book of Leviticus. Henry's thoughts on Leviticus 8:35 were the following:

> *"We shall every one of us have a charge to keep, an eternal God to glorify,*
> *an immortal soul to provide for, one generation to serve."*

Wesley's inspiration led him to write:
> *A charge to keep I have, a God to glorify,*
> *Who gave His Son my soul to save, and fit it for the sky.*
> *To serve this present age, my calling to fulfill,*
> *O may it all my powers engage to do my Master's will.*
> *Arm me with jealous care, as in Thy sight to live,*
> *And O Thy servant, Lord, prepare a strict account to give.*
> *Help me to watch and pray, and on Thyself rely.*
> *By faith assured I will obey, for I shall never die.*

Henry's commentary, as well as Wesley's hymn text, can very easily become the battle cry for our generation of mature Black men. Every one of us has a charge of the Lord: a Christian, cultural and civic responsibility to serve our generation. In a time when our society is becoming more self-centered and less community-oriented, the charge given to us by the Lord must be kept.

Wesley's reading of Henry's commentary inspired his writing a four-stanza hymn text; my reading of Isaiah 1:23 had a similar effect on me.

Thy princes are rebellious, and companions of thieves: every one loveth gifts, and followeth after rewards: they judge not the fatherless, neither doth the cause of the widow come unto them.

Reading this Scripture brought about tremendous conviction in me and yielded the *Talks* curriculum. The *Talks* curriculum has as its goal the challenge for mature men to judge the fatherless young men of this day. Isaiah's message, although written generations ago, has very close parallels with our present generation. We live in a time where there has been a tremendous breakdown of communication between the generations. There is very little intellectual, cultural, moral or spiritual sharing going on. Isaiah's message serves as a chilling reminder of what happens when mature, spiritual men abdicate their responsibilities.

Having realized and understood the magnitude of our current problem, I submit the need for an appropriate response. The Black Church, and Black men in particular, are the only hope for our young men. The only power sufficient for the task at hand is the power of God through His Holy Spirit working in spiritual, mature men. I am fully persuaded that God has a special anointing for those men who will take ownership of this problem and become vessels to be used in His service.

> *What shall we then say to these things? If God be for us, who can be against us?*
> Romans 8:31

We must accept this challenge as an opportunity, despite the formidable obstacles.

> *Lift up your eyes, and look on the fields: for they are white already to harvest.*
> Luke 10:2

Let us not surrender our future husbands and fathers because of the present challenge. The act of mentoring (that is, counseling, teaching, or tutoring) is a divine deed. Scripture is replete with examples of elders teaching (passing on the torch) and building into the lives of the younger.

> *Joshua the son of Nun was full of the spirit of wisdom; for Moses had laid his hands upon him: and the children of Israel hearkened unto him, and did as the Lord commanded Moses.*
> Deuteronomy 34:9

> *Moses my servant is dead; now therefore arise, go over this Jordan, thou and all this people, unto the land which I do give to them, even to the children of Israel.*
> Joshua 1:2

> *And it came to pass, when they were gone over, that Elijah said unto Elisha, ask what I shall do for thee, before I be taken away from thee. And Elisha said, I pray thee, let a double portion of thy spirit be upon me. And he said, Thou has asked a hard thing: nevertheless, if thou see me when I am taken from thee, it shall be so unto thee; but if not, it shall not be so. And Elisha saw...And he took the mantle of Elijah, that fell from him...And when the sons*

of the prophets which were to view Jericho saw him, they said, The spirit of Elijah doth rest on Elisha.

selected passages from II Kings 2:9, 10, 12, 14, 15

Wherefore I put thee in rememberance, that thou stir up the gift of God, which is in thee by the putting on of my hands.

II Timothy 1:6

To Titus, mine own son after the common faith:

Titus 1:4

Upon whom will your spirit rest? Who will continue your legacy and work? Seize this opportunity to make an impact that will resound throughout all eternity. You are not alone in this venture. You have God's divine presence. God is with you every step of the way.

Lo, I am with you alway, even unto the end of the world.

Matthew 28:20

Be assured of God speaking to you for your personal edification and through you as you minister to others. It is impossible to share God's Word and not receive a blessing. There have been countless testimonies of individual men and men's groups who have been radically changed as a result of going through the "Talks" curriculum with some young men.

As you spend time with the boys, remember that you are not alone in this venture. As you work to give, build and empower young men, your adversary will seek to steal, kill and destroy your effort and influence. Expect to encounter disruptions in your personal life. As I worked to complete this book, my computer broke down and had to be replaced. When I took the book to the printer, the motor on his printing press stopped working, which caused another delay. The enemy will attempt to divert your time, energy and resources in a frantic attempt to thwart your effectiveness. Be not dismayed whatever betides; God will take care of you. Be assured of God's divine power on your behalf.

Be strong and of a good courage; be not afraid, neither be thou dismayed: for the Lord thy God is with thee withersoever thou goest.

Joshua 1:9

Enlist the aid of partners who will support you in prayer and fortify your efforts. Our success comes not from power or might, but by God's Spirit. He is a heart-fixer and a mind-regulator. Who knows this better than the mothers of the Church? Mothers, grandmothers and prayer warriors of the Church should be engaged.

The effectual fervent prayer of a righteous man availeth much.

James 5:16b

You are not alone in this venture. You are equipped with a wealth of experience from which to share. At this point, you have probably forgotten more than the student has learned. You are the master-teacher in the relationship. Listen to what is being said, but be emphatic about the fact that you have lived long enough to understand the consequences of certain behaviors.

My ministry to young adults on the University of Illinois campus addresses a number of areas, particularly life skills and interpersonal relationships. As I meet with these students week in and week out, I draw from my reservoir of life experience. As a husband of nineteen years, father of four children, and a gainfully employed, taxpaying citizen, I do not debate with them, weighing their opinions against mine. I am the authority on those matters, and I teach in the divine power of the Holy Spirit.

God has allowed us to have the experiences that we have had so that we may be prepared to help someone else.

> *Who comforteth us in all our tribulation, that we may be able to comfort them which are in any trouble, by the comfort wherewith we ourselves are comforted of God.*
> II Corinthians 1:4

Be assured of God's divine provision for you in your effort

Do not overlook the *personal benefit* to be derived from your participation as a mentor. The Scripture passages that you share with others will bless you as well. You may experience some discomfort as you study and teach these lessons. Rejoice! You may have scars and some of the principles may irritate your sore spots. Again, I say, Rejoice! Be assured that God desires to heal you. He wants to make you whole, complete and mature. God in His infinite wisdom knows the **how**, the **when** and the **why** concerning the dysfunction of your past. Allow Him to work His work in your life as you invest in the lives of others.

> *Now the God of peace...make you perfect in every good work, to do his will working in you that which is well-pleasing in his sight, through Jesus Christ, to whom be glory for ever and ever. Amen.*
> Hebrews 13:21

Our God To Glorify (The Ministry Of The Word)

The main objective and ultimate goal of mentoring young men is to empower them with a personal relationship with Jesus Christ.
> *To open their eyes, and to turn them from darkness to light, and from the power of satan unto God, that they may receive forgiveness of sins, and inheritance among them which are sanctified by faith that is in me (Christ).*
> Acts 26:18

The way to lead young Black men to Christ is to expose young men to God's Word and to be an example of what a mature, Black Christian man should be.

For the Word of God is quick, and powerful, and sharper than any twoedged sword, piercing even to the dividing asunder of soul and spirit, and of the joints and marrow, and is a discerner of the thoughts and intents of the heart.

Hebrews 4:12

Those things, which ye have both learned, and received, and heard, and seen in me, do: and the God of peace shall be with you.

Philippians 4:9

This book is packed with Scripture for a purpose. When a person reads or hears Scripture, God has entry into that person's heart and mind from that point on. When children memorize Scripture, they are changed for the rest of their lives. A Scripture in the heart of a child is a watchman in the heart of that child. The watchman will sound an alarm when a Biblical principal is violated. A Scripture in the heart of a child has a greater impact than any other source of teaching.

Thy word have I hid in mine heart, that I might not sin against thee.

Psalm 119:11

My son, forget not my law; but let thine heart keep my commandments; for length of days, and long life, and peace, shall they add to thee.

Proverbs 3:1-2

Train up a child in the way that he should go: and when he is old, he will not depart from it.

Proverbs 22:6

The Importance Of Reading

You may encounter situations where young men will be unable to read and comprehend at their grade level. Actually, they may read several grades below grade level. Please approach these instances prayerfully. Be certain to establish a comfortable, non-threatening environment for the young men. Coax them to read or follow along with you as your read. Urge and encourage their participation, even if they are uncomfortable with the idea. Having them read will open their ears and accomplish several things:

1. Enhance their reading ability and endear the book to them.
2. Aid the retention of the principles shared.
3. Reinforce what you are telling them.
4. Stimulate them academically.

5. Encourage them to begin a personal library.

When reading a Scripture passage, be careful to take your time. Remember that what is familiar to you may be quite foreign to the students. Refrain from glossing over the Scripture as if on automatic pilot. Give the students time to digest what is being said and read. Quiz their comprehension with open-ended statements and questions. Remember that if you don't use the boys in the discussion, you will more than likely lose them in the demonstration. Below are some ice-breaking statements to encourage discussion:

1. I don't believe the author said that!
2. Look at what that says right there on page 32.
3. Did you see that word on the third line down in the middle?
4. If I hadn't read this for myself, I would not have believed it.
5. I really wish page 97 was not in this book because it really challenged me.

Your goal is to get the principles from the book in the students, not to just get them through the book. Spend as much time as needed on one chapter or subject. Move on only when you feel the subject has been adequately discussed.

I have used the 1611 King James Version of the Bible for consistency and because of its rich vocabulary. Much of the vocabulary used in the King James Bible is also used in the legal profession. I have also included in this guide Scriptures from the Living Bible. When you have any doubt about the meaning of a verse or wish to have additional insight or clarification, use the Living Bible version. In some cases you may want to read from additional translations. I suggest you consider the New International Version, The New King James, The New Revised Standard Version and the Amplified Bible.

I believe that every student should have a personal copy of *Talks My Father Never Had With Me.* He should be taught the importance of building a personal library with materials that will help him now and serve him as resources and references in the future. I feel that the student or his parents should purchase the book if they are able. In my opinion, the inability to pay should not keep the student from having a personal copy. If the boy or his parents cannot afford the text, the Church should defray the expense if necessary. While it is widely believed that where there is no sacrifice (cost), there is little appreciation, appreciation, regard and respect can be taught as part of the curriculum. Ponder creative ways for the student to pay for the text. Use preparedness for the lesson, promptness and punctuality to the scheduled sessions and positive, active participation at the meetings as forms of payment, as well as having the Church employ the students for various chores on the Church grounds or for elderly Church members.

To Serve This Present Age

Ministry to the Black family must be the thrust of the 90's and beyond. If the family crumbles, everything else will fall apart. The Church must adopt a holistic approach to ministry which serves

14

the physical, spiritual, social, emotional and economic needs of Black families.

The *Talks* approach to evangelism and discipleship addresses head-on the total needs of young Black men. It is designed as a tool to equip and assist the Church in fulfilling the Great Commission. The *Talks* mentoring curriculum is a viable program which seeks to remedy the destruction of our Black youth by providing positive peer influence, parental involvement, inter-generational sharing and development in social, spiritual and scholastic areas.

> *For God is not unrighteous to forget your work and labor of love, which ye have shown toward his name, in that ye have ministered to the saints, and do minister.*
> Hebrews 6:10

> *Be not deceived; God is not mocked: for whatsoever a man soweth, that shall he also reap.*
> Galatians 6:7

When you bless others, God will bless you (Luke 6:38; Heb. 6:10)

Part Two

Up to this point I have written of the responsibility we have to keep the charge given to us by God. I now want to give you the specific fundamentals for implementing the program. Part One of this guide listed five fundamental directions for the village: Praying, Recruiting, Enlisting, Securing, and Scheduling. If we take the initial letter from each word, we form the acronym PRESS. The PRESS represents the five fundamentals of the Talks Mentoring Program.

I. Praying

Prayerfully seek God's divine intervention for good success with the program. Prayer must undergird all of your efforts. Much prayer, much power; little prayer, little power; no prayer, no power. Assign mothers of the Church to pray for the men and boys.

> *If my people, which are called by my name, shall humble themselves, and pray, and seek my face, and turn from their wicked ways; then will I hear from heaven, and will forgive their sin, and will heal their land.*
> II Chronicles 7:14

It is my strong conviction that prayer will make a big difference as you work with these young men. In the event that you are not comfortable with praying, use the sample prayer below for you personal devotion.

Heavenly Father, thank you for this opportunity to serve you. I recognize that all that I am and ever hope to be I owe to you. I ask your forgiveness of sins that I may have committed against you and my fellow man in word, thought or deed. Thank you for forgiveness of sin and the assurance that you hear and answer prayer. As I have freely received, help me, Lord, to freely give. Empower me that I might empower others.

In Jesus' Name, Amen.

Prayer is fundamental and foundational. We must seek God's will concerning every detail of the ministry. Prayer must undergird everything: planning, implementation, administration and evaluation. Prayer should open every session, lead every session and close every session.

Leading young Black men in prayer is essential for their success. They need to see a Black man who is not the Pastor pray. They will learn more from hearing you pray than from hearing you talk about prayer. As you relationship develops, encourage the young men to submit their prayer requests and join in the praying. Maintain a prayer list (form in the addendum). As you proceed through the chapters, different concerns and problems will surface. Keep a list of each young man's struggles and pray for them daily. This information should be kept in strictest confidence and only shared with your prayer partner.

Here are two sample prayers for you to adapt for use with your time with the young men.

Sample Opening Prayer:
Heavenly Father:
Thank you for allowing us to spend this time together. Bless us as we look at our lesson today. Speak to our hearts individually and teach us what You would have us to know.

In Jesus' Name, Amen.

Sample Closing Prayer
Heavenly Father:
Thank you for this time we have had together discussing your principles. Please burn these principles into our memory so that we can walk in victory today and for the rest of our lives. Bless our families and take us home safely.

In Jesus' Name, Amen.

The earnest prayer of a righteous man has great power and wonderful results.
James 5:16b TLB

II. Recruiting Men

The harvest truly is plenteous, but the laborers are few; pray ye therefore the Lord of the harvest, that he will send forth laborers into his harvest.
Matthew 10:37-38

There have been cases where men from the community have used this program, but the curriculum stands on the strength of the men of the Church. The Church should look within her doors initially for qualified mentors. There are several advantages to this:

    1. You know the men personally.

    2. You are aware of strengths and weaknesses.

    3. Your church will benefit from active male leadership and evangelistic involvement.

Young men of character may also participate. Mature high school seniors should be considered to mentor sixth graders. Some of the benefits for involving young men are:

    1. They have energy.

    2. They are challenged to grow and mature.

    3. They will develop a love for evangelism and discipleship.

    4. You are building into the lives of the next generation of leaders.

The high school component of the mentoring ministry could be set up as a class at the church where high school youth teach elementary school youth. A Deacon or mature adult should oversee the ministry. The sessions could be part of the Sunday school curriculum.

The mentors must be prepared to take on a mission of this nature. To mentor a young Black man is to do spiritual warfare with our enemy, satan. The mentoring ministry is designed to break down negative strongholds that have been set up in a young man's life. "The devil thought he had me, but the Lord delivered me" should be the testimony of the young men upon completion of the program. The Pastor or a mature spiritual leader should meet with the mentors to prepare them for what lies ahead. A thorough training session with the men should be completed before embarking on the mission. This training session should follow a format similar to the one provided below.

A Sample Format For A Training Session Is Below:

1. Open with prayer.
2. Discuss the thesis of the program and "A Charge To Keep We Have."
    a. Share your heart's burden surrounding the condition of our boys.
    b. Discuss the role and responsibility of the Church.
3. Read or summarize the mentor's guide.
4. <u>Responsibilities for the Mentor</u>
    a. Commit to completing the program which could possibly last for as long as 40 weeks.
    b. Stress that the mentors respect the students' time by keeping appointments or notifying them of a conflict at least 24 hours before the scheduled meeting. Call until you contact him. Do not rely on an answering machine, voice mail, or family member.
    c. Share from your rich experience at the sessions, even if it is painful. God will bless you.
    d. When it is your turn, participate in field trips and outings.
    e. Serve as a source of wise counsel in the future.
    f. Include your students in your prayers.
5. <u>Rewards for the Mentor</u>
    a. Have the blessed assurance that you have done all that is within your power to impact the

life of someone. You have not disassociated yourself; rather, you have given back to your community.

    b. The Law of the Harvest (you reap what you sow, you reap more than you sow, and you reap after you sow) can be applied to your account. (Gal. 6:7-9)
Choose from this selection of Scriptures and share with mentors as the Lord leads. You can also encourage the mentors to read these Scriptures when they need encouragement: Hebrews 6:10; Prov. 11:30; Ps. 68:5; Matt. 28:19-20; Matt. 28:19-20; Matt. 24:34-40; Isa. 1:17; Luke 1:37; Luke 11:9; John 17:17; Romans 5:8; II Cor. 10:4; II Tim. 1:7; Rev. 20:11-15.

6. Review of the do's and don'ts of mentoring.

Do. . .

    1. Pray before each meeting with the young men, asking God to use you.
    2. Remember the influence that you are having may not become visible for many years.
    3. Be sure to read the chapter guide before picking your boys up.
    4. Leave any field trip plans with someone and make sure that you have a signed permission slip before you take the boys anywhere.
    5. Counsel with another spiritual, wise man when you encounter problems you can't solve.
    6. Be dependable. Keep your promises. Be there if you say you are going to be there.

Don't . . .

    1. Allow fear to stop you. It is normal to fear some aspect of this commitment, but feel the fear and keep on pushing. (I Jn. 4:18)
    2. Exceed your 90-minute per week time commitment.
    3. Compromise your integrity at any time.
    4. Involve yourself emotionally, financially or otherwise with unwed mothers.
    5. Neglect to read each Scripture in the lesson and ask the questions.

Remember that you have made a ninety (90) minute weekly commitment. Think of it as a weekly business appointment:
    15 minutes to pick the young men up.
    15 minutes to read the lesson.
    30 minutes to discuss the lesson, sharing the questions at the end of the chapter and from your rich personal experience.
    15 minutes to be used at your discretion.
    15 minutes to take the young men home.

The time commitment should not exceed 90 minutes for three reasons:
    1. Most men can find that amount of time in their schedule.
    2. The time commonly allotted for a business appointment is 90 minutes.
    3. It will protect you from burning out.

Transporting The Young Men:

Some prayer, thought and wisdom should be involved when transporting the young men. In some cases, a man should not be alone with a boy, especially a troubled youth. In some areas of the country this is more of a concern than others. The concern also varies based on the attitude and reputation of the youth. You may want to have a rider in the car if you are concerned about the stability and truthfulness of any of the young men. When I mentor my group of three, I always pick up the most stable boy first and the most difficult boy last. The most challenging boy asked me why he was picked up last and dropped off first. I told him that I didn't know but actually it was by design.

A Quick Word For The Mentor's Wives:

If the wives of the mentors would view their husband's involvement as a spiritual activity, they would more clearly see the blessings that will come to their homes as a result of their husbands' involvement. God is also aware of the sacrifice of the wives and will bless them for their sacrifice. As Christian men, God holds us responsible for the spiritual training of the next generation (not just the children in our house). If the man will commit to a 90-minute-per-week involvement, this should minimize any conflict from home. I also sincerely believe that the wives will be blessed by the spiritual growth that their husbands experience as a result of participating in this ministry. I have letters from men and churches from around the nation testifying of how their involvement blessed them.

III. Enlisting

Enlist young men who are in need of positive interaction with mature men.

Brethren, my heart's desire and prayer to God for Israel is that they may be saved.
Romans 10:1

1. Begin at home. It is often very easy to assume that family relationships are healthy and that values are being taught and embraced. Although easily assumed, it is not often the case. Look within your doors first, then extend your hand to relatives, friends and others in the 'hood, the church, the school system and social service agencies. God will direct your path and provide you with someone who needs you—someone only you can help. Be alert to God's providential leading.

2. Ask the boys that you know to identify additional young men who would benefit from the ministry. Get their phone numbers and call them. If they don't have phones, set aside a Saturday morning to go visit their homes.

3. Find boys at the mall. The mall ministry is when mature men walk the mall in an attempt to identify young men who should participate in this ministry. Check with your mall to determine the day and time when the largest number of teenagers are present. Then walk the mall introducing yourself, your church and your program.

4. Involve your congregation. Most congregations know of a number of young people who need help. Often when members identify young people for the ministry, they are more likely to participate as prayer partners.

IV. Securing

Inasmuch as you are dealing with minors, be certain to secure parental approval and consent before any interaction with the students. Explain in detail the program and request a written, legally approved document granting you permission to interact with their child. Using permission (consent) forms is encouraged for these reasons:
>   1. It diminishes the possibility of unwarranted legal challenges.
>   2. It gives professional credibility to you, the church and the program.

Use the following procedures to secure young men:
>   1. Write the parents or guardians seeking their support and permission. (A sample letter is included in the appendix of this guide).
>   2. Follow up the letter with a phone call.
>   3. Receive a written consent form.
>   4. Put the written consent form on file for your protection.
>   5. Contact the student by letter.
>   6. Follow up the student's letter with a phone call.
>   7. Schedule the first meeting.

Specific permission forms should be signed and on file before you take the students on any field trips or outings. Sample permission forms are included n the appendix section of this guide. Please consult with a lawyer if you have any legal concerns.

V. Scheduling: Initiating A Large Group

Schedule the initial meeting with mentors, students and parents. If the program is implemented by a church, then the Pastor, a Deacon or a church officer should be present at the first meeting. Below is a recommended agenda for the first meeting. This could be an occasion where you have a simple meal like spaghetti to facilitate fellowship.
1. Welcome
2. Opening prayer
>   a. Should be short
>   b. Should be simple (avoid using terminology that only Church folk understand because you are in a mixed group of Christians and non-Christians)
3. Introductions
>   a. Mentors should be introduced and addressed by their surname or professional title at all times (Mr., Dr., Rev., Brother, etc.).
>   b. Students should be introduced and addressed by their legal names (no nicknames).

Maintaining formality will greatly benefit the relationship in the long run. It helps the young student learn respect for his elder and reminds the elder of his responsibility to the young student.

4. Responsibilities for the Students
    a. Make a commitment to complete the 28-week program.
    b. Respect the time of the mentor by notifying him of a conflict 24 hours in advance of the scheduled meeting time. Call until you make contact. Do not rely on an answering machine, voice mail, secretary or family member.
    c. Cooperate and participate in all sessions and planned activities.

5. Rewards for the Students
    a. Upon completing the program, the student will receive the support of the mentor, the support of the Church, and the support of his family in his endeavors.
    b. Support will include, but is not limited to, letters of recommendation, on-going counsel, opportunities for employment and scholarships.

6. Assign three students to each mentor.
    a. Give the mentors copies of the students' registration forms.
    b. Commit to resolving personality conflicts.

7. Have the mentors break off for 5 minutes with their students to coordinate schedules.
    a. Determine the best time to meet. Select a time when there will be no conflicts.
    b. Determine the best place to meet. Select a neutral place for the initial meetings. A Church may be extremely intimidating to those who have never been in one. A room in a community center would be wonderful.

8. Reassemble the group.

9. Explain the Covenant (found in the back of this guide).
    a. Covenant: a solemn agreement between two or more persons or groups to do or not to do a certain thing.
    b. Read the covenant.
    c. Ask if there is agreement to abide by the terms of the covenant.

10. Sign the Covenant.
    a. Make this a very special time.
    b. Use elaborate paper for the covenant.
    c. Have the mentor and the students sign the covenant to seal the commitment.

11. Exchange Covenants.
    a. Have the mentors present their covenant to the students.
    b. Have the students present their covenant to the mentors.

12. Distribute books.
    a. Assign the first chapter for the first session.
    b. Have them keep a journal and write down any questions or comments.
    c. Insist that they keep up with the books.
        (1) They will use them as a reference in the future, a trusted friend and a source of wisdom.
        (2) They will soon be mentoring others.

13. Close with prayer.

VI. Scheduling: Initiating A Small Group

One mentor paired with three boys comprises a **mentoring cell**. Cells may be implemented very simply by having the Pastor or designated leader of the ministry accompany a mentor and three boys to a fast-food restaurant. Over a milk shake or soft drink, the Pastor or leader will explain the business of the mentoring program. This can be done by simply reading the covenants to the participants. Use the following procedure to establish a single mentoring cell:

1. Introduce the boys to their mentor (use the formal procedure as described previously).
2. Explain to the boys the 90-minute weekly investment of sharing wisdom with them— wisdom that has been tried and tested by great men in history, i.e. Martin Luther King, Jr., George Washington Carver and countless Black American heroes.
3. Explain the covenant that is being made.
4. Read the covenant and answer any questions regarding rights and responsibilities therein.
5. Sign the covenants.
6. Exchange the covenants.
7. Present the students with their books. Challenge them to keep up with them and bring the books to every session.
8. Have the mentor and students schedule the first appointment. You may want to present each boy with an inexpensive calendar.
9. Solidify the agreement with a firm handshake and/or hug as you leave the restaurant.
10. Take the students home (use a church van whenever possible).

WARNING: Expect disruptions from the enemy that are designed to discourage your consistency. While disruptions are normal when attempting to do something that will change your life for the better, not all disruptions will be negative. Expect some disruptions to come in very enticing forms: a good job offer, a fiiine woman you've been trying to talk to who is suddenly interested and has time for you (the time of your mentoring sessions, of course!), opportunity to work overtime, etc. Be careful not to trade what is best for what is only very good. We cannot compare anything that we can see or experience to how God will honor and reward our faithfulness.

Paperwork

Paperwork is a necessary inconvenience. You must document your activities for two basic reasons: protection and evaluating progress. I recommend that you be as detailed as possible. Secure the assistance of the church secretarial staff or some qualified volunteer to send letters to teachers and parents, photocopy forms and so forth. Make sure that all correspondence is well written. Remember that your materials reflect on and are representative of you, your church, and God.

The administrative duties of the person who serves as secretary include, but are not limited to, the following:
1. Prepare the initial letter to parents and permission slip.

2. Prepare letter to the student.
3. Prepare letter to the school (dean, principal, teachers, or counselor).
4. Maintain student files such as a file of reach student which contains all pertinent personal information.
5. Serve as the contact person for the mentoring ministry.
6. Serve as the liaison between the mentor, students and parents.
7. This designated leader should keep statistics on how well the program is going.

The administrator of the ministry should set up a system whereby the progress and consistency of the mentors is monitored on a regular basis. Each mentor should submit monthly progress reports to the leader of the mentoring program. The reports should include weekly entries on the attendance, lessons and activities held (see forms in the addendum). Each mentor should also record thoughts and concerns in a personal journal. The leader should schedule a monthly or bi-monthly session with the mentors to edify and encourage them in the ministry and deflect any symptoms of burn-out or feelings of being overwhelmed. Share journal notes and insights about your progress, problems, procedures and prognosis. These sessions may be around a meal or can be very brief. Let me stress the importance of this time together to strengthen the bond of the men of the Church and the men of the community.

Explanation of the various forms: See addendum in the back of this guide for the forms.

1. **Mentor and student applications:** You should have applications on file for your men and boys for legal reasons.
2. **Mentor Report Form:** This form will serve as your official notes from each meeting. This form is to be turned in to the coordinator of the program. The concerns that you have may also be turned in to those designated to pray for you and your young men.
3. **Monthly Report Form:** This report will summarize your activities for each month. The facts and victory reports from these forms can be used to encourage others to get involved. A good place to share is in the Sunday morning service.
4. **Book purchase form:** Some young men may not be able to purchase a book. This form makes it possible for you to document those who wish to assist this ministry by donating a book.
5. **Prayer Partner form:** *Each mentor should have someone praying for him!* This is very serious! **_MUCH PRAYER, MUCH POWER, Little Prayer, Little Power,_ no prayer no power.** We teach this to children in Sunday school and it is very true. Not only can these individuals pray for you, but there are other ways that they can assist you, such as preparing food for gatherings, writing letters to the young men, doing correspondence for the mentor, etc.
6. **Prayer List:** If you make a list of your prayers and check them off when God answers them you will be surprised to see just how many prayers that God does answer. As you spend this time with the young men, write down their prayer requests and watch God impress them. If you would like to have all of the necessary forms personalized with your Church name, address and phone number, call or write "Talks Mentoring" at the address in the front of the book.
7. **Participation permission slip:** We live in a day and age where it is necessary to have written documentation when interacting with a minor. This slip is for your protection.

8. Field trip permission slip: This is for your protection and should be filled out before you take the young men anywhere.

Ministering To The Community

As we work in our individual vineyards, the local churches who have implemented the program should fellowship periodically for reinforcement and refreshment. The community of believers should also consider hiring a church-school liaison so as to have a visible and viable presence in the local public schools. This individual should meet the following criteria:

1. Be a Christian.
2. Possess character and integrity. Be honest!!!
3. Have earned a high school diploma or its equivalent.
4. Have initiative and energy.
5. Be self-motivated and need a minimum amount of supervision.
6. Be punctual.
7. Be professional in demeanor (actions), attitude and appearance (dress).

A stringent interview process should be conducted and considerable prayer offered up so that God may direct the decision. The duties should have two components:

1. Daily visits to the local schools (classrooms, detention rooms, etc.).
2. Administrative work which includes phone calls and letters to local pastors and parents about the progress of their students.

Field Trips

Scheduling field trips. For young people, a trip is a big deal! Once a month, there should be an outing planned for the young men. The best trip would be to fellowship with a sister church which is doing the same thing that you are doing. This is good because it creates an environment of positive peer pressure for the young men. It is not necessary for all of the mentors to go on these trips. Rotate chaperons duties among the various mentors and no one will get tired. It is possible for two mentors to take ten boys to a game or four mentors to take twenty. The individual mentor's involvement on field trips will depend on how big your program is. There are many things that can be done for free. See the following list.

Places To Visit And People To See:
- A College class room
- The County Jail
- The home of a senior citizen to talk with them
- A Nursing Home
- The Police station
- A Bank
- Various businesses

- A Lawyer's office
- Fishing
- A Funeral Home
- Basketball game
- A Church that has a totally different worship style
- A local Principal

Discussions:
- Talk with the funeral home director and get his perspective on funeralizing a young person.
- View the area where bodies are embalmed.
- Talk with a college student to find out what it is like to be in college or a professor.
- Talk with an emergency room doctor.
- Schedule a conversation with an Asian-American and let the boys hear his views about America and how they see Blacks.
- Schedule a conversations with a victim of crime who can discuss their hurt with the young men.
- Visit the State's Attorney's office and get an understanding of what he does.
- Talk with the oldest person you can find.
- Visit a Judge to get his perspective on what he sees each day.
- A candid conversation with the Pastor.
USE YOUR SPECIFIC GEOGRAPHIC AREA TO ITS FULLEST BENEFIT. EACH AREA OF THE COUNTRY HAS HISTORICAL, CULTURAL, INDUSTRIAL SIGHTS THAT WOULD BE EDUCATIONAL.

All Our Powers Engage / It Takes A Whole Village To Raise A Child

The Talks Mentoring Ministry is not designed to be a solo effort. It promotes partnering with parents by providing positive experiences for the child. One goal of this approach is to build a sense of community and involve the entire "village" (community) in the rearing of its children.

One Thought That You Must Remember As You Proceed: The principal goal of this ministry is to plant seeds of Scripture in the hearts and minds of these young men that will be available for the Holy Spirit to call upon. Please be sure to read the Scripture with the young men. I believe what God said about His Word:

> *So shall my Word be that goeth forth out of my mouth: it shall not return unto me void, but it shall accomplish that which I please, and it shall prosper in the thing whereto I sent it.*
> Isaiah 55:11

> *For the Word of God is quick, and powerful, and sharper than any two-edged sword, piercing even to the dividing asunder of soul and spirit, and of the joints and marrow, and is a discerner of the thoughts and intents of the heart.*
> Hebrews 4:12

Notes:_____

_____

_____

_____

_____

_____

_____

_____

_____

_____

_____

_____

_____

_____

_____

_____

_____

_____

_____

_____

_____

WARNING!!

Before you turn this page and begin your first lesson, remember that your faithfulness is EXTREMELY important! What the young men see in you on a regular basis will tear down negative memories and build positive ones. When a conflict arises on a scheduled meeting day, make every effort to contact your young men! You may not be rich, famous, brilliant or good looking but you can be faithful!   Don't be a 25:19. If you are a 25:19, you will do more damage than good.

> *Confidence in an unfaithful man in time of trouble is like a broken tooth, and a foot out of joint.*
>
> *Proverbs 25:19*

INTRODUCTION TO CHAPTER GUIDES

The following section provides an overview of each chapter with some suggestions for teaching. Also included is a duplicate list of Scriptures used in the chapter from the New International Version of the Bible and the Living Bible. In the event that a Scripture in the book is not clear, the leader can turn to the other versions for clarification. Make sure that you read ALL OF THE PRINTED SCRIPTURES. Doing this will have an impact that is beyond man's immediate understanding. This section also gives the leader additional insights for each chapter. Where applicable, use the insights. If they don't fit your particular need, use your own creativity.

Mentor: Read this page before you meet with your boys.

1 The Importance Of Understanding Your Orientation

Definition: Your orientation is the manner in which you were raised. This would include your home structure, economic status, and any dysfunctional family traits.

CONNECTING WITH AND LEARNING FROM YOUR RICH, PERSONAL, PAINFUL, PRODUCTIVE PAST: Before you teach this lesson, examine your past and recall those areas of your upbringing that were not good. We all have some aspects of our past that were painful and that we would like to forget. For the sake of this lesson, I am asking you to remember your orientation so that you can empathize with the young men (put yourself in their shoes).

You could easily spend a year talking about this subject. If this young man has been abandoned by his father or mother, he has tons of pain and hurt to unload. Be sure not to rush when you can discern that he needs to talk or linger at an issue while he sorts his feelings out.

CAUTION: This is a very delicate chapter that goes to the very foundation of our self-worth. Don't rush through this chapter, because most people are reluctant to open up regarding those things that have hurt them in their past. As painful as it may be, opening up and talking about your painful childhood hurts and disappointments is very important. It is the beginning of the healing process.

CHARGE: The young men will enjoy hearing about your painful orientations that you have struggled with and overcome. It is appropriate to some degree to share the ones that you are still struggling with. Be transparent. It will help encourage the young men and promote an open relationship.

ACTIVITY: If you know someone who has made many mistakes because of the manner in which they were raised, you may want to have them come and share their testimony with the young men. There are many people in this category, but not many that are willing to share. Make sure that the individual who shares will do so with sensitivity, leaving out any unnecessary, lurid and sinful details.

1 The Importance of Understanding Your Orientation

There are some fundamentals that a person needs to understand in order to be successful and stay successful. Fundamental number one is an understanding of how you were raised, and what those who raised you did right and what they did wrong. This is called YOUR ORIENTATION. **Gaining an understanding of your orientation is important because it will provide you with objectivity (fairness) when dealing with yourself and others.**

A few years ago, I purchased a run-down house that I intended to remodel and rent out. There was a lot of damage to the house, much of which was visible to the naked eye. What I did not know was that there was additional damage that I could not see. Not long after buying the house, I found out that the foundation under the middle wall of the house was cracked and sinking. It required going under the house, digging around the foundation and reinforcing it. It was very hard work, but necessary to make the house safe and liveable.

Your orientation is your foundation (how you were raised). It is what your life today and tomorrow is built upon. In most cases, foundations are covered up and not seen once a house is built. This can be tragic because some of our foundations (orientations) are faulty and need to be re-examined. As you read the next few pages, take a shovel, remove the hard soil from around your foundation and take a close look for cracks and defects.

My earliest memories are pleasant memories of spending time with my dad. My dad was and is a source of strength and wisdom that has been with me through the years. He always had time for me, and though he was not extensively verbal (he did not talk a lot), he did give me many insights into human nature.

On one occasion when I had a business deal that went sour, he heard me angrily tell the person over the phone that I was on my way to see him and would discuss the matter with him when I got there. My dad informed me that you don't tell people that you are coming over to discuss an issue with them, for if you do that, they will have time to prepare a defense. The way to do it is just to show up and discuss it with them. Then you have a better chance at success. I appreciated my dad's advice. Because of my relationship with my dad and watching him for years and years, there are some benefits that I picked up from being around a wise, older man who loved me.

It was not until I was grown that I began to understand the impact of my relationship with my dad. I attribute my desire to work to my dad. He modeled a strong work ethic for me. I learned at an early age to hustle because I saw my dad hustling. I thought that all men hustled. My dad never argued with my mother, even though he did get frustrated with her sometimes. As a result of living in that environment, I don't fuss and cuss with my wife, and to my knowledge, none of my brothers fuss and cuss with their wives. I don't know what your orientation has been, but one thing is for sure: It has affected you greatly. You are what you are largely because of your orientation or upbringing. Consider these words of wisdom:

> *If a child lives with criticism, he learns to condemn.*
> *If a child lives with hostility, he learns to fight.*
> *If a child lives with fear, he learns to be apprehensive.*
> *If a child lives with jealousy, he learns to feel guilty.*
> *If a child lives with tolerance, he learns to be patient.*
> *If a child lives with encouragement, he learns to be confident.*
> *If a child lives with praise, he learns to be appreciative.*
> *If a child lives with acceptance, he learns to love.*
> *If a child lives with approval, he learns to like himself.*
> *If a child lives with recognition, he learns it is good to have a goal.*
> *If a child lives with honesty, he learns what truth is.*
> *If a child lives with fairness, he learns justice.*
> *If a child lives with security, he learns to have faith in himself and those about him.*
> *If a child lives with friendliness, he learns the world is a nice place in which to live.*
> SINAI SENTRY

You need to be honest with yourself regarding what you have lived with and what you are living with. As a parent of four children, I am amazed at how my children have picked up the characteristics of their parents. My children are all musically inclined, just like their parents. The children have also developed a love of reading like their parents. There are many other characteristics that they have acquired as a by-product of growing up in our house. I know of unfortunate cases where the parents are doing all of the wrong things and their children are acquiring these traits as well.

Many males wait until they are 40 years old before they start to examine and correct the mistakes their parents made in raising them. Please note that there is a proper way to raise children. If the children are not raised properly, forms of dysfunction will follow. What I mean by dysfunction is that something in your family is not working right, such as divorce, abuse, violence, or extreme poverty. **Only <u>YOU</u> can figure out why you act the way you act and do the things you do. Only <u>YOU</u> can change you.** Here are some things to consider and think about:

1. What man has served as your role model while you were growing up? Every male is exposed to older men as he grows up. These men may be family members, neighbors or friends, but we all have had men in our lives that we learned from. Now that you are getting older, do you recognize the bad habits that you observed these men display that you should not copy? Have you noted how an older man's mistakes and bad choices have hurt him? Have you determined to avoid at all costs the traps that scarred his life?

My main role model was my father. He was a wonderful man and wonderful father, but he still was not perfect. There are habits that my father had that I fight whenever I see them developing in me. Are you fighting all known negative influences?

2. What were your role model's coping mechanisms? What did your role model do or turn to when he felt like he couldn't make it? Did he turn to alcohol, cocaine, marijuana, cussin', hittin' somebody, fussin', staying out late, prayer, or driving the car fast? There is an old saying: "Like father, like son," which has proven to be true in many instances. Older men make grooves, ruts, and paths in which young men follow. Sometimes it is very difficult to avoid these paths made by the men who went before us. **Coping mechanisms** is an area of need in the Black community. Men need to learn to find strength in the hard times without turning to drugs, abuse, sex, or running away. In the past, men coped by doing positive things, such as working hard, playing basketball, praying, talkin' it out, or dancing. Recreation served as an outlet to relieve tensions.

Today many of these coping skills have been pushed aside for coping mechanisms that are destructive to the man, his family and the community. All young men should learn to develop a variety of coping mechanisms that will provide strength when times get hard. I would like to suggest that all young men do these things:

1. Pray for and seek to develop wise, close friends who can help you keep perspective when you are having hard times. I have wise men that I can call day or night if I am having a problem, and they will give me a word of wisdom when I can't seem to think. Did you know that when you get mad, your thoughts are not always in your own best interest? So it is wise to have other men to help you think when you get mad. Have you ever noticed that on the basketball court, when the defense gets a player surrounded and he is clutching the ball, trying to get free, the other teammates will yell: "Throw me the ball"? As simple as that sounds, we often forget to throw the ball, and we also forget that we have someone to throw the ball to.

> *Faithful are the wounds of a friend; but the kisses of an enemy are deceitful.*
> Proverbs 27:6

> *Where no counsel is, the people fall: but in the multitude of counselors there is safety.*
> Proverbs 11:14

2. Avoid all inebriants (drugs). Avoid the gateway drugs such as cigarettes, marijuana, beer and wine. These drugs only lead you to harder drugs. That is why they are called gateway drugs. Get wise to the TV commercials that show young, athletic people drinking and go look in the alley at the drunk and see reality. One drink is too many and one thousand is never enough.

> *Who hath woe? Who hath sorrow? Who hath contentions? Who hath babbling? Who hath wounds without cause? Who hath redness of eyes? They that tarry long at the wine; they that go to seek mixed wine.*
> Proverbs 23:29-30

3. Seek the wisdom that God offers. God says that if you ask for wisdom, He will give it to you.

> *If any of you lack wisdom, let him ask of God, that giveth to all men liberally, and upbraideth not; and it shall be given him.*
>
> James 1:5

There is a difference between man's wisdom and God's wisdom. It is most beneficial to seek God's wisdom. I have met young men in their late teens who have done this. They have displayed the wisdom of 40-year-old men.

> *Happy is the man that findeth wisdom, and the man that getteth understanding. For the merchandise of it is better than the merchandise of silver, and the gain thereof than fine gold. She is more precious than rubies: and all the things thou canst desire are not to be compared unto her. Length of days is in her right hand and in her left hand riches and honor.*
>
> Proverbs 3:13-16

4. Learn how to handle your anger. Anger is a God-given emotion that is designed to protect us by keeping us and our world pure. Appropriate anger results when helpless people are abused or righteous standards are violated. Anger was never designed to destroy us, but that is what it will do if we do not learn how to handle it. Always seek to think before you talk when angry. Avoid getting physical when angry because angry people are out of control and can hurt others. Walk away from a situation that has made you angry. Realize that you don't have to fix the situation right now. Take time to analyze yourself to see what role you played in causing your anger.

> *A wrathful man stirreth up strife: but he that is slow to anger appeaseth strife.*
>
> Proverbs 15:18

5. Work on feeling good about yourself so that you are not crushed when you fail. The ability to keep standing when everything around you has fallen is the key to success. How you feel about yourself will greatly determine if you keep going after failure. Your orientation and how you deal with it holds the key to your future. The question on the floor is: "Are you man enough to look at your past, embrace the good and eliminate the bad?" We really don't have a choice. I challenge you to use wisdom and deal with your orientation, because when you do, the sky is the limit when it comes to your future. For the following questions, you may choose to use a private sheet of paper, or you may choose to discuss this section with an older man or a group.

Questions
for Introspection and Discussion (to make you think)

1. List five men who have contributed or are contributing to your orientation, personality, morals, habits and future success.

1._____
2._____
3._____
4._____
5._____

2. List five negative events from your orientation that have damaged you and need to be dealt with in order for you to function properly.

1._____
2._____
3._____
4._____
5._____

3. Give yourself credit and name some negative things from your orientation that you have faced and conquered.

1._____
2._____
3._____
4._____

4. List five qualities that you would like to eliminate from your personality, or habits that you would like to drop.

1._____
2._____
3._____
4._____
5._____

5. State to yourself and another person when you plan to start eliminating these negative qualities and the practical steps you plan to take to accomplish your goal.

_____
_____
_____

Applicable Scriptures: Please have a boy read the Scripture, then use the questions to facilitate discussion. Conclude by quoting the Scripture from the Living Bible, which was written for teenagers. *Please remember that the reading of Scripture according to Isaiah 55:11 is the most important thing you will do with the boys. This section is where the Holy Spirit really works in their hearts, so don't skip it.*

(1) *Train up a child in the way he should go: and when he is old, he will not depart from it.* Proverbs 22:6
[Question] **Do you feel that you have been raised in the way you should go? Explain.**
[Question] **How do you feel you will behave when you grow up?**
This is the way the Living Bible translates Proverbs 22:6: *Teach a child to choose the right path, and when he is older he will remain upon it.*

(2) *I can do all things through Christ which strengtheneth me.* Philippians 4:13
[Question] **Do you believe that Christ can really give you the power to do right?**
[Question] **Have you asked Jesus Christ to help you do right? Give an example.**
This is the way the Living Bible Translates Philippians 4:13: *For I can do everything God asks me to with the help of Christ who gives me the strength and power.*

(3) *Examine yourselves, whether ye be in the faith; prove your own selves.* II Corinthians 13:5a
[Question] **This chapter is really designed to make you think about how you are being raised. Do you find this topic painful?**
[Question] **Do you regularly examine your attitudes and actions and try to determine why you do the things you do? If no, why not? If yes, give an example.**
The Living Bible translates II Corinthians 13:5a like this: *Check up on yourselves. Are you really Christians?*

(4) *The heart is deceitful above all things, and desperately wicked: who can know it?* Jeremiah 17:9
[Question] **Do you feel that you understand your heart? Explain.**
[Question] **Who or what has trained your heart: TV, the Bible, friends, music?**
[Question] **Do you feel that your heart is wicked?**
The Living Bible translates Jeremiah 17:9 like this: *The heart is the most deceitful thing there is, and desperately wicked. No one can really know how bad it is!*

(5) *And I will restore to you the years that the locust hath eaten, the cankerworm, and the caterpillar, and the palmerworm, my great army which I sent among you.* Joel 2:25
[Question] **Do you feel that God can help you in those areas of life where you have been hurt?**
[Question] **Do you feel that if you work hard and with God's help you can have a better life in the future than you have had in the past?**
The Living Bible translates Joel 2:25 like this: *I will give you back the crops the locusts ate!—my great destroying army that I sent against you.*

Additional Scriptures Used In Chapter One As Found In The Living Bible

Wounds from a friend are better than kisses from an enemy.
                                                    Proverbs 27:6

Without wise leadership, a nation is in trouble; but with good counselors there is safety.
                                                    Proverbs 11:14

Whose heart is filled with anguish and sorrow? Who is always fighting and quarreling? Who is the man with bloodshot eyes and many wounds? It is the one who spends long hours in the taverns, trying out new mixtures.
                                                    Proverbs 23:29-30

If you want to know what God wants you to do, ask him, and he will gladly tell you, for he is always ready to give a bountiful supply of wisdom to all who ask him; he will not resent it.
                                                    James 1:5

The man who knows right from wrong and has good judgment and common sense is happier than the man who is immensely rich! For such wisdom is far more valuable than precious jewels. Nothing else compares with it. Wisdom gives: A long, good life, Riches, Honor, Pleasure, Peace.
                                                    Proverbs 3:13-17

A quick-tempered man starts fights; a cool-tempered man tries to stop them.
                                                    Proverbs 15:18

Make This Statement To The Boys:

Before we go on to the next chapter, tell me which Scripture made you mad, glad or made you think.

Note to the Mentor: As a result of this lesson, are there any prayer requests that should be added to your list and forwarded to your prayer partners?

Notes:_____

_____

_____

2 Ask Yourself The Question:

"Have I Been Properly Nurtured?"

Definition: To be nurtured is to be given love, support and encouragement while young.

CONNECTING WITH AND LEARNING FROM YOUR RICH, PERSONAL, PAINFUL, PRODUCTIVE PAST: An illustration from your personal life will go a long way with the young men. Can you remember when your family forgot your birthday, or that time when you made the winning shot in the game and your family's response was less than what you thought it should be? At what point of your childhood or even in your marriage were you slighted of the love, support and attention that you felt you deserved? When you identify this painful event and share it with the young men, they will be blessed and you will be blessed also.

CAUTION: This chapter also calls for self-examination and honesty. Very few young men will be willing to admit that they have not received enough love in their short lives. The fact of the matter is that we all would like to have received more love at various times during our formative years. The example of the young lady given in the text is a rare case in which this child told the adults that she was not getting enough attention. Her parents were sensitive to her needs and sought to meet them. If you have a young man in your group that has a deficit in the area of nurture, then you need to make him feel comfortable as you discuss this situation.

Stories are great for helping the other person see that you can relate to their situation. I am amazed how young people of all ages love a good story. When you tell a story about your own struggles with feeling unloved or under-loved at a particular time in your life, you will break down barriers and help the young man open up to you.

Please understand that you may not see immediate results from your efforts. You may have to wait until the seed that you are planting has time to germinate and grow, but believe me, there will be results from your sharing.

CONCERN: I am concerned that the young men will not open up to discuss their hurts and frustrations. The first step in dealing with deficits from our orientation is to talk about it.

CHARGE: I charge you as the older male to ask the Lord to give you creativity to help the young men open up. Ask the Lord to give you a heart for the young men that you will be MENTORING.

CURE: The cure for a deficit in the area of nurture is to give love, support and encouragement to others and it will come back to you. The cure for loneliness is to make friends.

2 Ask Yourself The Question:

"Have I Been Properly Nurtured?"

Young men need to come to grips with the fact that there may have been something missing in their upbringing. If you are the type of person who needs attention, feels unloved, suffers from low self-esteem, it is possible that you were not given enough attention as a child.

I was at a friend's house one day, visiting with him and his wife. We were involved in an adult conversation that we were enjoying very much. Our conversation was interrupted when his six-year-old daughter walked into the middle of the adults who were sitting around and spoke her mind. The child said: "*I'm* not getting enough attention." She was displeased with her parents' temporary abandonment of her needs to meet the needs of their guests. What I found most interesting was that she verbalized her concern. She didn't trip or act out her frustrations like many children and adults do; she very calmly said: "I'm not getting enough attention."

I like her approach. Some of us need to admit that we are not getting enough attention or that we did not get enough attention when we were younger. Have you experienced what it feels like to be loved by a father or a father-like person? Have you experienced the comfort of knowing that your dad would protect you from danger? Have you experienced the assurance of knowing that Dad would be there no matter what happened? Did you receive objective, fair, well-balanced discipline? Was there a grandmother or auntie in your life who offered you unconditional love and discipline? What amount of nurturing did you receive as a child?

As a child, my best friend was my white, female collie named "Bootsie." I loved Bootsie with all of my heart, and I know that she loved me just as much. I can distinctly remember how Bootsie would see me on the other side of the yard, come over to me and rub her neck against my leg. This was her way of saying: "I need some attention." I would then scratch her head between her ears and scratch her back, after which she was satisfied and would go and sit down.

People need love more than dogs do, and when it is not received, there can be strange repercussions. When love is not present in a person's life, some of the results can be:
- Limited appreciation of others.
- Inability to freely give love.
- The development of focusing on one's self.
- Limited experiential knowledge of love.
- Lack of trust for others.

Psychologists teach that all people have a need for significance and security. In order to be psychologically healthy, people must feel significant and they must feel secure. If you observe the people around you, it is easy to see that they are struggling with these needs. When people talk loud and cut up in public, it is obvious that they are in need of attention. They would NEVER admit it and probably don't even realize it. When people feel insecure, they act strangely and do strange things.

A wise young man seeks to understand himself and how he was nurtured because it will affect everything that he does in life. ANSWER THIS QUESTION: Have you been left to yourself as far as discipline goes? Did your mother or father go upside your head when you acted up, or did they just talk and let you get away with whatever you wanted to do?

The rod and reproof give wisdom: but the child left to himself bringeth his mother to shame.
Proverbs 29:15

I know that this may sound cruel, but it is not, believe me. All throughout our history, parents have gotten on the cases of their children with whatever means necessary to BREAK that mean, rebellious spirit in their children. Society today says that we should not "whip" (as we used to say) our children. They even put a big word on it to make it sound even more terrible, "CORPORAL PUNISHMENT!" Please note that proper discipline, administered by a loving parent, is not abuse. Please note the following passages.

He that spareth his rod hateth his son: but he that loveth him chasteneth him betimes.
Proverbs 13:24

This simply means that a man who hates his son will not discipline him. The man that loves his son will discipline him when he needs it. This instills in a young man a sense of consequences for his actions. When this is absent in young men, they fear nothing and as a result die early.

Foolishness is bound in the heart of a child; but the rod of correction shall drive it far from him.

Proverbs 22:15

Foolishness comes with childhood. Sometimes I think of the foolish things that I did as a child that I thought were funny. Just thinking about these things scares me now that I am grown.

When I was a child, we lived on a hill, and my dad told us not to roll tires down the hill. It was fun to roll tires down the hill, but we did not realize the danger involved. A tire rolling down the hill would have enough momentum to go through a house if it hit it. We didn't understand or perceive the danger involved, so we continued to roll tires down the hill. One day, Dad caught us rolling tires down the hill, and he almost killed us. After we recovered, we never touched a tire again, and now that we are grown, we agree with what Dad said. A good spanking, or whipping, or whatever you call it, will not hurt you if it is done in love.

Withhold not correction from the child: for if thou beatest him with the rod, he shall not die. Thou shalt beat him with the rod, and shalt deliver his soul from hell.

Proverbs 23:13-14

I must mention the fact that unfortunately many parents have taken the Biblical concept of discipline and abused it. Any time you are spanked or whipped for unclear reasons, or because your parents were in a bad mood, is an unhealthy situation. Abuse could be defined as punishment administered without love. If you are a victim of excessive punishment, there are some things that you must remember:

- God loves you and did not initiate the abuse.
- You must filter any negative feelings about the parent or adult that abused you so that you will be free from hatred and bitterness.
- Resolve to stop the abuse with your generation. When you get married talk about your abuse to your wife and ask her to help you to release any frustration before you have children so that you will not repeat the abuse.

Questions
for Introspection and Discussion (to make you think)

1. Tell the truth, shame the devil! Have you been disciplined enough by your parents? Yes___ No___ Are you, or were you, able to get away with MURDER? Yes___ No___

2. What makes you feel significant or important?_____

3. What makes you feel secure or safe?_____

4. Are you aware of any areas where you have not been properly nurtured? Yes___ No___ If so, what are you doing about it? _____

5. What one thing did your parent(s) do to make you feel nurtured or loved?_____

Applicable Scriptures: Please have a boy read the Scripture, then use the questions to facilitate discussion. Conclude by quoting the Scripture from the Living Bible which was written for teenagers. *Please remember that the reading of Scripture according to Isaiah 55:11 is the most important thing you will do with the boys. This section is where the Holy Spirit really works in their hearts, so don't skip it.*

(1) *For I was my father's son, tender and only beloved in the sight of my mother. He taught me also, and said unto me, Let thine heart retain my words: keep my commandments, and live.*
Proverbs 4:3,4

[Question] **Has your father or any other man ever told you that he is proud of you?**

[Question] **Do you have a saying, a sentence, or a statement that your father or a man taught you that is dear to you? What is it?**

[Question] **Has a man who loves you given you some commandments?**

The Living Bible translates Proverbs 4:3,4 like this: *For I, too, was once a son, tenderly loved by my mother as an only child, and the companion of my father. He told me never to forget his words. "If you follow them," he said, "you will have a long and happy life."*

(2) *The rod and reproof give wisdom: but a child left to himself bringeth his mother to shame.*
Proverbs 29:15

[Question] **Has a man whom you love ever put a belt on your butt?**

[Question] **If you have been spanked, was it done in love?**

[Question] **Did the adults in your life talk to you while they spanked you?**

[Question] **Did they hug you and tell you they loved you after the spanking?**

[Question] **Have you been left to yourself and do you bring your parents shame?**

The Living Bible translates Proverbs 29:15 like this: *Scolding and spanking a child helps him to learn. Left to himself, he brings shame to his mother.*

(3) *Hatred stirreth up strifes: but love covereth all sins.* Proverbs 10:12
[Question] **Have you grown up in an environment where there was a lot of hate?**
[Question] **Do you have people around you who love you and see the best in you?**
The Living Bible translates Proverbs 10:12 like this: *Hatred stirs old quarrels, but love overlooks insults.*

(4) *A friend loveth at all times, and a brother is born for adversity.* Proverbs 17:17
[Question] **What person loves you consistently?**
[Question] **What man can you go to when you are having hard times?**
[Question] **Do you feel that Jesus is there in the hard times?**
The Living Bible translates Proverbs 17:17 like this: *A true friend is always loyal, and a brother is born to help in time of need.*

(5) *For this is the message that ye heard from the beginning, that we should love one another.*
I John 3:11
[Question] **The true test of a Christian is his ability to love. Are you a loving person?**
[Question] **What person do you hate (parent, brother, homie) that you should love?**
[Question] **Have you asked Jesus to help you love others?**
The Living Bible translates I John 3:11 like this: *For the message to us from the beginning has been that we should love each other.*

(6) *And, ye fathers, provoke not your children to wrath: but bring them up in the nurture and admonition of the Lord.* Ephesians 6:4
[Question] **How has your father made you mad?**
[Question] **Your father is supposed to teach you to love Jesus and to read the Bible. Did he do this?**
[Question] **If your father did not do these things, what do you feel you should do?**
The Living Bible translates Ephesians 6:4 like this: *And now a word to you parents. Don't keep on scolding and nagging your children, making them angry and resentful. Rather, bring them up with the loving discipline the Lord himself approves, with suggestions and godly advice.*

(7) *When my father and my mother forsake me, then the LORD will take me up.* Psalm 27:10
[Question] **Do you look to Jesus to help when you can't find a parent to help you?**
[Question] **Do you believe that Jesus will consistently hold you up?**
[Question] **Do you understand that a father and mother can only do so much and that Jesus has to pick up where they fail?**
The Living Bible translates Psalm 27:10 like this: *For if my father and mother should abandon me, you would welcome and comfort me.*

Additional Scriptures Used In Chapter Three As Found In The Living Bible

If you refuse to discipline your son, it proves you don't love him; for if you love him you will be prompt to punish him.

Proverbs 13:24

A youngster's heart is filled with rebellion, but punishment will drive it out of him.

Proverbs 22:15

Don't fail to correct your children; discipline won't hurt them! They won't die if you use a stick on them! Punishment will keep them out of hell.

Proverbs 23:13-14

Make This Statement To The Boys:

Before we go on to the next chapter, tell me which Scripture made you mad, glad or made you think.

Note to the Mentor: As a result of this lesson, are there any prayer requests that should be added to your list and forwarded to your prayer partners?

Notes:_____

3 Brothers and Sisters (Siblings)

Definition: A sibling is one of two or more persons born of the same parents or, sometimes having one parent in common.

CONNECTING WITH AND LEARNING FROM YOUR RICH, PERSONAL, PAINFUL, PRODUCTIVE PAST: I am sure that if you have a brother or sister you will have plenty examples of negative and positive experiences to share with the young men. You may want to mention a specific hurt that you had to overcome and share it with them. From your experience, share the importance of resolving conflicts before you get old.

CAUTION: This subject may be painful for those from broken homes. This subject may also be painful for the mentor if he has unsettled scars from the past.

CONCERN: Be careful not to deceive yourself regarding the pain that you feel about this subject. Men frequently will lie and say: "It's not bothering me!" Be honest.

CHARGE: I challenge you and the young men to talk about it openly, for only then can you be healed.

CURE: Peace will come when a phone call is made and forgiveness is given or asked for. This may be the hardest task you have ever been asked to do, but it will set you free! Please note that it does not matter who started the conflict. What matters is that the ill feeling be resolved. If they started it, you still can call them and say: "Brother, I am sorry about what happened **(EVEN THOUGH YOU DIDN'T DO IT!).** I would like to clear the air between us on this issue. I want you to know that I forgive you and I would like for you to forgive me." It takes a REAL MAN to do this, and I believe that if your situation calls for this, you can do it.

3 Brothers and Sisters (Siblings)

It takes many years to understand how your relationship with your brothers and sisters affects you. There are many adults in their forties who are just beginning to understand how the problems they had with their brothers and sisters while young have affected them all of these years. We could say that they have unresolved **sibling rivalries.** It is quite normal for there to be tension between children in the same home, and when children fuss and fight, it is a normal part of growing up. The problem comes when you have adults in their forties and fifties who are holding things against each other because of something that happened many years ago. This is an unhealthy situation.

If you have brothers and sisters, you should study your relationships to make sure that they are healthy. Here are some things to consider when dealing with your brothers and sisters.

1. They are human and will make mistakes.
Ignorance means that you are not knowledgeable of a particular fact. It can also be used in the area of relationships by saying that "He was ignorant of how she felt." People can be ignorant of others and unintentionally harm them. While growing up, brothers and sisters do things that hurt each other, such as giving each other hurtful nicknames. It is possible to play a trick on a brother or sister that you feel is funny but that they remember painfully for many years. These things are usually done in ignorance, and we should consider them childhood mistakes.

2. In a moment of weakness, they may say or do something that will hurt you.
Everybody has a bad day, a weak moment, a time when they will step on the neck of a loved one just to save their own skin. Brothers and sisters do this all of the time. Usually they will realize that they were wrong and apologize, either audibly, through gestures or some other way. Some people say they are sorry without using the words "I'm sorry." Don't hold this against them forever. Ask God to help you forgive them.

3. If you feel that your parents treat them better than they treat you, seek to find out why.
Good parents know their children and deal with them according to their own personalities. Children don't usually understand this and will feel that the parents are choosing one child over the other. One child can handle money, so he gets money; the other child can't handle money and blows it, so he gets less money. One daughter knows how to come in when she is supposed to, so she gets to go out; the other daughter does not know how to come in, so she does not go out as much. There is generally a reason why parents treat one child differently from the other. Seek to find out why by observing the larger picture and listening when your parents give their responses to your requests.

4. If your parents actually do treat your brother(s) or sister(s) better than they treat you, be patient.

I would like to come to your house, take you by the arm, go to a room which gives us privacy, look you dead in the eye and yell at the top of my lungs: "YOUR PARENTS AREN'T GOING TO DO EVERYTHING RIGHT! THEY WILL MAKE MISTAKES!!!" Now, I admit that this is no excuse for the injustice that you will suffer, but the fact of the matter is that some parents prefer one child over another. In a dysfunctional family, there can be many reasons for this:

- One child may be more appealing than the other.
- One child may remind a parent of the other parent, which displeases the parent.
- The parent may fail to see the natural beauty in the child.
- Younger siblings may benefit because the parents may have more money now than they did when you were young.

5. Don't be jealous of your brother's or sister's successes.
When you are jealous of others, you are not focusing on your own God-given strengths. This jealousy will cripple you as you attempt to succeed in life.

6. Learn to talk objectively (with an open mind) with your brothers and sisters about the hurts that the two of you have suffered while growing up.
The worst thing that you can do is to hold in the fact that your brother *&%#@ you off because he broke your bicycle when you were in the fifth grade and never said he was sorry and didn't even pay for it. Sit your brother or sister down and say: "We need to talk."

7. Be sure to forgive them.
Forgiveness equals freedom for the one who forgives. To forgive is to free YOURSELF. satan wants to bind you with the hurts of the past. Refuse to be enslaved to negative childhood memories. Set yourself free by forgiving those who have offended you. If you don't feel that you can face the person who hurt you, then write a letter and send it to them. If the person is dead, then pull up a chair and talk to the chair. The point to remember is that you have to get it out. This is where healing begins.

8. See to it that the mistakes of the past are not repeated.
We should all take personal responsibility in seeing to it that we don't repeat the mistakes our parents made with us. We should also seek to limit the damage caused by mistakes and scars between our brothers and sisters. One thing I am doing with my children is, I am going to see to it that they study, participate in class and get their homework done even if I have to live at the school. I am sure you have some things that you would like to do differently when you have kids.

Seek to develop a better relationship with your brother(s) and sister(s). If they won't act right, you keep on loving them and seeking to develop a relationship with them and God will do the rest. If you are reading this book, God is trying to give you what you need to repair any broken relationships.

Questions
for Introspection and Discussion (to make you think)

1. Do you have any brothers? Yes___ No___ If so, how many? _____

2. Do you have any sisters? Yes___ No___ If so, how many?_____

3. Have they ever hurt you? Yes___ No___ If so, how?_____

4. How do you see yourself rating in the family? favorite___ average___ least favorite___

5. What coping skills did you develop to deal with your position in the family?_____

6. Do you understand why your parents treat you the way they do? Yes___ No___

7. Can you talk to your brother/sister about the things in your family that hurt you and you don't understand? Yes___ No___

8. Have you forgiven your brother/sister/parents for how they hurt you? Yes___ No___

9. Name or list three things that happened to you that you don't want to happen to your kids.
   1. _____
   2. _____
   3. _____

10. Do you need to call a brother/sister and settle some things with them? Yes___ No___

Applicable Scriptures: Please have a boy read the Scripture, then use the questions to facilitate discussion. Conclude by quoting the Scripture from the Living Bible which was written for teenagers. *Please remember that the reading of Scripture according to Isaiah 55:11 is the most important thing you will do with the boys. This section is where the Holy Spirit really works in their hearts, so don't skip it.*

(1) *A brother offended is harder to be won than a strong city: and their contentions are like the bars of a castle.* Proverbs 18:19
[Question] **Have you ever tried to make up with someone and they refused?**
[Question] **Because it is so difficult to make up once we offend someone, what should we do to try not to offend people?**
[Question] **Do your brothers and sisters forgive you when you ask them?**
[Question] **What family member do you need to make up with right now?**

The Living Bible translates Proverbs 18:19 like this: *It is harder to win back the friendship of an offended brother than to capture a fortified city. His anger shuts you out like iron bars.*

(2) *A man that hath friends must show himself friendly: and there is a friend that sticketh closer than a brother.* Proverbs 18:24
[Question] **Are you friendly?**
[Question] **Are you friendly with people who are not your homies?**
[Question] **Are you a faithful friend?**
The Living Bible translates Proverbs 18:24 like this: *There are "friends" who pretend to be friends, but there is a friend who sticks closer than a brother.*

(3) *And when his brethren saw that their father loved him more than all his brethren, they hated him, and could not speak peaceably unto him.* Genesis 37:4
[Question] **Joseph was the baby boy and his father made a fuss over him. As a result, the older brothers were jealous. Are you jealous over how your parents treat one of your siblings?**
[Question] **Do you understand that many times when your parents treat you different than one of your siblings it is because your personality is different and not because they love you less?**
The Living Bible translates Genesis 37:4 like this: *His brothers of course noticed their father's partiality, and consequently hated Joseph; they couldn't say a kind word to him.*

(4) *And Isaac loved Esau, because he did eat of his venison: but Rebekah loved Jacob.* Genesis 25:28
[Question] **Sometimes one parent will gravitate toward a particular child because their interests are the same. What skills, hobbies or interests do you have with your dad or father figure?**
[Question] **When boys are raised by their moms they often develop similar interests. What interest do you share with your mom?**
[Question] **Do you feel that your parents love you just as you are?**
The Living Bible translates Genesis 25:28 like this: *Isaac's favorite son was Esau, because of the venison he brought home, and Rebekah's favorite was Jacob.*

(5) *A friend loveth at all times, and a brother is born for adversity.* Proverbs 17:17
[Question] **Do you love your brothers and sisters all the time?**
[Question] **When was the last time you told your family you love them?**
[Question] **Can your brother/sister confidently come to you when they are having a hard time?**
[Question] **Have you made an agreement with your brother/sister to stay close as you grow up?**
The Living Bible translates Proverbs 17:17 like this: *A true friend is always loyal, and a brother is born to help in time of need.*

(6) *Then came Peter to him, and saith, Lord, how oft shall my brother sin against me, and I forgive him: till seven times? Jesus saith unto him, I say not unto thee, Until seven times: but, Until seventy times seven.* Matthew 18:21-22
[Question] **How many times have you forgiven your family?**

48

[Question] **Jesus commanded us to forgive every time your brother genuinely asks for it. Are you quick to forgive family?**

[Question] **Forgiveness is supernatural: it takes Jesus in your life to really forgive. To hate and hurt is natural, anybody can do that. Which do you choose, to be natural or supernatural?**

The Living Bible translates Matthew 18:21-22 like this: *Then Peter came to him and asked, "Sir, how often should I forgive a brother who sins against me? Seven times?" "No!" Jesus replied, "seventy times seven!"*

Make This Statement To The Boys:

Before we go on to the next chapter, tell me which Scripture made you mad, glad or made you think.

Note to the Mentor: As a result of this lesson, are there any prayer requests that should be added to your list and forwarded to your prayer partners?

Notes:_____

_____

_____

_____

_____

_____

_____

_____

_____

_____

_____

_____

Mentor: Read this page before you meet with your boys.

4 Living In The Projects: A Housing Development

(Or Living In The Trap Of A Poor Hood)

Definition: A neighborhood is a community district or area, especially with regard to some characteristic or point of reference (a bad neighborhood or a good neighborhood).

CONNECTING WITH AND LEARNING FROM YOUR RICH, PERSONAL, PAINFUL, PRODUCTIVE, PAST. Share with the young men where and how you grew up. You may be able to relate to the slum and you may not. Nevertheless, you can share struggles that you faced.

CAUTION: For those currently living in poverty, be sure to keep the focus of the lesson on their potential for positive change.

CONCERN: Be sensitive to those who are already ashamed of their living conditions.

CHARGE: Charge the young men to determine to make a change when they grow up. If they start planning now, they can get an education that will help them work their way out of poverty.

CURE: Strive to avoid the traps that keep so many in poverty such as drugs, crime, and teen pregnancy, etc.

ACTIVITY: Have the young men request a meeting with the school counselor to determine just what it takes to get into college and where they stand. Have them discuss the results with you.

4Living In The Projects: A Housing Development

(Or Living In The Trap Of A Poor 'Hood)

Recently I was spending some time in a housing project in our city. As a grown man, I am fascinated with the projects because I lived in one as a child. I now spend time there seeking to enrich the lives of children who live there. When I lived there as a child, I learned how to be amused with whatever was lying around. I made toys out of trash and entertained myself with whatever I found.

While in the neighborhood the other day, I found myself doing something that I had done as a child. I was looking at the ground. While looking at the ground, I found a quarter on the street and a cat's-eye marble partly submerged in the dirt outside of an apartment. I was excited with my discovery, and I found myself reliving part of my childhood. Even though I am many years removed from the "manor," as we used to call it, the "manor" is still very much in me. I have a fondness for the atmosphere that is found there. Even the negative aspects of the projects are firmly a part of my past that I think of occasionally.

If you are a young man who was raised or is being raised in the projects, there are some things that I learned as I grew up that you should be aware of now.

1. You can work your way out of the projects. We know about sports as a way out, but we need to consider some additional ways that are less based on chance.
- Education will get you out of the projects, and it will enrich your personal life.
- The army will get you out of the projects, but without the education you may end up right back.
- Musical talent may get you out of the projects, but without an education you may end up right back.
- There are many illegal ways to get out of the projects, but you may die or go to jail in the process.

My wife and I made it out of the projects and out of poverty through education. With an education, you have a better chance of getting a job, and the education helps you better understand the world in which you live.

2. Turn any anger into positive energy. I used to watch my dad clean toilets with his hands, and it made me angry because racism limited him to that job. I grabbed that anger and refused to throw bricks during the riots but instead took that energy and channeled it into building my own business and getting an education.

Look around you. Does what you see (drugs, crime, despair, poverty) make you angry? If it does, good! Take the energy that results from that anger and channel it into those things (education, integrity, love, prayer, work) that will make a difference. NEVER WASTE YOUR ANGER! Seek to develop the habit of directing the energy that comes from your anger in positive ways.

3. Refuse to be apathetic. Apathy is when you just don't care. Many people die in projects in poverty because they became apathetic ("ain't no use tryin', they ain't gonna let us get nowhere"). Say to yourself: "I can do all things through Christ who strengthens me, and I can work my way out of here."

Black folks created the blues, and we could sing them because we were oppressed. I feel that the blues as an art form is an important part of our history which should be maintained. On the other hand, singing the blues will not help you elevate your thinking to where it should be maintained. Learn to cultivate a passion toward improving your status in life. Don't hang around negative, lazy, apathetic people who are going nowhere.

4. Don't be stingy. Learn to become a flowing brook and not a stagnant pond. Water flows in and out of a brook, and it stays fresh. Water flows into a pond, stays there and gets stale.

> *The liberal soul shall be made fat: and he that watereth shall be watered also himself.*
> Proverbs 11:25

Learn to give and be sure not to step on people as you rise out of poverty. When you step on people to get ahead, you will find yourself standing on shaky ground.

> *Give, and it shall be given unto you; good measure, pressed down, and shaken together, and running over, shall men give into your bosom. For with the same measure that you mete withal it shall be measured to you again.*
> Luke 6:38

I am sure that you have heard people say: "You reap what you sow." This simply means what you dish out will come back to you. This applies to the good as well as to the bad.

5. Develop an empowerment mentality now. Just because you live in the ghetto does not mean that you need to have a ghetto mindset. When you open your mouth, people should not be able to tell what part of town you are from. No one can imprison your mind. "Kunta Kinte" was a slave in body but never in his mind. Our problem today is that many men are slaves in their minds, which also puts their bodies into slavery.

6. Determine only to open your mouth with wisdom or keep it shut. Some people talk too soon, too loud, too fast, too much and about nothin'. James Brown had a popular song a few years ago titled "Talkin' Loud and Sayin' Nothin'."

Even a fool, when he holdeth his peace, is counted wise: and he that shutteth his lips is esteemed a man of understanding.
                                                    Proverbs 17:28

There is a time to be quiet and there is a time to display wisdom.

Pleasant words are as an honeycomb, sweet to the soul, and health to the bones.
                                                    Proverbs 16:24

When people observe your wisdom, discernment and discretion, they will pay attention. Webster defines wisdom as the quality of being wise or the power of judging rightly and following the soundest course of action, based on knowledge, experience, understanding, etc. Discernment is defined as the power of discerning; keen perception or judgment; insight; acumen. Discretion is defined as the freedom or authority to make decisions and choices; power to judge or act. Your gift of wisdom will work on your behalf if you let the right people see it.

A man's gift maketh room for him, and bringeth him before great men.
                                                    Proverbs 18:16

Strive to develop the gift of wisdom, which will help guide you as you seek to make money off of your other gifts. We all know of many young, gifted men who were destroyed because they did not have the wisdom to handle success and the money that came with it.

Wisdom is the principle thing; therefore get wisdom: and with all thy getting get understanding.
                                                    Proverbs 4:7

7. Resolve to take every opportunity to help others better themselves. There is a rich, gratifying sense of accomplishment you get when you help others. When you help others, you are planting seeds in your flower garden that will one day bloom and bless you. There is a law or principle that you employ when you help others. It is the principle of reaping and sowing. The fact that you reap what you sow can work to your own good if you sow good things.

So, where do you live? If you live in the projects, it is possible to move out right now simply by changing your thinking. If you don't take the time and effort to learn how to lift your thinking to a higher plane, it is possible that you will never leave the projects. In order to escape poverty, you must first enrich your mind.

Questions
for Introspection and Discussion (to make you think)

1. Have you ever lived in the projects in or poverty? Yes___ No___

2. If so, how long?_____

3. What were your plans for getting out of the situation? _____

4. What steps have you already taken toward that goal? (write or discuss them)_____

5. Who have you discussed your plans with and allowed to evaluate them?_____

6. Of the seven suggestions given in this chapter to help you get out of the 'hood, which of the seven

do you need to work on?_____

Applicable Scriptures: Please have a boy read the Scripture, then use
the questions to facilitate discussion. Conclude by quoting the Scripture from the Living Bible, which was written for teenagers. *Please remember that the reading of Scripture according to Isaiah 55:11 is the most important thing you will do with the boys. This section is where the Holy Spirit really works in their hearts, so don't skip it.*

(1) *Wisdom is the principal thing; therefore get wisdom: and with all thy getting get understanding* Proverbs 4:7
[Question] **Do you feel that you are wise? Where do you get your wisdom from?**
[Question] **It takes years to understand life. What are you doing to gain understanding?**
The Living Bible translates Proverbs 4:7 like this: *Determination to be wise is the first step toward becoming wise! And with your wisdom, develop common sense and good judgment.*

(2) *Trust in the LORD with all thine heart; and lean not unto thine own understanding. In all thy ways acknowledge him, and he shall direct thy paths.* Proverbs 3:5-6
[Question] **Who do you trust in to help you make it through the day?**
[Question] **Do you have any idea how limited your own understanding is?**
[Question] **What do you know about your path in life? Do you feel you need direction?**
The Living Bible translated Proverbs 3:5-6 like this: *If you want favor with both God and man, and a reputation for good judgment and common sense, then trust the Lord completely; don't ever trust yourself. In everything you do, put God first, and he will direct you and crown your efforts with success.*

(3) *Give, and it shall be given unto you; good measure, pressed down, and shaken together, and running over, shall men give into your bosom. For with the same measure that ye mete withal it shall be measured to you again.* Luke 6:38

[Question] **Do you believe that giving is related to getting?**

[Question] **Have you ever noticed that stingy people are never happy?**

[Question] **Do you feel that this applies only to money?**

The Living Bible translates Luke 6:38 like this: *For if you give, you will get! Your gift will return to you in full and overflowing measure, pressed down, shaken together to make room for more, and running over. Whatever measure you use to give—large or small—will be used to measure what is given back to you.*

(4) *I can do all things through Christ which strengtheneth me.* Philippians 4:13

[Question] **Do you believe that Christ can help you do anything?**

[Question] **What one thing do you need Christ to help you do?**

[Question] **Are you willing to be obedient to Christ's commands before you ask Him to help you?**

The Living Bible translates Philippians 4:13 like this: *For I can do everything God asks me to with the help of Christ who gives me the strength and power.*

(5) *But seek ye first the kingdom of God, and his righteousness; and all these things shall be added unto you.* Matthew 6:33

[Question] **Is doing God's will the most important thing in your life?**

[Question] **Have you thought about the benefits of living a right or righteous life?**

[Question] **If God becomes your priority, things will come. What things do you need today?**

The Living Bible translates Matthew 6:33 like this: *So don't worry at all about having enough food and clothing. Why be like the heathen? For they take pride in all these things and are deeply concerned about them. But your heavenly Father already knows perfectly well that you need them, and he will give them to you if you give him first place in our life and live as he wants you to.*

(6) *Seest thou a man diligent in his business? He shall stand before kings; he shall not stand before mean men.* Proverbs 22:29

[Question] **Do you take care of business, school business, personal business?**

[Question] **Are you a diligent person or a lazy person?**

[Question] **Do you believe that if you work hard you will eventually hang out with important people?**

The Living Bible translates Proverbs 22:29 like this: *Do you know a hard-working man? He shall be successful and stand before kings!*

Additional Scriptures Used In Chapter Four As Found In The Living Bible

It is possible to give away and become richer! It is also possible to hold on too tightly and lose everything. Yes, the liberal man shall be rich! By watering others, he waters himself.
Proverbs 11:24-25

The man of few words and settled mind is wise; therefore, even a fool is thought to be wise when he is silent. It pays him to keep his mouth shut.
Proverbs 17:27-28

Kind words are like honey—enjoyable and healthful.
Proverbs 16:24

A bribe does wonders; it will bring you before men of importance!
Proverbs 18:16

Make This Statement To The Boys:

Before we go on to the next chapter, tell me which Scripture made you mad, glad or made you think.

Note to the Mentor: As a result of this lesson, are there any prayer requests that should be added to your list and forwarded to your prayer partners?

Notes:

Mentor: Read this page before you meet with your boys.

5 Blocks (Our Fears And Anxieties That Stop Us In Life)

Definition: A block is an obstacle or obstruction; a hindrance, the state or condition of being obstructed.

CONNECTING WITH AND LEARNING FROM YOUR RICH, PERSONAL, PAINFUL, PRODUCTIVE PAST. Unfortunately, a large number of our childhood blocks are still with us— academic blocks, relational blocks, financial blocks and many others. I have recently decided to deal with a block that has affected my business dealings over the years. I have attacked this block many times, making some headway, but I have not completely destroyed this particular block. I pray that God will help you conquer the block that you choose to share as an example with the young men.

CAUTION: Be careful not to confuse lifes natural obstacles with blocks. It is a fact that if you want to get ahead in this life, you will have struggles. Those struggles will come from external forces and internal forces. Obstacles are not blocks! Poverty, a broken home and limited opportunities are not blocks! A block is what you tell yourself about these things.

The key to success is to always speak victory to yourself regarding those things that attempt to become blocks in your life.

CONCERN: I am sure that many young men will deny being "punked out" by another male. When this happens, make the transition to other things that they have been punked out by, such as: English literature, science, algebra, trigonometry, etc. The fact of the matter is that we have all been punked out by something if not by somebody.

CHARGE: I charge you to challenge the young men to identify their blocks and develop a strategy to overcome them. Ask them to write this goal down with a date they expect to be free from that specific block.

CURE: Encourage the young men to face all blocks regardless of how frightening they are. Seek the help and assistance of God, friends, and family to help you heal from these blocks. If you refuse to face your blocks, then they have won and punked you out.

ACTIVITY: Have a black man share how he overcame his blocks for the young men. This can be done at a gathering of the larger group.

5 Blocks (Our Fears And Anxieties That Stop Us In Life)

In the summer of my sixth year of life, my family moved from a house to a large public housing complex (the projects). The first day there, I was pleased and surprised when a group of kids came to my front door and asked my mom if I could come out and play. She responded positively, and I soon found myself outside with a group of young people, playing and having big fun. All of a sudden, without any warning, the kids stopped playing and I found myself in the middle of a circle that they had made around me. The leader of the group was a kid named Mikey. He walked up to me, grabbed me by the collar and said: "I heard that you think you are baad?!!," to which I quickly replied: "Who told you that? I never said that I was bad." At that point he let me go, and everyone returned back to their fun and games.

I had learned an important lesson about my new neighborhood. If I was to have any clout in the neighborhood, I would have to work my way up the ladder, one kid at a time. As time passed, I found out that Carl was no problem because he was a crybaby. BoBo was big, but he was slow; I learned to hit him several times real fast and the fight would be over. But there was a problem when it came to Mikey. I had what is called a mental block when it came to Mikey. This mental block led me to believe that I would never be able to overcome his meanness and power.

Mikey did a good job of making a lasting first impression when I was most vulnerable. When we are vulnerable, we remember events very well that in a different setting would not bother us. Mikey, in my face on my first day in the 'hood, is stamped on my memory for the rest of my life. I firmly believe that if Carl or BoBo had gotten to me on that first day, I would not have been able to beat them and move up in rank. **The fact that I had the opportunity to study them without fear allowed me to accurately assess their strengths and weaknesses and to challenge them with confidence.**

I must say that I never beat Mikey. I never got up enough nerve to overcome the mental damage that he did to me on my first day in the 'hood. Now that I am grown, I understand that **I HAD A MENTAL BLOCK.**

1. The Dawning Of Blocks

Blocks are most dangerous during the formative years (childhood). This is why it is so important for little children to be treated fairly. When I was in the first grade, a White kid hit me in the nose and it hurt. I can remember going to the White teacher and through tears telling her what happened. Her response was: "Shut up and get in line." As a first grader, I immediately determined that several things were true:

- This White woman did not care about my nose.
- If this thing called education, which to me meant getting fair treatment from this White

woman, is going to be so painful, I DON'T NEED IT!

- I had better protect myself and keep my mouth shut. Therefore while in class, I'll be quiet, but on the playground while the White teacher ain't lookin', I will rule the class.

Blocks that occur during the formative years (while you are growing up) do an extensive amount of damage. They are bad because children don't understand the importance of talking about those painful events so that they can heal from them.

2. The Danger Of Blocks

We can clearly see how blocks can cause a person to **FOREGO OPPORTUNITIES.** I personally feel that the damage I received while in the first grade caused me to miss many opportunities for academic advancement. It was not until I was older and understood what happened that I was able to heal myself and reteach myself. In my mind, I became the teacher and punished the child that hit me in the nose. Blocks will also make you **FOCUS ON FAILURE.** A block usually positions itself at a very busy intersection in your brain. It does this so that all of your positive thoughts will have to pass by MR. BLOCK. When the positive thoughts pass by MR. BLOCK, he reminds them that it is rough out there and you probably won't make it. Our blocks are one of the reasons we focus our attention on past failures.

3. The Desire Of Blocks

Blocks are **TOOLS OF TERRORISTS.** When people purposely or accidentally scar you, it is similar to a terrorist attack. The reason is that damage is not always immediately apparent, and it can be difficult to properly place the blame.

Blocks are also **TACTICS OF THE TORMENTOR.** Satan wants to ruin us all while we are young. If he can get us while we are young, he has us for a lifetime. Satan has servants (child molesters, mean adults, mean kids) whose job is to place a scar on young minds so that they will grow in a dysfunctional way.

4. The Demise Of Blocks

I am glad to report that we need not be controlled by our damage, scars or blocks. God is there to help us overcome them. Here is how you can destroy the blocks in your life.

- **Solicit the help of the Holy Spirit.** He is the one who helps us identify the blocks we picked up early in our lives. He will give you strength as you face those frightening scars of the past.
- **Make satan fight fairly.** Satan fights us every day. We must learn to detect illegal blows (below the belt) and make sure we get points for satan's illegal blows. Well, the question on the floor is: "What is an illegal blow by satan?" The answer is, any time satan tortures you with a failure from your past, it is an illegal blow. When this happens you must say: "THAT AIN'T FAIR!! THAT DIDN'T COUNT!!"

When satan tempts us to feel guilty about something that happened in the past, we should refuse to participate. It is spiritually illegal to feel guilty about something in the past that you can't change. We do need to feel guilty about it initially and then recover and move on. Don't fight satan's illegal battles; do fight his legal battles. There are temptations and battles that we do need to fight and cry about. Those are the battles that we can do something about. When satan tempts us right now, the bell has rung and the fight has begun. Please note that this is a fair fight. We must trust Christ to sustain us when we are tempted with the legal stuff, and the decision has to be made right then to do right.

5. The Dawning Of Freedom
Once you develop the art of consciously and actively identifying, confronting, and dealing with the scars and blocks in your life, you have developed a skill that will help you be free to reach your full potential. You can now become successful personally and professionally. More importantly, with your new-found freedom, you can really like yourself.

Questions
for Introspection and Discussion (to make you think)

1. What personal blocks are you aware of?_____

2. Have you analyzed how they paralyze you? Yes ___ No___

3. Are you prepared to deal with them or are you afraid to face them right now?_____

4. Discuss with a mature friend how your personal blocks have stunted your growth. Discuss what

steps you can take to overcome your blocks._____

5. What one thing makes you feel guilty or ashamed? _____

6. Have you figured out if this is something you should feel guilty about?_____

Applicable Scriptures: Please have a boy read the Scripture, then use the questions to facilitate discussion. Conclude by quoting the Scripture from the Living Bible, which was written for teenagers. *Please remember that the reading of Scripture according to Isaiah 55:11 is the most important thing you will do with the boys. This section is where the Holy Spirit really works in their hearts, so don't skip it.*

(1) *And I will restore to you the years that the locust hath eaten, the cankerworm, and the caterpillar, and the palmerworm, my great army which I sent among you.* Joel 2:25

[Question] **Do you have a situation, a memory, a hurt that you need for God to heal?**

[Question] **What thing that happened to you in the past, hurts you the most now?**

[Question] **Do you believe that God can heal you of past hurts?**

[Question] **Are you man enough to ask out loud for God to heal you right now?**

The Loving Bible translates Joel 2:25 like this: *And I will give you back the crops the locust ate!—my great destroying army that I sent against you.*

(2) *I can do all things through Christ which strengtheneth me.* Philippians 4:13

[Question] **Do you believe that Jesus will give you the power to get over your blocks?**

[Question] **Do you believe that Jesus can make you strong against your blocks?**

[Question] **There is power in the name of Jesus. Do you feel you can learn to say that name when you feel threatened?**

The Living Bible translates Philippians 4:13 like this: *for I can do everything God asks me to with the help of Christ who gives me the strength and power.*

(3) *Likewise the Spirit also helpeth our infirmities: for we know not what we should pray for as we ought: but the Spirit itself maketh intercession for us with groanings which cannot be uttered.* Romans 8:26

[Question] **Did you realize that when we don't know what to pray for, the spirit prays for us?**

The Living Bible translates Romans 8:26 like this: *And in the same way—by our faith—the Holy Spirit helps us with our daily problems and in our praying. For we don't even know what we should pray for, or how to pray as we should; but the Holy Spirit prays for us with such feeling that it cannot be expressed in words.*

(4) *Submit yourselves therefore to God. Resist the devil, and he will flee from you.* James 4:7

[Question] **According to this verse, what is the first thing we should do?**

[Question] **What should we do secondly?**

[Question] **After we have done steps one and two, then what happens?**

The Living Bible translates James 4:7 like this: *So give yourselves humbly to God. Resist the devil and he will flee from you.*

(5) *Ye are of God, little children, and have overcome them: because greater is he that is in you, than he that is in the world.* I John 4:4

[Question] **When you become a Christian, God's Spirit comes to live inside of you. God's Spirit** inside of you is more powerful than the devil's spirit that is trying to dog you out. Do you have God's Spirit in you?

[Question] **Do you feel that God's Spirit in you can help you overcome any blocks that you have?**

[Question] **Do you want to get to know God's Spirit better?**

The Living Bible translates I John 4:4 like this: *Dear young friends, you belong to God and have already won your fight with those who are against Christ, because there is someone in your hearts who is stronger than any evil teacher in this wicked world.*

(6) *For God hath not given us the spirit of fear; but of power, and of love, and of a sound mind.* II Timothy 1:7

[Question] **God does not want us to tremble at life's challenges. What makes you afraid?**

[Question] **What are the three things that God wants us to have?**

The Living Bible translates II Timothy 1:7 like this: *For the Holy Spirit, God's gift, does not want you to be afraid of people, but to be wise and strong, and to love them and enjoy being with them.*

(7) *No weapon that is formed against thee shall prosper; and every tongue that shall rise against thee in judgment thou shalt condemn. This is the heritage of the servants of the Lord, and their righteousness is of me, saith the Lord.* Isaiah 54:17

[Question] **A block is a weapon that your enemy wants to use to destroy you. What is the promise that this Scripture makes regarding satan's weapons?**

[Question] **It is important to live right and be right because when you do this no tongue can accuse you of wrong. Are you living right?**

The Living Bible translates Isaiah 54:17 like this: *But in that coming day, no weapon turned against you shall succeed, and you will have justice against every courtroom lie. This is the heritage of the servants of the Lord. This is the blessing I have given you says the Lord.*

Additional Scriptures Used In Chapter Five As Found In The Living Bible

And I will give you back the crops the locust ate!—my great destroying army that I sent against you.

Joel 2:25

For I can do everything God asks me to with the help of Christ who gives me the strength and power.

Philippians 4:13

And in the same way—by our faith—the Holy Spirit helps us with our daily problems and in our praying. For we don't even know what we should pray for, nor how to pray as we should; but the Holy Spirit prays for us with such feeling that it cannot be expressed in words.

Romans 8:26

So give yourselves humbly to God. Resist the devil and he will flee from you.
James 4:7

Dear young friends, you belong to God and have already won your fight with those who are against Christ, because there is someone in your hearts who is stronger than any evil teacher in this wicked world.

I John 4:4

For the Holy Spirit, God's gift, does not want you to be afraid of people, but to be wise and strong, and to love them and enjoy being with them.

II Timothy 1:7

Make This Statement To The Boys:

Before we go on to the next chapter, tell me which Scripture made you mad, glad or made you think.

Note to the Mentor: As a result of this lesson, are there any prayer requests that should be added to your list and forwarded to your prayer partners?

Notes:_____

_____

_____

_____

_____

_____

_____

_____

_____

_____

_____

_____

_____

_____

_____

_____

_____

_____

_____

6 What Kind Of Gang Are You In?

Definition: A gang is a group of people who are associated together in some way.

CONNECTING WITH AND LEARNING FROM YOUR RICH, PERSONAL, PAINFUL, PRODUCTIVE PAST. At some point most men have been forced to hang or run with a group of men. It may not have been called a gang but it actually was. Share from your experiences of gang or group involvement.

CAUTION: Black men working together for the common good is wonderful and we need to do more of it. Not everything that the media labels as a gang is a gang, but society has been conditioned to perceive it that way.

CONCERN: I am concerned that we, as Black Men strive to turn the negative gang stereotypes into positive images of Black men working within the boundaries of the law to bring about change.

CHARGE: Distance yourself from negative people, period. Strive to band with positive people who can support you and challenge you to strive for excellence. Please note that it is OK to try to help negative people if you are strong enough to avoid becoming negative with them.

ACTIVITY: While visiting the jail or prison, have an inmate discuss his gang experience. If there is not prison or jail available, it is not necessary to go into the prison. You may know an older man in the community who may have had experiences in prison that he can share, making a positive message out of his negative experience.

6 What Kind Of Gang Are You In?

The human being is a communal creature. In other words, we all like to have friends and associates. Young people are especially prone to feel that they need a friend or a clique to hang with. While all of this is natural and good, it can be taken to extremes.

The term "gang" carries with it the image of coercion, aggressive persuasion, violence and the reckless following of a misguided leader. Many young people who get involved in gangs make the mistake of going to the wrong people for support. There are a multitude of reasons people get involved in gangs, but none of the reasons can be justified when you consider the end result of much of the gang activity we see in society today.

Actually, there are associations that are established and accepted by society. We do not call them gangs, but they all meet the same fundamental need that a gang meets. Some of these organizations are called tribes, teams, clans, races, fraternities, sororities, and clubs. These organizations meet the need of providing a feeling of safety and giving credibility to one's existence. Things you should consider when you are tempted to become involved in a gang:

1. Ask yourself the question: "Why do I need to be involved?" If you have glaring unmet needs, it is easy to believe that those needs can be met through gang activity. Any time you are drawn to a group of people or an individual, you should seek to know why you are drawn in that direction.

2. What is it that the gang will supply that I cannot get in other places? Many young people find love, acceptance and a sense of belonging in a gang. I would like to submit that these fundamental needs can be found in other places. There is a principle that comes from this Scripture that tells us how to get friends.

> *A man that hath friends must show himself friendly: and there is a friend that sticketh closer than a brother.*
>
> Proverbs 18:24

It is a fact that if you need friends, the only way to get them is to be friendly. I challenge you to initiate friendship by showing yourself friendly. I have many friends, and the reason that I have them is that I am a very friendly person. I have cultivated the ability to go into a room of complete strangers and strike up a conversation, make them feel at ease and comfortable with me. With this ability I am never alone very long because people flock to kind, friendly persons.

3. Consider the long-term consequences of your involvement. Can you name three persons who were deeply involved in gangs and somehow got out of the gangs and lived happily ever after? The odds are against you naming three people. If you can name three people who are doing well, I am sure that you are aware that they were negatively impacted by their gang involvement. One of the greatest talents that a young man can develop is the ability to look at another's mistakes and learn from them. One of the perils of being young is that you have this false belief that somehow you will not get caught and that you will be successful doing something that you have seen others fail at. "Yeah, I'm not going to get caught, I'm too smooth." These are popular last words of many foolish young men.

4. Consider how your other family members will be impacted by your involvement. One of the terrible consequences of gang involvement is that your family will be affected. We all have heard of situations in which ruthless gang members have attacked innocent women and children because of a disagreement they had with another gang member. There is a saying that goes like this: There is no honor among thieves. The Scripture says it like this:

> *But evil men and seducers shall wax worse and worse, deceiving, and being deceived.*
> II Timothy 3:13

This Scripture states that evil men and those who seduce others will get worse and worse as time passes. It also goes on to state that they will deceive or run games on others and they will be deceived in the end. So, God says that if you deceive others, all you are doing is assuring that in the future you will be deceived. There is no escaping this principle or law! So, no matter how nice the gang members appear to be, there will be a deterioration in the relationship as time passes, and your family may be sucked into the confusion.

5. Ask yourself the question: "How will gang involvement restrict my thinking?" One characteristic of gang activity is that it restricts individuality. You must think like the gang and put the interests and mindset of the gang first. You must hate whom they hate and love whom they love. It is a fact that you will become like the people that you hang with. You may deny this all you want to, but the facts are in. I had an older dope addict tell me that: "You can't hang with the coolie boys and don't do dope." The Scripture says it this way:

> *Be not deceived: evil communications corrupt good manners.*
> I Corinthians 15:33

Before you join a gang, consider the mindset of those in the gang and ask yourself the question: "Do I want to think like they think?"

6. If you are being forced to join a gang, what alternatives do you feel you have?
    a. Move (a forced relocation)
    b. Resist involvement
    c. Join a local church
    d._____

The pressure placed on young people to join a gang can be immense. I feel that one of the first things you should do when this happens is to consult with an older, wiser person. If you don't do this, you may make the wrong decision under pressure. Consider having a pastor, police officer, teacher or relative assist you.

Questions
for Introspection and Discussion (to make you think)

1. Have you been pressured to join a gang? Yes___ No___

2. Do you have friends who are in gangs? Yes___ No___

3. Is your self-esteem high enough that you don't need to join a gang? Yes___ No___

4. Do you live in a gang-infested area? Yes___ No___

5. What do you feel are the best defenses against gang activity?_____

6. How do you feel that home life affects gang involvement? _____

7. On the positive side, what groups are you involved in that provide many of the things that a gang provides but without the negatives of gang association?_____

8. What suggestions would you have for the younger brother regarding gangs? _____
_____

Applicable Scriptures: Please have a boy read the Scripture, then use

the questions to facilitate discussion. **Conclude by quoting the Scripture from the Living Bible, which was written for teenagers.** *Please remember that the reading of Scripture according to Isaiah 55:11 is the most important thing you will do with the boys. This section is where the Holy Spirit really works in their hearts, so don't skip it.*

(1) *My son, if sinners entice thee, consent thou not. If they say, Come with us, let us lay wait for blood, let us lurk privily for the innocent without cause: let us swallow them up alive as the grave; and whole, as those that go down into the pit: We shall find all precious substance, we shall fill our houses with spoil: Cast in thy lot among us; let us all have one purse: My son, walk not thou in the way with them; refrain thy foot from their path: For their feet run to evil, and make haste to shed blood.* Proverbs 1:10-16

[Question] **Can you walk away from people who entice you?**

[Question] **It can sound good when people talk about the wrong that they are going to do. How do you avoid getting caught up in their talk?**

[Question] **Do you realize that if you are with a group of boys who commit a crime that you also get caught up in the legal proceedings to follow even if you did not participate in the crime?**

The Living Bible translates Proverbs 1:10-16 like this: *If young toughs tell you, "Come and join us"—turn your back on them! "We'll hide and rob and kill," they say. "Good or bad, we'll treat them all alike. And the loot we'll get! All kinds of stuff! Come on, throw in your lot with us; we'll split with you in equal shares." Don't do it, son! Stay far from men like that, for crime is their way, and murder is their specialty.*

(2) *Discretion shall preserve thee, understanding shall keep thee: To deliver thee from the way of the evil man, from the man that speaketh froward things;* Proverbs 2:11-12

[Question] **Discretion and understanding are worth more than millions of dollars. Do you feel that you have them, and if so, how do you know you have them?**

[Question] **I have seen young men destroyed over stupid stuff. What does this verse say that discretion and understanding will do for you?**

[Question] **Who will discretion and understanding deliver you from?**

The Living Bible translates Proverbs 2:11-12 like this: *You will be given the sense to stay away from evil men who want you to be their partners in crime—men who turn from God's ways to walk down dark and evil paths.*

(3) *Trust in the LORD with all thine heart; and lean not unto thine own understanding. In all thy ways acknowledge him, and he shall direct thy paths.* Proverbs 3:5-6

[Question] **How much are you asked to trust in the Lord?**

[Question] **Why do you feel the Scripture says that you should not lean on your own understanding?**

[Question] **What do you think "in all thy ways" means?**

[Question] **What does God promise to do once you acknowledge Him?**

The Living Bible translates Proverbs 3:4-6 like this: *If you want favor with both God and man, and a reputation for good judgement and common sense, then trust the Lord completely; don't ever trust yourself. In everything you do, put God first, and he will direct you and crown your efforts with success.*

(4) *Happy is the man that findeth wisdom, and the man that getteth understanding.* Proverbs 3:13
[Question] **What is it about having wisdom that can make a man happy?**
[Question] **Do you think it is possible to understand without having wisdom?**
[Question] **Where should a young man look for wisdom?**
The Living Bible translates Proverbs 3:13 like this: *The man who knows right from wrong and has good judgment and common sense is happier than the man who is immensely rich!*

(5) *Strive not with a man without cause, if he have done thee no harm.* Proverbs 3:30
[Question] **Do you pick needless fights?**
[Question] **Do you stop the basketball game arguing, trying to make your point?**
[Question] **Do you dislike people for no apparent reason?**
The Living Bible translates Proverbs 3:30 like this: *Don't get into needless fights.*

(6) *Enter not into the path of the wicked, and go not in the way of evil men. Avoid it, pass not by it, turn from it, and pass away. For they sleep not, except they have done mischief; and their sleep is taken away, unless they cause some to fall. For they eat the bread of wickedness, and drink the wine of violence. But the path of the just is as the shining light, that shineth more and more unto the perfect day. The way of the wicked is as darkness: they know not at what they stumble.* Proverbs 4:14-19
[Question] **A person's path could be defined as their habits or behavior. Do you imitate the behavior of wicked people?**
[Question] **Do you feel that you can flirt with wickedness or wicked people and not get caught?**
[Question] **Do you know people who are not happy unless they are causing someone else pain?**
The Living Bible translates Proverbs 4:14-19 like this: *Don't do as the wicked do. Avoid their haunts—turn away, go somewhere else, for evil men don't sleep until they've done their evil deed for the day. They can't rest unless they cause someone to stumble and fall. They eat and drink wickedness and violence! But the good man walks along in the ever-brightening light of God's favor; the dawn gives way to morning splendor, while the evil man gropes and stumbles in the dark.*

7 How Does Your Size Affect You?

(Endomorph–Ectomorph–Mesomorph)

Definition: Size is the spatial dimensions, proportions, or extent of anything.

CONNECTING WITH AND LEARNING FROM YOUR RICH, PERSONAL, PAINFUL PRODUCTIVE, PAST. Regardless of what body size you have, we all can remember instances where our body size was instrumental in us being perceived a particular way. For example, we all have had to endure the choosing of sides in gym class or in an after-school playground game. Whether you were picked first or last was greatly impacted by your body size. Pick a situation from your past in which your body size was the major reason you were put in that situation. Share with the young men how you have compensated for and used your body to the best advantage.

CAUTION: No body size should be used as an excuse for failure!

CONCERN You should rejoice with the body that you have. God does not make mistakes! A love for yourself and your body is all-important.

CHARGE: If you have neglected or abused your body, ask God to forgive you and stop doing it! If you need help, seek out a professional or someone who has recovered from what you are struggling with.

7 How Does Your Size Affect You?

(Endomorph–Ectomorph–Mesomorph)

I had just passed to the 7th grade when my family moved from the west side to what we called the uptown area of my city. All of my life I had lived on the west side, and at this critical period in my development, we moved. It was very difficult because I had to start all over making new friends on a new side of town.

On one particular day, I rode my bicycle through the neighborhood, hoping to find a friend. I came across some people my age sitting on the loading dock of a paper company. As I pulled up on my bike, I noticed that they were ratting each other or playing the dozens. This was quite amusing until an older, bigger guy named Kenny looked at me and said: "What you laughing at? You need to go home and jump out of those dingaling pants!" (My pants were hand-me-downs from my older brother.) I quickly came back and told him: "I <u>CAN</u> go home and jump out of these dingaling pants, but you <u>CAN'T</u> go home and jump out of those dingaling lips." Everybody laughed, and I had obviously scored a significant point. The only bad part was that Kenny got mad. Now, Kenny was too big and old to jump on me, but there was a guy there who could, named Magoo.

They called him Magoo because he was big for his age and goofy. Kenny said to Magoo: "Hey Magoo, I bet you can't beat him" (talking about me). To this Magoo replied: "Yes I can," Kenny said: "No you can't," to which Magoo said: "Yes I can," and in a matter of seconds I was in a fight with a goofy FAT dude. I felt like I didn't have a friend in the world. There I was, a skinny dude in a fight with a fat dude which was started by an older muscular dude.

Size is very important when you are young. It is also very important to learn how to capitalize on the size that God gave you and use it to your best advantage. Endomorph, ectomorph, and mesomorph, respectively, are the technical names for fat, skinny and muscular body types. Whether or not you know it or want to acknowledge it, your body type has a lot to do with how you view yourself and how others view you. The goal of this chapter is to help you consider your attitude about your body size and help you determine what attitudinal adjustments you need to make in order to have a healthy self-esteem. Also, we want to examine how others (teachers, police officers, store clerks, etc.) relate to your body size.

Let's Consider The Endomorph (Fat Dudes)

Not too long ago, I was visiting with a youth group. There was a young man in the group who was very large. He was an endomorph, or we would say fat. To my amazement this brother was much younger than I thought he was. He appeared to be high school age, but he was only in elementary school.

It is a fact that young people are eating more today than they did in years past, and it is also a fact that fast foods are high in fat content. For this and other reasons, there are many young men who are large for their age. If you are a large young man and have an endomorphic body type, you need to analyze how it has affected you. Is your self-esteem intact? Have you taken the time to analyze why you are big? Is it in your genes or do you just eat a lot?

Sometimes young men will eat when they feel depressed, defeated, helpless and hopeless. Friction in the home can lead young men to eat as a way to escape. When we add to that the various video games which tend to limit exercise, we see why the rate of obesity is increasing.

I want to challenge the endomorph to do several things:

1. Make sure that you are getting enough exercise. As you get older, this need will become more apparent.

2. Develop a discipline regarding your eating habits. Don't eat late at night. Try to eat healthy foods (fruits, vegetables, etc.). If you do this, you will thank yourself for it later.

3. Determine not to be defeated by a weight problem. Never give up. Remember that everyone is struggling with some real or imagined deficiency. Some deficiencies are more visible than others. Remember that your problem is common, and if it is caused by your bad habits, God can help you get over it.

4. Decide where you want to excel in life and pursue excellence with all of your might. You must believe that you are gifted and good at something. Seek to find what that is and get even better at it. I grew up with a friend who had a physical deformity. He was not able to play ball and do many of the things that other young people did. His hobby was collecting model airplanes. While other kids were out playing, he would be inside studying the various types of planes. He learned so much with his childhood hobby that he was able to get a job as an adult with an aerospace company.

5. If you are really bothered by your weight, seek out someone you can talk to about it. This will help you overcome the mental blocks about your weight. Some have overcome the anxiety regarding their weight, and others have learned how to manage their weight. The worst thing that can happen with a weight problem or any other problem is to keep it to yourself.

6. Strive to break the standard stereotypes regarding fat people by being neat, well groomed, and a hard worker. When you conform to the negative stereotypes, people see you as one who is molded by his situation or controlled by others.

7. If you need help, go to an adult and openly express your concern to them and ask them for help. If they don't help you, go to another adult. I know of a child that used to worry me to death about her needs. I did not always have the time or cash to help her, but I appreciated her gumption, zeal, nerve, aggression and goal-oriented personality. She knew that I wanted her to succeed in life, and she challenged me to help her.

Remember, your size will not cause you to fail in life, but your attitude about your size could be your downfall!!

The endomorph should consider how others view fat young men. Consider these facts:

- You look older than you are. Remember that older people aren't exactly sure how to treat you.
- Strive to make your behavior match your perceived age. For example, if you are 12 years old and you look 15, act more mature when in the presence of strangers.
- Remember that if you act aggressive or violent, you will be dealt with as an adult. People are generally afraid of you, so be sure not to give any indication that you are violent.

Let's Consider The Ectomorph (Little Dudes)

Ectomorphs are little dudes. Little dudes have a totally different set of problems than fat dudes. I have a little friend who is an ectomorph. As I have observed him over the years, I have learned some interesting things about ectomorphs from my little friend. I also know a lot from experience because I was an ectomorph as a young man.

Ectomorphs must be careful not to work hard just so that others will accept them. It is characteristic of little dudes to try to overcompensate for their size. It seems like they are always trying to prove something. Little dudes also have been known to have limited patience. When threatened, they will go on the offensive very quickly.

In some cases, ectomorphs retreat from sports and physical activity to the academic arena. The stereotypical 90-pound weakling who makes straight A's is generally an ectomorph. He is the one that the girls look at last, and he may struggle to get a date. Please note that these are just stereotypes and don't have to be true if you are an ectomorph.

I want to challenge the ectomorph to do several things:

1. Take time to stop and consider any feelings of inferiority you have when you are around bigger guys. You will never reach your full potential if your path is lined by negative thoughts regarding those who are bigger than you are.

2. Work to develop the attitude that your size is a unique asset as opposed to a liability. You should view life like you view basketball. Because of my size, there are some positions on the court that I do not play well. On one occasion while playing basketball, I found myself in the hole (under the basket) with the big men. I saw the ball coming down and I jumped up to get it. The only problem is that the big men (some weighing 100 pounds more than I do) saw the ball also, and they jumped to get it. At that moment, I realized that I was not playing the game wisely. So I moved outside and started working on my killer jump shot while using my speed to out-maneuver the big dudes.

75

3. Make a list of the many things that you can do well. To focus on the positive gifts and abilities that you have is a healthy habit. It helps you see the positive side of your existence rather than focusing on what you can't do. You should take the time to write your strengths down on a sheet of paper. Writing these things down will further enhance your understanding and awareness of the areas in which you are strong.

4. Don't be afraid to be smart. Anyone who does not appreciate your God-given brains is either jealous or is not your friend. In either case you should not concern yourself with how they feel about you. I know kids who are so insecure about themselves that they will purposely not do their best in order to fit in with some of the kids who put pressure on them.

5. Be sensitive to the temptation to overcompensate for your size by doing things such as having three girlfriends, dressing crazy or any such thing. To **overcompensate** for your size is to say to the world: "I don't like myself or I'm not satisfied with myself." People can see how you are behaving and will believe that you have a weak personality. Resist the temptation to over-compensate for your size. Please, always do your best, but don't overcompensate.

The small dude needs to consider how others view him. Generally, ectomorphs are seen as less of a threat than endomorphs or mesomorphs. It is advisable for the small dude to have a healthy vocabulary and learn how to use it wisely. Ectomorphs have a tendency to run their mouths. Try to control that temptation and attempt to speak with wisdom. This can help you gain the respect that you may not otherwise get. It is possible for ectomorphs to gain access to positions and opportunities that others may not get because of the fact that they are not physically threatening. Be sure to take advantage of this.

Let's Look At The Mesomorph (Muscular Dudes)

The mesomorph is the muscular type. I live in a college town, and there are a lot of athletes in this town. I frequently watch the University of Illinois football and basketball teams on television to see how the season is going. Not long ago, I was in the grocery store when a van load of athletes came into the store. At first I thought it was an invasion of giants. When they came in the store, it was as if everybody else in the store shrank. Mesomorphs are imposing people.

I have a good friend who is muscular. One day while we were playing, I jumped on his back and wrapped my arms around him in an attempt to hold him. He simply exhaled and lifted his arms, breaking my hold with little to no effort.

In our society, people are impressed with muscular men. It has always been that way with human beings. I think of the children of Israel, who, when they wanted a king, looked on the physical stature of a man named Saul. The Bible says of Saul that from his shoulders up he was higher than any of the people. He was chosen to be the king when the people wanted a king. The interesting thing is that he did not make a good king. You see, a man must be a king on the inside before he can ever be a good king, regardless of what he looks like on the outside.

I want to challenge the mesomorph to do several things:

1. Take advantage of the mystique that comes with having a mesomorphic body type. This mystique can help you get jobs and positions of leadership. There have been many studies done showing that the tall, dark, handsome men get the best jobs. I know that it is unfair, but it is a fact of life that is a plus for the mesomorphs and causes others to work a little harder.

2. Remember that as you get older, the mystique and its advantages will diminish. As with Saul, the mystique wore off and the people were depending on his character, wisdom, integrity, and courage to lead them. Saul was lacking in these areas. Although others may be impressed with your size, don't you be impressed; instead, prepare for your future when size is no longer an asset.

3. Don't neglect to get an education. Once you and your admirers become adults, the fascination over your body will diminish and you will need to be qualified to get a job. This is particularly important with the young males who only want to be in the NFL or NBA. There is nothing sadder than a 6'3" male with no education who almost made it to the big money arena of professional sports. This brother's past great moments on the court are now forgotten, because people will forget quickly. The only thing that can help him now is an education or a rich uncle.

4. Don't allow the athletic community to push you if you don't feel gifted in that area. Just because you are muscular does not mean that you should be an athlete. You will never be a great athlete unless your heart is in it. Another sad situation is the males who play sports and get hurt because they really weren't gifted athletes.

5. Make sure that any woman that you are with has considered your personality as well as your physical attraction. It is a fact that men want beautiful women and women want handsome men. This natural tendency can get you into big trouble in the long run. If she is only interested in you while the crowds are shouting and there is a chance for a professional career, then you are in trouble. You will be better off with a woman that you seek out rather than a woman who seeks you out. (I know I'm right about it.)

Questions
for Introspection and Discussion (to make you think)

1. What is your body type?_____

2. What are you doing to take advantage of it? _____

3. Can you name a specific occasion when your body type came in handy? Explain_____

4. Can you name an occasion when your body type was a source of trouble? Explain_____

5. Have you considered the negatives of your body type?_____

6. Have you talked to someone about any concerns you may have in this area?_____

7. Are you prejudiced against a particular body type? If so, have you figured out why?
Yes___ No___

8. Do your friends represent a variety of body types? Yes___ No___

Applicable Scriptures: Please have a boy read the Scripture, then use the questions to facilitate discussion. Conclude by quoting the Scripture from the Living Bible which was written for teenagers. *Please remember that the reading of Scripture according to Isaiah 55:11 is the most important thing you will do with the boys. This section is where the Holy Spirit really works in their hearts, so don't skip it.*

(1) *The glory of young men is their strength: and the beauty of old men is the grey head.*
Proverbs 20:29
[Question] **Do you consider yourself strong, average or weak?**
[Question] **Are you aware that if you keep living that you will one day be weak?**
[Question] **Are you taking care of your body so that you will one day have gray hair?**
The Living Bible translates Proverbs 20:29 like this: *The glory of young men is their strength; of old men, their experience.*

(2) *Give not thy strength unto women, nor thy ways to that which destroyeth kings.*
Proverbs 31:3
[Question] **Are you wise in your dealings with women?**
[Question] **Do you know the things that destroy Kings, Presidents or NBA stars?**
[Question] **How do you plan to protect yourself from making these mistakes?**
The Living Bible translates Proverbs 31:3 like this: *Do not spend your time with women—the royal pathway to destruction.*

(3) *Then said I, Wisdom is better than strength:* Ecclesiastes 9:16a
[Question] **Which would you prefer to be, the strongest man or the wisest man?**
[Question] **Is it kool to be smart or are you considered weak when you study?**
[Question] **What do you tell yourself about wisdom?**
The Living Bible translates Ecclesiastes 9:16a like this: *Then I realized that wisdom is better than strength,*

(4) *And there we saw the giants, the sons of Anak, which come of the giants: and we were in our own sight as grasshoppers, and so we were in their sight.* Numbers 13:33
[Question] **There is not a lot that you can do to change your body type. Are you satisfied with your body type and determined to work with what you got?**
[Question] **The sons of Anak were giants. There will always be big men in our world. What do you say to yourself when you stand beside a big man?**
[Question] **Are you a grasshopper in your sight?**
The Living Bible translates Numbers 13:33 like this: *And we saw some of the Anakim there, descendants of the ancient race of giants. We felt like grasshoppers before them, they were so tall!*

(5) *And Jesus increased in wisdom and stature, and in favor with God and man.* Luke 2:52

[Question] **Are you wiser today than you were last year?**

[Question] **Give me one reason why you feel you are wiser.**

[Question] **Are you physically stronger this year than you were last year?**

[Question] **Do people enjoy your presence more this year than they did last year?**

The Living Bible translates Luke 2:52 like this: *So Jesus grew both tall and wise, and was loved by God and man.*

(6) *And he had a son, whose name was Saul, a choice young man, and a goodly: and there was not among the children of Israel a goodlier person than he: from his shoulders and upward he was higher than any of the people.* I Samuel 9:2

[Question] **Saul was chosen to be King because he looked good. Do you feel our President was elected because he looks good?**

[Question] **Being tall, dark, and handsome has its benefits. How can you compensate if you are short, light and ugly?**

The Living Bible translates I Samuel 9:2 like this: *His son Saul was the most handsome man in Israel. And he was head and shoulders taller than anyone else in the land!*

Make This Statement To The Boys:

Before we go on to the next chapter, tell me which Scripture made you mad, glad or made you think.

Note to the Mentor: As a result of this lesson, are there any prayer requests that should be added to your list and forwarded to your prayer partners?

Notes:

Mentor: Read this page before you meet with your boys.

8 Drugs (The Contemporary Slavemaster)

Definition: A drug is a habit forming medicinal substance, especially a narcotic.

CONNECTING WITH AND LEARNING FROM YOUR RICH, PERSONAL, PAINFUL, PRODUCTIVE, PAST. Most mature men have known friends who did drugs and are no longer with us. As I write this, I am sad as my mind views faces that are no longer among the living. Maybe you personally experimented with drugs. If you feel led, you may want to be transparent with the young men and share how you overcame your involvement with drugs.

CAUTION: Be sure to present this chapter with mercy in your heart for those who seem to be hopelessly hooked on drugs. At the same time, freely show your disapproval of Blacks who for a dollar sell others into a slavery that is worse than what was endured under the White plantation master. **SHAME ON BLACK MEN WHO SEND OTHER BLACK MEN, WOMEN AND CHILDREN INTO ADDICTIVE BONDAGE FOR THE DOLLAR!!!!**

CONCERN: I want the young men to see that drugs comprise one aspect or front in the attack against the black male. In my opinion, if we could begin to see today's drugs and those who push them in the same light as we saw the White slavemaster, we could kick the habit sooner.

CHARGE: Resolve to never experiment with drugs. From cigarettes to cocaine, a drug is a drug is a drug. Your body will begin to demand any drug that it becomes biologically dependent upon.

ACTIVITY: A visit to prison or jail or drug treatment wing of a hospital would be appropriate. Discuss those who have lost everything as a result of drug activity.

8 Drugs (The Contemporary Slavemaster)

When a person gets high, that person alters his state of consciousness. When young people drink alcohol, smoke pot or even do 'caine, they are altering their state of consciousness. This is accomplished in many cases by decreasing the amount of oxygen that goes to the brain. For each drug, the body's function is altered in a manner in which the conscious state of the individual is altered. In many cases, people think this is fun, and they will laugh and giggle while high; but in reality serious damage is being done to the body while in this state.

So I would like to suggest to you today that when we consider the issue of drugs, we should look at ourselves and determine how do we handle reality. Do we seek to escape from our world and problems by any means? Here are some things to consider:

How Healthy Is Your Personal Esteem?
A person's self-esteem will affect their need for crutches. I was always amazed by people that I grew up with who could look at temptation (drugs, women, money) in the eye and say: "I don't want any!" This would always blow my mind. In most cases, the reason a person can say this is that they know who they are and know what they want in life. Earlier chapters in this book have pointed out the need to really search to determine strengths and weaknesses so that we are aware of our areas of vulnerability.

How Do You Cope With Personal Problems?
Problems can be devastating! The problems of youth only compound themselves in later life. One of the greatest gifts you can give yourself is the gift of studying and applying problem-solving skills. No problem should be allowed to have a greater influence on you than it deserves. Many times it is our inappropriate response to a minor problem that creates a bigger problem. I have learned (as ridiculous as this sounds) to view each problem as an opportunity to grow, especially in the area of relationships.

How Aggressively Do You Shun Drugs?
Just the other day, I was talking to a young man who had been on drugs for two years. He stated that it all started when he innocently went to a party. As the party progressed, the drugs were put on the table. He stated that he knew he should have left immediately. Unfortunately, he didn't leave and his life is currently in shambles as a result.

It is a wise man who walks away from drugs and any form of pressure from "friends" who would bring drugs into his presence. A simple point to remember is that anyone who would attempt to get you high is not a friend but a minister (servant) of satan. Have predetermined boundaries or limits when it comes to dealing with drugs. Those boundaries should be to go to all lengths to avoid them.

Understanding The Bigger Picture.

Drugs are destroying Black communities and weakening the strength of the United States of America. The question has been asked: "Is there a conspiracy against Blacks and have drugs been used to do Blacks in?" Well it doesn't take a rocket scientist to figure out that drugs have always been sent to the ghetto. It was never intended for cocaine to hit the suburbs, but if you dig one ditch, you had better dig two. The bigger picture shows that there are people who would like to destroy the Black community but they can only do it with our cooperation.

Planned Parenthood's goal in the beginning was to limit the number of undesirables (Blacks and Hispanics) so they placed the abortion clinics in Black neighborhoods and made abortion free. The liquor companies don't place advertisements in the suburbs but in the Black communities so that the weak are constantly bombarded with visuals to stimulate their weaknesses. Morality in America in general, and in Black America particularly, is at an all-time low.

So, the big picture is one of rapid moral, civil, social, and religious degeneration of a country which is affecting all. The greatest damage is being done to those who have the least power to resist, the minorities. The only redeeming fact in this whole scenario is that YOU CAN CHOOSE NOT TO PARTICIPATE IN THE DESTRUCTION.

I have decided that I am not going to be poor, illiterate, uneducated, deprived, abused, victimized, oppressed and many other things. Inasmuch as I have control of my life and can do as I please, I have chosen the route of success. You can too.

A Drug Is A Drug Is A Drug

Crack cocaine is not the only drug. Cigarettes, alcohol, snuff, and beer are all drugs. If you are addicted to one drug, you are no better than a person who is addicted to another drug. Don't seek to rate drugs according to their destructive qualities but according to their addictive qualities. I have been told that it is just as hard to get off of cigarettes as it is to get off of cocaine.

Remember that the only successful approach to drugs is never to introduce your body to them.

84

Questions
for Introspection and Discussion (to make you think)

1. Are you committed to staying drug-free? Yes___ No___

2. Do you see drugs as the enemy of yourself and your community? Yes___ No___

3. Are you developing coping mechanisms so that you will not need to find relief through drugs? Yes___ No___ If so, name some of your coping mechanisms_____

4. How many people can you name who have been destroyed by drugs? _____

5. Is there anything in your life now that is controlling you? If so, what?_____

6. Do you feel that a personal relationship with Jesus Christ compares to getting high on drugs? Yes___ No___

> *The thief cometh not, but for to steal, and to kill, and to destroy: I am come that they might have life, and that they might have it more abundantly.*
> John 10:10

Applicable Scriptures: Please have a boy read the Scripture, then use the questions to facilitate discussion. Conclude by quoting the Scripture from the Living Bible which was written for teenagers. *Please remember that the reading of Scripture according to Isaiah 55:11 is the most important thing you will do with the boys. This section is where the Holy Spirit really works in their hearts, so don't skip it.*

(1) *All things are lawful unto me, but all things are not expedient: all things are lawful for me, but I will not be brought under the power of any.* I Corinthians 6:12

[Question] **It is a fact that you have the right to take drugs. The question is, are you prepared to deal with the consequences of drug consumption?**

[Question] **Do you focus on the things in life that are expedient like: staying alive, getting an education, helping others or do you focus on self pleasure?**

[Question] **Many people are under bondage to (slaves to) habits that they started in fun. I know drug addicts who say: "the first train ride to hell is free, but you pay for the rest." Are you under bondage to anything right now?**

The Living Bible translates I Corinthians 6:12 like this: *I can do anything I want to if Christ has not said no, but some of these things aren't good for me. Even if I am allowed to do them, I'll refuse to if I think they might get such a grip on me that I can't easily stop when I want to.*

(2) *Wine is a mocker, strong drink is raging: and whosoever is deceived thereby is not wise.* Proverbs 20:1

[Question] **You have the right to drink, but you also have the right to act like a fool. Do you feel you can drink and not eventually become a slave to the bottle?**

[Question] **This Scripture says that strong drink is _____? Have you ever seen anyone in a drunken rage?**

[Question] **This Scripture says that it is not wise to do what?**

The Living Bible translates Proverbs 20:1 like this: *Wine gives false courage; hard liquor leads to brawls; what fools men are to let it master them, making them reel drunkenly down the street!*

(3) *Hear thou, my son, and be wise, and guide thine heart in the way. Be not among winebibbers; among riotous eaters of flesh: For the drunkard and the glutton shall come to poverty: and drowsiness shall clothe a man with rags.* Proverbs 23:19-21

[Question] **In the first sentence of this Scripture, the son is asked to do three things. What are they?**

[Question] **"Be not" is a command. You are commanded not to be among winebibbers. How would we say that today?**

[Question] **In the last sentence of this Scripture a promise is made to the drunkard which also applies to the person who smokes cocaine.**

The Living Bible translates Proverbs 23:19-21 like this: *O my son, be wise and stay in Gods paths; don't carouse with drunkards and gluttons, for they are on their way to poverty. And remember that too much sleep clothes a man with rags.*

(4) *Pride goeth before destruction, and a haughty spirit before a fall.* Proverbs 16:18

[Question] **Sometimes pride keeps us from listening to wise advice. Are you receiving the advice that your mentor is giving or are you being prideful?**

[Question] **What do you think that "pride goeth before destruction means?"**

[Question] **What do you think a haughty spirit is and do you have one?**

The Living Bible translates Proverbs 16:18 like this: *Pride goes before destruction and haughtiness before a fall.*

(5) *He that is soon angry dealeth foolishly: and a man of wicked devices is hated.* Proverbs 14:17

[Question] **Do you have a quick temper?**

[Question] **Is it wise to make decisions while you are angry?**

The Living Bible translates Proverbs 14:17 like this: *A short-tempered man is a fool. He hates the man who is patient.*

(6) *Lest satan should get an advantage of us: for we are not ignorant of his devices.*
II Corinthians 2:11

[Question] **Drugs are satanic in origin. Do you see drugs as spiritual in nature or do you see them as something that people just choose to do?**

[Question] **What do you think the term "not ignorant of his devices" means?**

[Question] **Are you wise to the tactics of satan?**

The Living Bible translates II Corinthians 2:11 like this: *A further reason for forgiveness is to keep from being outsmarted by satan; for we know what he is trying to do.*

Make This Statement To The Boys: Before we go on to the next chapter, tell me which Scripture made you made, glad or made you think.

Note to the Mentor: As a result of this lesson, are there any prayer requests that should be added to your list and forwarded to your prayer partners?

Notes:_____

_____

_____

_____

_____

_____

9 My First Job

Definition: A job is a post of employment.

CONNECTING WITH AND LEARNING FROM YOUR RICH, PERSONAL, PAINFUL, PRODUCTIVE, PAST. A person's first job is an experience that few forget. Be honest, was your first job a disaster? If it was, share the bad and tell how you worked it out and learned from it. Share your current struggles and how you are seeking to overcome them.

CAUTION: It is a normal process to begin a job as the lowest-paid worker. This should not cause any one to slack on their work or to have a bad attitude.

CONCERN: The development of a company mindset is extremely important if you are to be successful on your job. Never isolate the work that you do from the work of others. You are part of a team that will benefit from your positive attitude.

CHARGE: Trust God to promote you as you work hard. Remember that even if your boss is not the best, God observes how you work and HE promotes us when HE feels that we can handle it.

> *For promotion cometh neither from the east, nor from the west, nor from the south. But God is the judge: he putteth down one, and setteth up another.*
> Psalm 75:6-7

ACTIVITY: Arrange a mock job interview with a businessman who will take them through the ropes. Give them a taste of what it will be like.

9 My First Job

I had hung out in the music store for some time now. I loved music, played several instruments and loved to hang out in the store. On this particular day, I was on my way to find a job when the store owner asked me what I was doing. I told him that I was on my way to get a job, and he stated that I could work for him. This was a dream come true!

What I did not anticipate was Mr. Pratt. Mr. Pratt was my immediate supervisor. Mr. Pratt was a White man about 6'2" tall and right at 300 pounds. At 15 years old, I was 120 pounds soaking wet. As I look back, I appreciate Mr. Pratt, for he solidified many basic principles that my dad taught me which have contributed to my success in life.

I am going to share with you some basic things that young men need to incorporate into their success plans that I learned on my first job.

The Handshake (the fine line between firmness and arrogance)
In this world of fickleness, there is a need for genuine commitments. When two men shake hands, a lot of information is transmitted. A handshake can tell you if a person is genuinely glad to meet you or if they are shaking just as a formality.

Mr. Pratt, my 6'2", 300-pound boss, taught me how to shake hands when I was 15 years old. He met me as I came to work each day, extended his huge hand to me and shook it. His grip was almost unbearable. He would tell me: "When you shake a man's hand, look him in the eye!" I learned how to do that. After some practice, I learned how to confidently shake the hand of a man who:
- was bigger than I was.
- held the power to fire me, and
- Presented a challenge because of his high expectations of me.

The ability to shake hands properly can determine if you get a job and how others treat you, and it also gives an indication of the spirit that lies within you. A famous blind musician stated that he could shake a woman's hand and tell how tall she was and how much she weighed, and the texture of her skin told him additional things. Well, I am not talking about shaking a woman's hand. I am talking about shaking a man's hand. Be careful to be genuine when you shake hands with someone, because a discerning person can tell when you are not genuine. Also, don't overdo the macho handshake. In other words, don't try too hard to impress another man by squeezing his hand.

It is not how hard you squeeze his hand, it is simply being firm and genuine that conveys through your handshake a sense of purity of character that will impress men of integrity. Your handshake can convey to some degree the content of your character.

The Importance Of Being Dependable

> *Confidence in an unfaithful man in time of trouble is like a broken tooth, and a foot out of joint.*
>
> Proverbs 25:19

This proverb very accurately describes how it feels to be let down when you are depending on someone. An employer is dependant on those who work for him. Each man is like a link in a chain that depends on the strength of the other links to successfully complete the task at hand.

Just the other day, I watched one of my favorite football teams in a playoff game. The score was tied with seconds to go, and it was up to the punter to kick an easy field goal. He missed! His failure, though unintentional, let the whole team down. When someone depends on you, don't let them down. If you develop the discipline of being dependable, you will have in your possession part of a strong foundation to build a successful life upon. Don't ever allow yourself to be like <u>a broken tooth or a foot out of joint.</u>

The Importance Of Being Punctual

Any event that I am involved in I strongly insist on starting on time. The reason is that it helps develop a positive attitude about what you are doing. In the business world, you don't get ahead by being on time—you get ahead by being **early**! Your punctuality speaks volumes about you before you ever open your mouth. When you are punctual, people perceive you as:

    1. Organized
    2. Prepared
    3. Anxious for the task at hand
    4. A potential leader

While in school, be at least three minutes early for each class and take that time to get yourself together for the class. Please believe me when I tell you that teachers notice this and that it will help you in the long run.

The Importance Of Being Trustworthy

> *A wise servant shall have rule over a son that causeth shame, and shall have part of the inheritance among the brethren.*   Proverbs 17:2

Not long ago, a business in my town went bankrupt. The reason that the owner gave for going under was that his employees ripped him off. Employers are frantically searching for trustworthy employees to man their businesses. We live in an age when respect for the possessions of others is at an all-time low. When you determine that you will be trustworthy, you have increased your marketability. It is still possible to get a job and be promoted because you can be trusted. Trust is something that is invaluable.

> *A good name is rather to be chosen than great riches, and loving favour rather than silver and gold.*   Proverbs 22:1

Here is a good place to make the point that it is important to establish yourself with a group of reputable, responsible persons who will attest to your trustworthiness. This can be done by establishing your integrity in school, becoming an active member in a local church or some reputable civic organization, or establishing any affiliation that is positive. You never know when you will need people on your side. Your first job is very important because it is the beginning of a lifetime of work. If you take the time to work on these basics that we are discussing, your working career will get off to a good start.

The Importance Of Being Professional On The Job

I stopped by a fast food restaurant the other day because I needed some food in a hurry. The brother who was flippin' the burgers was involved in a heated discussion with his woman about a problem they had had the night before. I was not interested in their personal problems because I wanted a double burger, fries and a large drink (in a hurry). The brother stood there talking to his woman for at least three minutes (which is a long time) during the peak lunchtime rush hour. Now, check this out: If I had been his boss, I would have fired the brother on the spot!! He was acting unprofessionally on the job. He was causing the customers to become dissatisfied, which translates into lost funds for the business.

There is a time to talk to your woman, and it is not while you are being paid to work. I know that there are emergencies, but I am not talking about an emergency. What I am talking about is displaying the attitude that the boss should pay you regardless of how hard you work and how bad your attitude is. The bottom line is to give the man a good day's work for your pay. This is how you get ahead in life.

The Importance of Being Able To Take A Rebuke

It amazes me how so many young people have so much pride that they cannot receive a rebuke (correction). A rebuke properly given is in your best interest. Let me say that I appreciate rebukes because I know that they are designed to eliminate future mistakes and pain.

> *Reprove not a scorner, lest he hate thee: rebuke a wise man, and he will love thee.*
> Proverbs 9:8

> *A wise son heareth his father's instruction: but a scorner heareth not rebuke.*
> Proverbs 13:1

> *Poverty and shame shall be to him that refuseth instruction: but he that regardeth reproof shall be honored.*
> Proverbs 13:18

When a young person says: "Kaint nobody tell me what to do but my momma!" that young person IS A FOOL! When the momma says: "Kaint nobody tell my baby what to do!" that momma is a fool. The wise person knows that rebukes come from all people. As an adult, I am frequently rebuked by children. Not long ago, I was worried about a situation. I was not trying to solve it—I was just worrying about it. A child said to me: "Don't worry about it. It will be all right." I received the rebuke.

Rebukes come from a variety of sources, even strangers. Those who you come in contact with on a daily basis are in your life to help mold you. When their comments or criticisms are right, learn to listen to them and respond appropriately, and you will be a wiser man in the end.

Questions
for Introspection and Discussion (to make you think)

1. Have you had your first job? Yes___ No___

2. On my first job, Mr. Pratt was on my case. Who was on your case on your first job?_____

3. I stated how I learned from Mr. Pratt. What did you learn from your situation?
_____
_____

4. How do you shake hands with a male your own age?_____
_____

5. How do you shake hands with a man who is more powerful than you are?_____
_____

6. Tell the truth, shame the devil! Are you dependable? Yes___ No___

7. Can you be counted on to fulfill responsibilities that are not your favorite things to do?
Yes___ No___

8. What do you feel are some of the benefits of being on time?_____

9. Tell the truth, shame the devil! If you worked in a store and you were left all alone in the store with $200.00 cash (that nobody knew about), could you be trusted? Yes___ No___ Please remember that it is normal to consider taking the money. That is called temptation, but because you know that it is wrong, you don't take the money. That's called integrity and self-control.

> *There hath no temptation taken you but such as is common to man: but God is faithful, who will not suffer you to be tempted above that ye are able; but will with the temptation also make a way to escape, that ye may be able to bear it.* I Corinthians 10:13

10. If you were picked up tonight by the police because you looked like the 5'9" Black male who robbed a little old lady today, how many older people (with integrity, not your homeys) could come to the police station and say: "I KNOW HE DIDN'T DO IT!! Not this guy, you MUST!! have the wrong man!" List the people:_____
_____

11. Are you able to take a rebuke when it is properly given? Yes___ No___

12. Can you think of a time when you refused a rebuke which you should have received?_____

Applicable Scriptures: Please have a boy read the Scripture, then use the questions to facilitate discussion. Conclude by quoting the Scripture from the Living Bible, which was written for teenagers. *Please remember that the reading of Scripture according to Isaiah 55:11 is the most important thing you will do with the boys. This section is where the Holy Spirit really works in their hearts, so don't skip it.*

(1) *Confidence in an unfaithful man in time of trouble is like a broken tooth, and a foot out of joint.* Proverbs 25:19

[Question] **Are you an unfaithful man?**

[Question] **A broken tooth and a foot out of joint are worthless and painful. Do you know of any brothers who are not worth anything?**

[Question] **Do people call on you when they are in trouble?**

The Living Bible translates Proverbs 25:19 like this: *Putting confidence in an unreliable man is like chewing with a sore tooth, or trying to run on a broken foot.*

(2) *A wise servant shall have rule over a son that causeth shame, and shall have part of the inheritance among the brethren.* Proverbs 17:2

[Question] **Do you feel it is possible to move up in a company if you work hard?**

[Question] **Some sons of rich fathers grow up with a wasteful attitude. Why do you think this is?**

The Living Bible translates Proverbs 17:2 like this: *A wise slave will rule his master's wicked sons and share their estate.*

(3) *A good name is rather to be chosen than great riches, and loving favour rather than silver and gold.* Proverbs 22:1

[Question] **Do you have a name (reputation) that is positive?**

[Question] **How do you feel it affects you when you walk around with an attitude?**

[Question] **Which would you rather have, a good name or money?**

The Living Bible translates Proverbs 22:1 like this: *IF YOU MUST choose, take a good name rather than great riches; for to be held in loving esteem is better than silver and gold.*

(4) *Reprove not a scorner, lest he hate thee: rebuke a wise man, and he will love thee.* Proverbs 9:8

[Question] **Can anybody tell you anything?**

[Question] **Would you have problems taking directions from your boss?**

[Question] **What man loves you and gives directions to you?**

The Living Bible translates Proverbs 9:8 like this: *If you rebuke a mocker, you will only get a smart retort; yes, he will snarl at you. So don't bother with him; he will only hate you for trying to help him. But a wise man, when rebuked, will love you all the more.*

(5) *A wise son heareth his father's instruction: but a scorner heareth not rebuke.* Proverbs 13:1

[Question] **Are you a wise son?**

[Question] **A father is not only your biological dad, but other men who care about you. Do you hear their instruction?**

The Living Bible translates Proverbs 13:1 like this: *A WISE YOUTH accepts his father's rebuke; a young mocker doesn't.*

(6) *Poverty and shame shall be to him that refuseth instruction: but he that regardeth reproof shall be honored. Proverbs 13:18*

[Question] **Do you see any relationship between poverty and stubbornness?**

The Living Bible translates Proverbs 13:18 like this: *If you refuse criticism you will end in poverty and disgrace; if you accept criticism you are on the road to fame.*

Additional Scriptures Used In Chapter Nine As Found In The Living Bible

But remember this—the wrong desires that come into your life aren't anything new and different. Many others have faced exactly the same problems before you. And no temptation is irresistible. You can trust God to keep the temptation from becoming so strong that you can't stand up against it, for he has promised this and will do what he says. He will show you how to escape temptation's power so that you can bear up patiently against it.

I Corinthians 10:13

Only a fool despises his father's advice; a wise son considers each suggestion.

Proverbs 15:5

Make This Statement To The Boys:

Before we go on to the next chapter, tell me which Scripture made you mad, glad or made you think.

Note to the Mentor: As a result of this lesson, are there any prayer requests that should be added to your list and forwarded to your prayer partners?

Mentor: Read this page before you meet with your boys.

10 Your Concept Of The Work Ethic

Definitions: Work is exertion or effort directed to produce something.
An ethic is a body of moral principles or values.
Work Ethic in everyday language is how you feel about work.

CONNECTING WITH AND LEARNING FROM YOUR RICH, PERSONAL, PAINFUL, PRODUCTIVE PAST. How were you indoctrinated to work? Did you learn the value of work early in life or later? Did you have someone to model work for you, or did you grow up with a check coming to your house? Share the development of your work ethic with the young men.

CAUTION: Help the young men understand that there is no escaping work in this life. To refuse to develop a work ethic will make you miserable when you eventually do have to work. To continue to reject the development of a healthy work ethic will eventually lead you to crime.

CONCERN: I am worried about any young man who rebels at this point. When this happens the young man and his problem should be privately placed on the prayer list.

CHARGE: Don't strive for quick money, because there is no such thing. The only way to get quick money is to hurt someone.

ACTIVITY: When going through a mock job interview, ask the employer about his concept of a healthy work ethic.

10 Your Concept Of The Work Ethic

A man or young man who does not have a healthy work ethic is ruined, messed up, and going nowhere fast. A work ethic can be defined as "the knowledge and acceptance of the fact that work is necessary for survival." This ethic is in grave danger today. One of the factors that has contributed to the demise of the work ethic is welfare and invisible dads. When a child grows up in a home in which a check comes in the mail each month without any effort on the part of his mother, this child will not see the immediate benefits of labor.

The concept of getting something for nothing can be more powerful than the concept of working for your money. In reality, what we see and experience generally has more influence than what we are told to do. So, in this sense welfare is bad because it has erased the work ethic from much of the younger generation of American youth.

I firmly believe that young people should be taught that if you are not willing to work for what you want, then you won't get it. Let's look at some specific guidelines that will help you develop a good work ethic:

1. Nobody owes you anything!

> *For even when we were with you, this we commanded you, that if any would not work, neither should he eat.*
>
> I Thessalonians 3:10

Even your parents aren't required by God or the government to supply all of your wants, but only your needs (food, clothing, shelter, etc.). If you have had the benefit of a generous upbringing, please note that it won't last. After I found out about Santa, my Christmas list almost disappeared. There is going to come a time in your life when nobody will foot your bill and you will have to decide to work or to steal.

My suggestion is that you develop a strong work ethic now so that you can survive in the future. I was blessed to have a father who was a jack-of-all-trades. As a result I learned to paint, wax floors, cut grass, do basic carpentry and so forth. Let me make a RADICAL suggestion to you: Find an adult male and help him work.

Help him for FREE if you have to so that you can get some experience!

You will be the richer as a result. As an adult, I purchased a run-down house to remodel. I did the plumbing as a result of watching a plumber and the painting as a result of watching a painter.

I repeat (in case you fainted the first time), find an adult to learn a skill from. Let me put it like this. Have you ever seen those pictures that people take with books in the background? The books are fake, but they are designed to make it look like you are standing in a law library. When you stand there in front of the books, it is implied that you have read many of them. People want to have a lot of knowledge in their brains. Well, when you are born, your brain is like a library with just a few books on the shelves. Every time you learn something new, you place a new book on the shelf in the skills section of your brain's library. Please note that all books are not the same, but everything that you learn in life represents a book in your mental library. Try to avoid placing worthless books on the shelves in your mind's library because in the future, all that you can get out of life will be based on what you have on the shelf in that library. I would like to repeat my radical statement: FIND AN ADULT MALE TO LEARN A SKILL FROM EVEN IF YOU HAVE TO WORK FOR FREE!!

2. Evaluate what you have seen modeled.

When it comes to your work ethic, you need to analyze what you have seen modeled while you were young. I can remember my dad coming home at the end of the day after a hard day of physical labor. On one particular day, my mother met him at the door and with a sad face informed him that we had no dinner. My dad sighed, looked at me and said: "Come on Bud, let's go." We then walked to one of his many side jobs, cleaned and cut grass for enough cash for dinner.

This memory is indelibly, irrevocably, ineffaceably, ineradicably stamped on my memory. In other words, I won't forget it. I was impressed with my dad and consider his example of true manhood one of my greatest assets. What about you? What did you see as a child?

> ...Did your parents work?
> ...Did a check come to the house each month?
> ...Do you get angry when you think about the fact that you must work now in school and

someday in the market place?

As you ask yourself these questions, you can begin to identify any unhealthy attitudes in your mind and then challenge them.

3. Work hard in college now or work hard for the rest of your life.

Our society values a college education. Though it is true that a college education does not guarantee a good job, it does give you a better chance of getting a good job than you have with just a high school diploma. With this in mind, it pays to suffer through college with the hopes of a better-paying job after college. I guess this thought could be summarized by saying that you should work with a future goal in mind as opposed to working just for a check today. If you work just for a check today, you limit your chances for advancement and may still be on the same level years from now.

4. Never quit a job for these reasons:

A. You don't like it. This is not a good enough reason to quit a job. As a matter of fact, most of the jobs you will have in this life you won't like. So it comes down to discipline. If you have a job, you should do a good job and exhibit a good attitude even if you don't like the job. When you do this, you develop skills which prepare you for a better job.

B. Somebody made you mad. This is no reason to quit because no matter where you work, somebody will eventually make you mad. In some cases they will make you mad hoping that you will quit. God wants to use the situation even if it is UNFAIR to teach you, so don't quit!

C. You think they are prejudiced. Despite all the laws and attempts by our government and the Church, prejudice is here to stay. Want to hear something that will surprise you? Even Black people are prejudiced toward other Black people, so it is impossible to escape. The reality of the matter is that the work environment is usually a hostile environment where people are out for themselves. As a result of this, you will have problems whether they are racially motivated or not. Now that I am grown, I know of many situations where because of my youth I have accused a White man of being prejudiced when I now realize that he was just doing his job. Be careful not to use a claim of prejudice as a crutch for your ineffectiveness.

D. You are the only Black. In this situation, you must learn to capitalize on this and not let it work against you. When I am in these situations, I see myself as a teacher because everyone there will be taught by me. Staying in this environment will cause you to be alert and work for perfection, so don't quit!

5. Never quit until you have another job!
    A. Always give proper notice before quitting. This is very simply having a professional attitude about yourself. Not only is it a professional attitude, but it is a polite attitude. Be considerate.

    B. Don't burn bridges. Young people too often leave a situation in anger, cussin' someone out or doing something that would leave a bad memory in the minds of those at the job. This can work against you when you go to your next job. Employers talk and share the good and bad about past employees. Not only this, but you may need to go back to that previous employer in the future for employment or for a recommendation for another job.

God will honor you if you work hard on your job. Please realize that men may diss you for flippin' burgers, but if you do it with the right attitude, you will get opportunities for advancement.

For promotion cometh neither from the east, nor from the west, nor from the south. But God is the judge: he putteth down one, and setteth up another.
        Psalm 75:6-7

Questions
for Introspection and Discussion (to make you think)

1. How would you describe your work ethic?_____

2. Are you satisfied with your work ethic? Yes___ No___

3. What have you been told by your parents or family about your work ethic?_____

_____

4. What have you been told by teachers and others about your work ethic?_____

5. Tell the truth, shame the devil: Are you l-a-z-y? Yes___ No___

6. If so, what do you plan to do about it?_____

7. Would you rather have someone give you something or work for it?_____

8. Name five men that you know who display a good work ethic:

       a_____

       b_____

       c_____

       d_____

       e_____

Applicable Scriptures: Please have a boy read the Scripture, then use the questions to facilitate discussion. Conclude by quoting the Scripture from the Living Bible, which was written for teenagers. *Please remember that the reading of Scripture according to Isaiah 55:11 is the most important thing you will do with the boys. This section is where the Holy Spirit really works in their hearts, so don't skip it.*

(1) *Go to the ant, thou sluggard; consider her ways, and be wise: Which having no guide, overseer, or ruler, provideth her meat in the summer, and gathereth her food in the harvest. How long wilt thou sleep, O sluggard? When wilt thou arise out of thy sleep? Yet a little sleep, a little slumber, a little folding of the hands to sleep: So shall thy poverty come as one that travelleth, and thy want as an armed man.* Proverbs 6:6-11

[Questions] **What do you feel we can learn from an ant?**

[Questions] **What ant characteristics should we imitate?**

[Questions] **According to this Scripture, what causes poverty?**

The Living Bible translates Proverbs 6:6-11 like this: *Take a lesson from the ants, you lazy fellow. Learn from their ways and be wise! For though they have no king to make them work, yet they labor hard all summer, gathering food for the winter. But you—all you do is sleep. When will you wake up? "Let me sleep a little longer!" Sure, just a little more! And as you sleep, poverty creeps upon you like a robber and destroys you; want attacks you in full armor.*

(2) *He becometh poor that dealeth with a slack hand: but the hand of the diligent maketh rich. He that gathereth in summer is a wise son: but he that sleepeth in harvest is a son that causeth shame.* Proverbs 10:4,5

[Questions] **How would you describe your hand?**

[Questions] **Gathering in the summer means preparing while you are young. How are you preparing for your future?**

[Questions] **Many of our young men are sleeping (goofing off, doing drugs, in prison) during their most productive years. What do you plan to be doing between your 25th and 45th birthdays?**

The Living Bible translates Proverbs 10:4-5 like this: *Lazy men are soon poor; hard workers get rich. A wise youth makes hay while the sun shines, but what a shame to see a lad who sleeps away his hour of opportunity.*

(3) *He that tilleth his land shall be satisfied with bread: but he that followeth vain persons is void of understanding.* Proverbs 12:11

[Questions] **Are you a hard worker? Do you understand that while you are young, school is your most important job? Are you doing your job?**

[Questions] **Do you believe that if you work hard, you will have the things you need?**

[Questions] **Do you believe that it is stupid to run after the party crowd?**

The Living Bible translates Proverbs 12:11 like this: *Hard work means prosperity; only a fool idles away his time.*

(4) *The labour of the righteous tendeth to life: the fruit of the wicked to sin.* Proverbs 10:16

[Questions] **Do the things that you like to spend your time doing lead to a better quality of life?**

[Questions] **Each life produces fruit. When you think of a person who is dead, you think of the fruit of their life. What type of fruit is your life producing?**

[Questions] **Wicked fruit flows naturally from a wicked person's life. God specialized in using young people's lives to produce good fruit. Are you willing to let Jesus produce good fruit in your life? If you are, don't be ashamed, say it out loud: "Jesus, I give you my permission to produce good fruit through my life!"**

The Living Bible translates Proverbs 10:16 like this: *A good man's earnings advance the cause of righteousness. The evil man squanders his on sin.*

(5) *For even when we were with you, this we commanded you, that if any would not work, neither should he eat.* II Thessalonians 3:10

[Questions] **Do you believe that healthy people should be given a check each month when there is nothing wrong with them?**

[Questions] **Should a rich person be required to give to a poor person who will not work?**

[Questions] **Is it cruel to let people who refuse to work get hungry?**

The Living Bible translates II Thessalonians 3:10 *Even while we were still there with you, we gave you this rule: "He who does not work shall not eat."*

Make This Statement To The Boys:

Before we go on to the next chapter, tell me which Scripture made you mad, glad or made you think.

Note to the Mentor: As a result of this lesson, are there any prayer requests that should be added to your list and forwarded to your prayer partners?

Notes:_____

_____

_____

_____

_____

_____

_____

_____

_____

_____

_____

_____

_____

_____

_____

_____

_____

_____

Mentor: Read this page before you meet with your boys.

11 I Was Treated Unfairly Today (Prejudice)

Definition: Prejudice is an unfavorable opinion or feeling formed beforehand or without knowledge, thought, or reason.

CONNECTING WITH AND LEARNING FROM YOUR RICH, PERSONAL, PAINFUL, PRODUCTIVE PAST. As a Black man in America, I have had to deal with prejudice daily! I am sure that you have too. Share a personal experience with the young men in which you were treated unfairly. Be sure to share an experience in which you used wisdom to effect a good outcome.

CAUTION: Don't allow this lesson to degenerate into a pity party.

CONCERN: I am concerned that many Blacks use prejudice as an excuse for inactivity or laziness. I personally know Black folks who failed in business and they blamed it on prejudice. I happened to be close enough to the situation to know that they did not manage the business or their money well, which resulted in failure.

CHARGE: I charge you to succeed in spite of any prejudice that you may encounter!! The fact of the matter is that prejudice will always be with us, so overcoming it must become a life skill that we develop. Our country has overcome many things, but many Black men still have not experienced personal victory in their lives. Don't be one of them!

ACTIVITY: Discuss the prejudice that you experience that is not race-related: gangs, churches, fraternities, schools, west side vs. south side etc.

11 I Was Treated Unfairly Today (Prejudice)

Recently, I was in a mall with my two youngest children. On this particular day, I had on a suit and tie and was dressed very professionally. As I approached the cosmetics counter, I noticed a woman that I had previously worked with was at the counter making a purchase.

This woman was a tall, attractive, White woman with blue eyes and flowing blond hair. I had worked with the woman every day for a number of years, and I was more impressed with her character than I was with her carriage (body). As I approached her to say hello, her back was turned, so I cleared my throat to get her attention. Upon seeing this, the saleslady dissed me. She frowned, looked at me and said: "Sir, go on down the aisle, just! go! on! down! the! aisle!" I was shocked. My female associate, standing at the counter and not knowing what was going on, turned around, saw me, smiled and we talked like two friends who had not seen each other for a while.

The question on the floor now is: What should I say to the saleslady who dissed me? With the look on her face, you could have bought her with a wet food stamp. What should I say? WHAT SHOULD I SAY! Should I just walk away and forget that she said anything? Should I make a face? Should I walk away with my nose in the air? Or should I diss her like she dissed me?

When you are treated unfairly, you should seek to respond knowledgeably. A wise response is the best response because it will bring the most good from the situation.

In order to respond wisely, there are some things you should consider first. To check yourself, ask yourself these questions before you respond:
- Am I in a bad mood or having a bad day?
- Did I do something wrong to provoke this person?

Regarding the other person, ask yourself these questions:
- Is this person crazy?
- Has this person been exposed to intelligent Black folks?
- What would I have done if the situation was reversed?
- How can I do the right thing and come out ahead in this situation?

A proper assessment of the situation is necessary before you say anything.

> *He that keepeth his mouth keepeth his life: but he that openeth wide his lips shall have destruction.*
>
> Proverbs 13:3

The most effective way for you to help people realize that they have wronged you is for you to let God show them. In my situation, the saleslady knew she was wrong. At that point, for me to say anything would have been anticlimactic. Nothing I could have said would have made her feel any worse than she felt nor further impress upon her how wrong she was. So I suggest that the best approach is to let God fix it and don't plead your own case. This is not always easy, but I challenge you to look at history and see how people who were dissed eventually shined because the truth will eventually come forth.

> *If thou hast done foolishly in lifting up thyself, or if thou hast thought evil, lay thine hand upon thy mouth.*
>
> Proverbs 30:32

> *If thine enemy be hungry, give him bread to eat; and if he be thirsty, give him water to drink: For thou shalt heap coals of fire upon his head, and the LORD shall reward thee.*
> Proverbs 25:21-22

I know that kindness to people who are dissin' you may be a difficult concept to embrace, but it clearly is the best policy. Well, what about those situations where the person is going off and it seems like there is no justice and the person seems to be getting away with it? Shouldn't I go off then?

> *If it be possible, as much as lieth in you, live peaceably with all men.*
> Romans 12:18

Let me confess for a minute. I don't want you to think that I don't struggle with what I am trying to share with you. Just the other day, I blew it. My day was not going well, and I encountered a situation at the bank where it seemed like the teller was trying to diss me. Yes, I am sorry to say that I went off (a little bit) and said to the woman: "Is there a problem? I've been banking here for five years. IS THERE A PROBLEM?!" As I write this, I am still sorry that I went off (a little bit) on the teller. The bad thing is that my going off did not help me get my money any faster and now the people at the bank look at me funny.

I believe that the best way to handle ignorant people and abusive situations is to walk away from them. You should have enough self-esteem and confidence to know that the actions of another person will not hurt you. The danger in saying something and not walking away is that the situation may escalate.

> *Surely the churning of milk bringeth forth butter, and the wringing of the nose bringeth forth blood: so the forcing of wrath bringeth forth strife.*
> Proverbs 30:33

When you provoke an ignorant (ignent), evil person, you are asking for more trouble. With men this can only lead to violence, bloodshed and death. Now, don't get me wrong. There is a time to fight and a time to die for what you know to be right, but that time is not when someone hurts your feelings. If someone threatens your life or the life of your family, then is the time to protect yourself.

Anything short of a life-threatening situation should be walked away from!!
Remember, we live in a sin-sick, sin-cursed society. People will always diss other people. The question on the floor still remains: "How will you handle it?"

Questions
for Introspection and Discussion (to make you think)

1. What did you do the last time you were treated unfairly? (explain)_____
_____

2. When you are treated unfairly in school, do you assess the situation before you go off?
Yes___ No___

3. Have you dissed anybody lately? Yes___ No___

4. Are you secure enough in yourself to get dissed and ignore it? Yes___ No___

5. Do you really believe that people will reap what they sow? Yes___ No___

6. Do you believe that you respond to people based on how you feel about yourself? Yes___ No___

7. Why do you feel that strong people can ignore the insults of the weak?_____

8. In dealing with people, what characteristic in people makes you like them the most?
    ___ race
    ___ religion
    ___ sex
    ___ how pretty they are
    ___ how much money they have
    ___ where they live
    ___ other?

Applicable Scriptures: Please have a boy read the Scripture, then use the questions to facilitate discussion. Conclude by quoting the Scripture from the Living Bible, which was written for teenagers. *Please remember that the reading of Scripture according to Isaiah 55:11 is the most important thing you will do with the boys. This section is where the Holy Spirit really works in their hearts, so don't skip it.*

(1) *He that keepeth his mouth keepeth his life: but he that openeth wide his lips shall have destruction.* Proverbs 13:3

[Question] **Do you talk negatively about people of different races?**

[Question] **Have you used your mouth to get things started with people?**

[Question] **The mouth can provide many positive opportunities for you or it can ruin you. How do you feel you will use your mouth?**

The Living Bible translates Proverbs 13:3 like this: *Self-control means controlling the tongue! A quick retort can ruin everything.*

(2) *If thou hast done foolishly in lifting up thyself, or if thou hast thought evil, lay thine hand upon thy mouth.* Proverbs 30:32

[Question] **Do you feel that because of your race you are better than someone else?**

[Question] **Do you feel that someone owes you something because of your race?**

[Question] **Do you challenge the negative thoughts about others that pass through your mind?**

The Living Bible translates Proverbs 30:32 like this: *If you have been a fool by being proud or plotting evil, don't brag about it—cover your mouth with you hand in shame.*

(3) *If thine enemy be hungry, give him bread to eat; and if he be thirsty, give him water to drink: For thou shalt heap coals of fire upon his head, and the LORD shall reward thee.* Proverbs 25:21-22

[Question] **This is the approach that Rev. Dr. Martin Luther King took to solve race problems. Do you feel that loving your enemies makes any sense?**

[Question] **Do you feel that God rewarded Dr. King for his approach?**

The Living Bible translates Proverbs 25:21-22 like this: *If your enemy is hungry, give him food! If he is thirsty, give him something to drink! This will make him feel ashamed of himself, and God will reward you.*

(4) *If it be possible, as much as lieth in you, live peaceably with all men.* Romans 12:18

[Question] **I am not asking you to be a sucker, but do you feel that you can take the role of peacemaker in racial disputes?**

[Question] **What is the most you feel a person should take from someone before they snap?**

The Living Bible translates Romans 12:18 like this: *Don't quarrel with anyone. Be at peace with everyone, just as much as possible.*

(5) *Surely the churning of milk bringeth forth butter, and the wringing of the nose bringeth forth blood: so the forcing of wrath bringeth forth strife.* Proverbs 30:33

[Question] **Some people just pick, pick, pick, pick, pick until a fight is started. Why do you feel they do that?**

[Question] **To force wrath is to pick on another person until they snap. Have you ever done this?**

The Living Bible translates Proverbs 30:33 like this: *As the churning of cream yields butter, and a blow to the nose causes bleeding, so anger causes quarrels.*

Make This Statement To The Boys:

Before we go on to the next chapter, tell me which Scripture made you mad, glad or made you think.

Note to the Mentor: As a result of this lesson, are there any prayer requests that should be added to your list and forwarded to your prayer partners?

Mentor: Read this page before you meet with your boys.

12 A Proper Attitude About Money

Definition: Money is property, possessions or wealth.

CONNECTING WITH AND LEARNING FROM YOUR RICH, PERSONAL, PAINFUL, PRODUCTIVE PAST. It is not unusual in the Black community to find people who struggle to maintain the proper attitude about money. When you have never had much of anything, it is easy to lose perspective regarding it. Share your personal attitudinal history about money with the young men.

CAUTION: It is not how much you have, but your attitude about it that is important. If your attitude about money is not right, you will never have enough money. The proper attitude is to live for Jesus, work hard and trust God to give you all that you need.

CONCERN: How the influence of the media and the portrayals of lavish lifestyles fuel young people's passion for money.

CHARGE: Choose honesty and morality over money. Work hard to better yourself and refuse to compromise your character.

ACTIVITY: 1. Plan an interview with a rich person to see how they view money. 2. Show how compound interest will work for them when they start a savings account.

12 A Proper Attitude About Money

A very popular Bible verse is often misquoted like this: "Money is the root of all evil." The verse, I Timothy 6:10a, actually says: *"For the love of money is the root of all evil."* So, it is not money but the love of money that gets people into trouble. Please be advised that there is nothing inherently wrong with money. Money is AMORAL, which means that it is not good and it is not bad. Money becomes a factor only if we have an unhealthy attitude about it.

When a man loves money, he becomes a candidate for all types of traps. A man's attitude about finances or money is a CRITICAL factor in his future success. Those who are crazy about getting money will take one of several courses:

1. Become a crook to get it.

I am amazed at the many times I have had the opportunity to get money dishonestly. I have had opportunities to do almost everything wrong that you could think of. Most of you who read these pages will be presented with many opportunities to do wrong. What saves you at this point is what could be called internal restraints (something inside of you that keeps you in check when you are tempted). One restraint that has always helped me when it comes to getting money illegally is the fact that I know if I get it illegally, I won't be able to keep it without a lot of sorrow. You may not see the sorrow immediately, but it will come.

> *The blessing of the Lord, it maketh rich, and he addeth no sorrow with it.*
> Proverbs 10:22

> *Wealth gotten by vanity shall be diminished: but he that gathereth by labor shall increase.*
> Proverbs 13:11

> *Better is a little with righteousness than great revenues without right.*
> Proverbs 16:8

Those who get their money illegally will eventually suffer the consequences for their deeds.

2. Work so hard that they forget God in the process.

Dig this. God will not let a Christian forget that HE is God. God will get your attention when you ignore Him while making your fortune. I have learned from experience that God loves you and wants to use you. He will not allow you to have money or possessions that take the focus off of Him. He has a way of allowing your money to evaporate like a drop of water on a hot summer sidewalk. Look at what this Scripture says:

Ye have sown much, and bring in little; ye eat, but ye have not enough; ye drink, but ye are not filled with drink; ye clothe you, but there is none warm; and he that earneth wages earneth wages to put it into a bag with holes.

Haggai 1:6

What this Scripture means is that the people were spending all of their money on their houses and were neglecting God's house, the church. When God is neglected, He can bring a leanness to the situation. God can put holes in our money bags. So, workaholism at the expense of a relationship with God will not solve your money problems.

3. Allow their quest for money to separate them from family and friends.

He that is greedy of gain troubleth his own house; but he that hateth gifts shall live.
Proverbs 15:27

This is the common story of the man that works hard to give things to his family and neglects to give himself to his family. Children resent this later in life, and the financial stability that is gained is not worth the loss of wife or children. Again, it is not the money that is bad but the love for that money that is destructive. So, the wise man disciplines himself regarding money.

Now let's look at some common problem areas that young men have with money.

Credit
I remember when I was first granted credit privileges. I had never had much, and now the man says: "All you have to do is sign on the dotted line and it is yours." Name it, sign on the dotted line and claim it. I got in big trouble fast. I had to pay for everything that I signed for. Look at what the Bible says about credit:

The rich ruleth over the poor, and the borrower is servant to the lender.
Proverbs 22:7

Any man, woman, boy or girl who does not know how to use credit will soon be a servant to Visa, Mastercard, or your favorite clothing store.
- Never sign for what you can pay for.
- Never buy it when you first see it. Always go back a day or two later after you've cooled off.
- Remember, they will smile when you sign for it but take you to court and sue you when you are late with your payment.

He who borrows becomes the servant. Seek to be a free man. I know there are times when we all borrow to buy big ticket items such as cars, homes, or a college education, but it should never be for stuff we really don't need. Borrowing has been presented by credit card companies and others who loan money as glamorous, but in reality it is a form of enslavement that we should seek to avoid.

112

Loaning to Friends

This is something that we should do if we can and if we feel that God wants us to. Consider these things before you loan to friends:

- Is it a legit' loan? Don't be afraid to ask a lot of questions.
- Be sure to pray about it. People can be good liars when it comes to getting money.
- Get a CLEAR understanding up front if this is a loan or a gift. People get amnesia from time to time.
- We should not charge Christians interest. If you take the money out of savings to loan it to them, you may ask them for what you lost in interest while it was out of the bank but no more than what you would have gotten from the bank. In other words, don't try to make money off of fellow Christians or friends who are in need.

Borrowing from Friends

Friends who are always borrowing money will stretch the friendship to its limits. One who is constantly borrowing money gets on your nerves. If you borrow all of the time, it gives others the indication that:

- You are a poor manager of money.
- You need to work harder.
- You need to get a better job.

Keep your friendships strong by sparing your friends the burden of supporting you financially.

Co-Signing

It is very risky to co-sign for others. This should be done with extreme caution. Ten years ago, I co-signed for a friend against the advice of my wife to the tune of $2,500.00 (two thousand five hundred dollars). My friend paid two payments and I had to pay the rest while listening to my wife say: "I told you so." Tell people that you don't co-sign for others. Say it is a policy of yours. Many people will not understand this, but you can't worry about that.

> *A man void of understanding striketh hands, and becometh surety in the presence of his friend.*
>
> Proverbs 17:18

This verse is saying that a man who does not know any better will become surety or co-sign for his friend.

Compounded Interest

I can vividly remember my childhood. We never seemed to have enough money. My dad often borrowed money from a local finance company. It seemed like he was always late with the payments. They were always calling and he never seemed to get them paid off. As an adult, I now understand what was going on. They were charging him a high interest rate that compounded. They used to call it <u>add-on interest</u>. For example, he would borrow $300.00 to be paid back in one year. The interest was 21% annually, which meant that on the day that he took out the loan he owed

$363.00 total. So when he paid his first payment of $30.25, which went to pay the interest, he had a balance of $332.75. At this rate it took forever to pay off the loan.

Let me give you another example of how interest works. A friend of mine purchased a new car with a sticker price of $16,500.00. When the sticker price is computed at 11% interest, the total cost of the car comes to $18,315.00. The first payment is $600.00, of which $432.00 is paid on the car and $168.00 is payment on the interest. So, the $168.00 goes to the bank as interest and payment for services.

Now, please note this point: most Black people are on the wrong side of compound interest! Look at this example of how you can use compound interest to your advantage. Let's say you are 15 years old and you save $5.00 a month or $60.00 per year at 6 % interest. Look at what your returns will be five, ten, fifteen, and twenty years from now. Look at the following figures and see how a compounded interest rate of 6% will work for you.

Amount Returned in:

Amount Saved	5 years	10 years	15 years	20 years
$5 a month or $60 a year	$338	$791	$1397	$2208

I want to encourage you to strive to make compounded interest work for you by starting and developing consistent saving patterns NOW!

Tithing

To tithe means to give God 1/10 of your gross income. In the Christian Church, there are those who tithe and others who have a problem with this principle. I am not going to go into a long theological discussion of the matter other than to say that I tithe and I have prospered financially. Please note that I am not rich, but I have everything that I need and most of my wants. God does not need our money, but what He does desire is our obedience in the area of finances. When we tithe, He has our obedience and He is then free to bless us.

> *Will a man rob God? Yet ye have robbed me. But ye say, Wherein have we robbed thee? In tithes and offerings. Ye are cursed with a curse: for ye have robbed me, even this whole nation. Bring ye all the tithes into the storehouse, that there may be meat in mine house, and prove me now herewith, saith the Lord of hosts, if I will not open you the windows of heaven, and pour you out a blessing, that there shall not be room enough to receive it.*
> Malachi 3:8-10

Women and Money

Don't fall into the trap of thinking that you have to have a lot of money to get a good woman. A good woman is more impressed with your character than with your cash. A good woman values a man who has integrity more than the brother who can buy her everything. Please note that you should work hard to provide for yourself and a woman, but never seek for cash to be the criteria by which a woman chooses you or you choose a woman.

Questions
for Introspection and Discussion (to make you think)

1. Tell the truth, shame the devil! Do you love money? Yes___ No___

2. Have you ever cheated someone out of money? Yes___ No___

3. Do you consider God when you think about money? Yes___ No___

4. How many people owe you money right now? _____
What is your attitude toward them?_____

5. What is the largest sum of money you have ever had in your pocket at one time? $_____
Where is the money now?_____

6. Who do you owe money to right now? _____
Do you plan to pay it back? Yes___ No___ Find a Bible and look up Psalm 37:21.

7. Do you give money freely to God? Yes___ No___ To the poor? Yes___ No___

8. Do you know an adult who will co-sign for your car? Yes___ No___ Have you ever asked them to? _____ Would you understand if they said NO? _____

9. Can you imagine saving money even when you don't have enough? Yes___ No___

10. What one concept in this chapter do you have the greatest problem with? _____
What do you plan to do about it? Check all that apply:
____ A. Not adopt the concept as your own.
____ B. Pray about it.
____ C. Discuss it with an older, wiser man.

Applicable Scriptures: Please have a boy read the Scripture, then use the questions to facilitate discussion. Conclude by quoting the Scripture from the Living Bible, which was written for teenagers. *Please remember that the reading of Scripture according to Isaiah 55:11 is the most important thing you will do with the boys. This section is where the Holy Spirit really works in their hearts, so don't skip it.*

(1) *The blessing of the Lord, it maketh rich, and he addeth no sorrow with it.* Proverbs 10:22

[Question] **Do you believe that there is a difference in money from crime and money you earned?**

[Question] **Why do you think there is sorrow associated with illegal money?**

[Question] **The riches that this Scripture is speaking of goes beyond money. Name some other riches that the Lord gives.**

The Living Bible translates Proverbs 10:22 like this: *The Lord's blessing is our greatest wealth. All our work adds nothing to it!*

(2) *Wealth gotten by vanity shall be diminished: but he that gathereth by labor shall increase.* Proverbs 13:11

[Question] **This Scripture also speaks of the problem of ill-gotten gains. Do you plan to get your money honestly?**

[Question] **Why do you feel the dope pushers have such a hard time staying wealthy?**

[Question] **What is the promise made to the working man?**

The Living Bible translates Proverbs 13:11 like this: *Wealth from gambling quickly disappears; wealth from hard work grows.*

(3) *Better is a little with righteousness than great revenues without right.* Proverbs 16:8

[Question] **Do you feel it is better to be poor and happy or have money and have to constantly watch your back?**

[Question] **What do you think righteousness means? (Right standing with God)**

[Question] **Are you righteous?**

[Question] **How many people can you name who have died over money?**

The Living Bible translates Proverbs 16:8 like this: *A little, gained honestly, is better than great wealth gotten by dishonest means.*

(4) *Ye have sown much, and bring in little; ye eat, but ye have not enough; ye drink, but ye are not filled with drink; ye clothe you, but there is none warm; and he that earneth wages earneth wages to put it into a bag with holes.* Haggai 1:6

[Question] **This Scripture talks about what happens to people who ignore God in the area of finances. Do you give regularly to God's church?**

[Question] **Materially minded people are rarely satisfied. Why do you think this is so?**

[Question] **God can allow you to have holes in your pockets when you ignore Him. How much do you feel you should give God?**

The Living Bible translates Haggai 1:6 like this: *You plant much but harvest little. You have scarcely enough to eat or drink, and not enough clothes to keep you warm. Your income disappears, as though you were putting it into pockets filled with holes!*

(5) *He that is greedy of gain troubleth his own house; but he that hateth gifts shall live.* Proverbs 15:27

[Question] **Are you greedy for money?**

[Question] **Do you fall out with your parents over money and stuff you want?**

[Question] **What thing or things do you put before money?**

The Living Bible translates Proverbs 15:27 like this: *Dishonest money brings grief to all the family, but hating bribes brings happiness.*

(6) *The rich ruleth over the poor, and the borrower is servant to the lender.* Proverbs 22:7

[Question] **Did you realize that you are a servant to the person you borrow money from?**

The Living Bible translates Proverbs 22:7 like this: *Just as the rich rule the poor, so the borrower is servant to the lender.*

(7) *A man void of understanding striketh hands, and becometh surety in the presence of his friend.* Proverbs 17:18

[Question] **This verse means that you should not co-sign for someone. Have you ever co-signed for someone to buy something or has someone co-signed for your?**

[Question] **To say that a man is void of understanding is to say that he is stupid. It is stupid to co-sign for someone. Why do you think the Bible says we should not co-sign?**

The Living Bible translates Proverbs 17:18 like this: *It is poor judgment to countersign another's note, to become responsible for his debts.*

(8) *Will a man rob God? Yet ye have robbed me. But ye say, Wherein have we robbed thee? In tithes and offerings. Ye are cursed with a curse: for ye have robbed me, even this whole nation. Bring ye all the tithes into the storehouse, that there may be meat in mine house, and prove me now herewith, saith the Lord of hosts, if I will not open you the windows of heaven, and pour you out a blessing, that there shall not be room enough to receive it.* Malachi 3:8-10

[Question] **Did you know that ignoring God with your money is the same as robbing Him?**

[Question] **Do you rob God?**

[Question] **God forgives you when you don't know any better, but once you learn what you should do and don't do it, it is a different story. Tell the truth, shame the devil. Now that you know that you should give to God some of what He has given you, do you plan to do it?**

The Living Bible translates Malachi 3:8-10 like this: *Will a man rob God? Surely not! And yet you have robbed me. "What do you mean? When did we ever rob you?" "You have robbed me of the tithes and offerings due to me. And so the awesome curse of God is cursing you, for your whole nation has been robbing me. Bring all the tithes into the storehouse so that there will be food enough in my Temple; if you do, I will open up the windows of heaven for you and pour out a blessing so great you won't have room enough to take it in!"*

Mentor: Read this page before you meet with your boys.

13 The King's English and Employment

Definition: The King's English is standard or accepted English usage in speech or writing; so called from the royal sanction.

CONNECTING WITH AND LEARNING FROM YOUR RICH, PERSONAL, PAINFUL, PRODUCTIVE PAST. We have all been in a situation when we felt that our vocabulary was inadequate. We have all faced a situation when we could not find the words to express ourselves. Share such an occasion with the young men.

CAUTION - We live in two worlds, the Black one and the White one. I want to prepare the young men to be functional in both worlds. You compromise none of your Blackness when you speak the King's English.

CONCERN: As your vocabulary increases, there will be those who no longer want to talk to you. That's OK, move on!

CHARGE: Buy a dictionary and use it. I own a dictionary that I have had for years! It is my friend who has given me a richness that has contributed to my success in life. I challenge you to buy a dictionary or claim one that is in your house.

CURE: The development of a love for reading will strengthen your vocabulary in a marvelous way. Become a reader, for readers ARE leaders.

13 The King's English and Employment

I was assisting a young brother who was in search of a job. He had put in applications all over town when one day he received a call at the church because he didn't have a phone. I went and found him and took him to the prospective employer and stood there while the prospective employer talked to him. The employer asked him: "Why do you want to work here?" The brother replied: "I need a job." The employer continued to ask the brother questions, and each answer was about the brother's personal problems and not about solving the problems of the potential employer. Needless to say, he didn't get the job.

The brother talked with his prospective employer as if he was talking with his homey in the hood. When a man does this, his value and worth diminish in the eyes of his employer. Young people must learn that people are put at ease when you talk in a manner that they are comfortable with. I had the opportunity to go to another country where the people talked differently than I do. It was very difficult to order food and to be understood and understand others. I was very glad to get back to the States where I could understand and be understood. Don't put your employer in a foreign country every time he tries to talk with you. The ability to speak "Standard English" is a skill that will take you far in life, and many young men don't see the value in it. Here are some things to consider:

1. Standard English will get you noticed and listened to.
Not too long ago, I was at a local housing complex on a Saturday afternoon, where I came upon a young man leaning against a car with a wine bottle in one hand and his woman in the other. As it so happened, I was waiting on someone, and while waiting, I got into a conversation with the young man, who was extremely cool, laid back, and in his own world. During the conversation, the brother looked at me and said something like this:

> "Yo man, it be rough on the street
> trying to get enough to eat
> kids gettin' me down
> don't wanna mess around
> job's hard to find
> got my woman on my mind
> can't seem to get straight
> got to stop and meditate
> I'm going to give you the spiel
> I know the real deal...."

He continued on and on and finally stopped. After he stopped, he hugged his woman, sat back and grinned, taking pride in his linguistic accomplishment. I looked at him and said something like this: "I understand that the vicissitudes of life can be contentious and contrary, assailing and assaulting the ego and retiring a man's monumental efforts to a condition of ignominious invalidation. I also understand that the daily doldrums of sustaining this diminutive existence can be very exasperating, but I conclude that to retreat into a cocoon of inebriation in an attempt to incapacitate and invalidate life's incessant blows will not be efficacious."

At this point, the brother stood up straight, his countenance (face) changed and he looked at me and said: "Who are you?" I told him who I was, and he began to listen to the wisdom of one who was older and wiser than he was.

Now, I want you to realize that because of how I answered him, he wanted to know who I was. With my vocabulary, which is accepted wherever the English language is spoken, I challenged the brother to perform on the world's stage rather than only on the stage in his head.

2. An increased vocabulary will point out to you that the world is a huge place.
Many of the words we use come from other countries and maintain their native pronunciation. The word "kindergarten" is a German word that means the children's garden; however, in America, we never translated it for usage. There are other words which are transliterated, which means the spellings may differ somewhat but the pronunciation and meaning is nearly the same. The word Hallelujah (Praise the Lord) is one such word.

3. An enhanced vocabulary will make you wise beyond your years.
Words stimulate thought, and when you study their origins, it gives you extra power when you use them. Every new word you learn opens the door to many other words, and the cycle is endless.

4. An enhanced vocabulary comes from using a dictionary.
It is common knowledge that Malcolm X read the dictionary while in prison. It may be difficult to see the gain from such activity, but stop and think of the great men who had significant vocabularies: Martin Luther King Jr., Jesse Jackson, and Thurgood Marshall, just to name a few, were men of significant vocabularies. These men could think on their feet because they had words to express their thoughts. We have many great young thinkers today who will never be great because they can't express their thoughts. The newspaper is another place to pick up additional words. Read the paper and write down all the new words you come in contact with.

5. An enhanced vocabulary will help you get better grades in school and will help you get promoted on your job.
The ability to articulate your thoughts is power and money in the bank. Think about this. musicians struggle to get what they hear in their heads recorded on their new CD. Fashion designers struggle to get what they see in a new dress manufactured and on the rack. Athletes struggle to make the play that is in their mind work on the field. You and I struggle to get what we are thinking out of our minds and into our conversation. An enhanced vocabulary will help you get those valuable thoughts

conveyed to other people. When this happens, you become more valuable and wise in the sight of others.

6. Each field of study (discipline) has its own vocabulary.
Doctors talk doctor talk, lawyers talk lawyer talk, and so forth. I was impressed the last time I was in the courtroom by the vocabulary that was used there. I know a preacher who can take words and paint a picture so vividly that everyone in the congregation can see the picture.

The other day, I put my car in the shop. I told the mechanic that there was a low point on the front disc and that the disc needed to be turned. I LOVE to be able to speak the vocabulary of whatever we are talking about. Sometimes life forces us to learn new terms (vocabulary).

If you notice the handsome picture on the back of the book, you will see that this handsome author is bald. Well, my hair fell out after a very stressful period in my life. When this happened, I had to learn a new term, *alopecia*. This term is what doctors use for baldness. My condition was *alopecia totalis,* which means bald all over. My hair is now beginning to grow back, so my condition has become *alopecia areata*, which means bald in some areas.

When I buried my father, I talked to the funeral director, who had a whole new vocabulary: embalming, vaults, sealers, visitation, expired, etc. I pray that you have a good vocabulary, other than what is common on the streets. You need a street vocabulary, but you also need to be knowledgeable of the vocabulary of various disciplines or professions.

7. In addition to enhancing your vocabulary, learn the proper structure of the English language.
If you are a citizen of the U.S.A., English is your official language. While there are numerous dialects, Standard English is what's completely accepted. Discipline yourself and master the fundamentals of effective communication, which include subject-verb agreement and proper use of adverbs, adjectives, and prepositional phrases.

Questions
for Introspection and Discussion (to make you think)

1. When was the last time you learned a new word? _____

What was that word? _____

2. Name someone of your age who has an impressive vocabulary. _____

3. How many vocabularies or disciplines can you speak in? _____

4. Can you talk to a professional person without feeling intimidated? Yes___ No___

5. State your specific plans to increase your vocabulary. _____

6. The Scriptures in this book are taken from the King James Version of the Bible. There are several versions of the Bible that are easier to read, but I like the challenge that comes with reading the King James Version because of the words that it contains. Have you used a dictionary to look up any words from the Scriptures that you have read so far? Yes___ No___

As you read the rest of this book, when you come to a word that you don't know, stop and say: "What does that word mean?" The courage to admit that you don't know something and the humility to ask what it means are the signs of a leader.

Applicable Scriptures: Please have a boy read the Scripture, then use the questions to facilitate discussion. Conclude by quoting the Scripture from the Living Bible, which was written for teenagers. *Please remember that the reading of Scripture according to Isaiah 55:11 is the most important thing you will do with the boys. This section is where the Holy Spirit really works in their hearts, so don't skip it.*

(1) *For my mouth shall speak truth; and wickedness is an abomination to my lips.* Proverbs 8:7

[Question] **Do you regularly tell the truth?**

[Question] **Do you feel guilty when you lie?**

[Question] **Do you use profanity?**

The Living Bible translates Proverbs 8:7 like this: *Listen to me! For I have important information for you. Everything I say is right and true, for I hate lies and every kind of deception.*

(2) *A man's gift maketh room for him, and bringeth him before great men.* Proverbs 18:16

[Question] **Do you believe that intelligent speech can open doors for you?**

[Question] **Who would you feel more comfortable speaking to, the MVP of the NBA or the VP of the First National Bank?**

[Question] **Do you have good verbal skills?**

The Living Bible translates Proverbs 18:16 like this: *A bribe does wonders; it will bring you before men of importance!*

(3) *Let your speech be always with grace, seasoned with salt, that you may know how ye ought to answer every man.* Colossians 4:6

[Question] **What do you think it means to have graceful speech?**

[Question] **What do you think it means to have speech that is seasoned with salt?**

[Question] **Do you know how to answer men who talk to you?**

The Living Bible translates Colossians 4:6 like this: *Let your conversation be gracious as well as sensible, for then you will have the right answer for everyone.*

(4) *How forcible are right words: but what doth your arguing reprove?* Job 6:25

[Question] **Has anyone ever put you in your place with choice words?**

[Question] **Job was good with words and was able to make his point with his friends. How do you make your point with friends?**

The Living Bible translates Job 6:25 like this: *It is wonderful to speak the truth, but your criticisms are not based on fact.*

(5) *And Samuel grew, and the Lord was with him, and did let none of his words fall to the ground.* I Samuel 3:19

[Question] **Fools' words don't travel far before they hit the ground. Do you feel that your words travel far?**

[Question] **Your words become powerful when they speak the wisdom of God. Do you speak God's wisdom or your wisdom?**

[Question] **Is the Lord with you?**
The Living Bible translates I Samuel 3:19 like this: *As Samuel grew, the Lord was with him and people listened carefully to his advice.*

(6) *The words of the Lord are pure words: as silver tried in a furnace of earth, purified seven times.* Psalm 12:6
[Question] **Did you know that it is possible to speak God's words?**
[Question] **Did you know that after the world as we now know it is gone, God's Word will still be around?**
The Living Bible translates Psalm 12:6 like this: *The Lord's promise is sure. He speaks no careless word; all he says is purest truth, like silver seven times refined.*

(7) *Let the words of my mouth, and the meditation of my heart, be acceptable in thy sight, O LORD, my strength, and my redeemer.* Psalm 19:14
[Question] **Do you feel that the words you have spoken in the last week have been acceptable to God?**
The Living Bible translates Psalm 19:14 like this: *May my spoken words and unspoken thoughts be pleasing even to you, O Lord, my Rock and my Redeemer.*

Make This Statement To The Boys:

Before we go on to the next chapter, tell me which Scripture made you mad, glad or made you think.
Note to the Mentor: As a result of this lesson, are there any prayer requests that should be added to your list and forwarded to your prayer partners?

Notes:_____

Mentor: Read this page before you meet with your boys.

14 The Importance Of Controlling Your Passions And Not Letting Them Control You

Definition: Passion is any powerful or compelling emotion. (2) strong affection; love, (3) strong sexual desire; lust.

CONNECTING WITH AND LEARNING FROM YOUR RICH, PERSONAL, PAINFUL, PRODUCTIVE PAST. Most men do battle with their passions. Generally we think of sexual passions when the word passion is mentioned, but I want you to show the young men that any passion that is out of control will destroy you. What have you done with great passion and later discovered that it was misdirected passion? The Biblical example that comes to mind is the Apostle Paul who passionately persecuted the Church and later found out that he was very wrong. Share an example from your rich experience of how you allowed your passion to get you into trouble.

CAUTION: The world has told our young men a lie! Our culture has told them a lie. The lie is: You should follow your passions and let them lead you because you are a man.

CONCERN: I am concerned that our young men learn to discern the subtle lie that is found in most movies and TV shows. Passion sells, and our media is saturated with shows that excite our passions. The danger is they don't show the full impact of unleashing passions. I am concerned that you just present the Biblical position and leave it at that. If you do that, you have done your job. Along with presenting the Biblical position, take the risk of being transparent and sharing with the young men how you have allowed your passions to get you in trouble. Be sure to speak of passions other than sexual passions, such as; anger, rage or fury.

CHARGE: Determine to decide how, where and when you will allow your passions to be manipulated. Not too long ago my wife and I went to a movie. The movie was controversial and I did not want to go; I just went with my wife. While in the theater watching the movie, a strange thing happened; I got caught up in the plot. The next thing I knew, I had allowed my passion to get involved and I was standing up yelling at a movie. When I realized that they had got me, I felt stupid to have allowed myself to be manipulated by a movie.

CURE: Don't go to movies or watch TV that will excite your passions to the extreme. Don't watch X-rated movies or even PG if they excite you. Be determined to protect the **passionate you** from unreasonable and unhealthy stimulus.

14 The Importance Of Controlling Your Passions And Not Letting Them Control You

I was called by a friend to give his elderly father a ride one day. After I picked his father up, it soon became apparent to me that the old man wanted to talk. He proceeded to expound on issues of life that he felt needed to be addressed. At one point he said something that I distinctly remember. He said, "There are three things that will kill you: women, money, and alcohol."

I later thought about what he said, and I feel that it is true; but I also would like to state that it is an unbridled (uncontrolled) passion toward these things that is deadly. Men have been destroyed for centuries because they could not control their passions. When I speak of passion, the mind automatically drifts toward sex. Passion is much broader than that, but because our society focuses on sex we need to be aware of the danger of **undisciplined** sexual passion.

There is a danger in not controlling your sexual passion. Unbridled sexual passion affects you in these ways:

1. Unbridled passion impairs decision making.
When you are in love, you don't think straight. When your passions are out of control, you don't think at all. Many men have made decisions in the heat of passion that controlled them for the rest of their lives. I was talking to a man the other day whose wife is making his life miserable. He married her based on the passion that he had for her when he first met her.

2. Unbridled passion impairs your vision.
When you are passionately looking at a woman, what you see is not what you see. What you see is being airbrush-painted in your mind to make it look better. This is why they turn the lights down low in the nightclub. They want the red lights, yellow lights, blue lights, and black lights to alter what things look like so that what you see is not really what you see. Never make a decision about a woman while viewing her through the eyes of passion.

3. Unbridled passion promotes situation ethics.
Situation ethics is when right and wrong are based on the situation or what looks good now. Passion has its own way of thinking, which usually goes like this: "Anything that feels this good can't be wrong." In the heat of passion, a man will say anything, promise anything, because the focus is on how to master the present situation.

4. Unbridled passion is ignorant of consequences.

Unbridled passion clouds your ability to see and think about tomorrow. In the heat of passion, caution is tossed to the wind.

5. Unbridled passion should be saved for your wife.

Your unleashed passion should be saved for your wife. The Bible teaches that the marriage bed is the place where you can go at it.

> *Marriage is honourable in all, and the bed undefiled: but whoremongers and adulterers God will judge.*
>
> Hebrews 13:4

How To Cool Your Passions

1. Don't excite them in the first place.

Don't involve yourself in sexually exciting activities. Pick the movies that you go to very carefully. Not only avoid X-rated movies, but avoid X-rated music also. These things only excite your passions. Reading *Playboy* or a girlie magazine is equivalent to a child reading a comic book. Both are fantasy. There are many beautiful young women out there, and looking at them is not a sin. The Bible says that Rebekah, Isaac's wife, was pleasant to gaze upon. It is OK to look at women, but don't undress them with your eyes. Jesus knew men very well because he said:

> *But I say unto you, That whosoever looketh on a woman to lust after her hath committed adultery with her already in his heart.*
>
> Matthew 5:28

Realize that passion comes from the inside, so it must be controlled from there. It can be fueled from the outside but not controlled from the outside.

2. Fortify yourself with the objective truth of God.

One of the best defenses I know of is a strong offense. Your best offense is Scripture memorization. Let me tell you how you benefit from Scripture memorization. Take the following steps:

     Step 1: You memorize some Scriptures.

     Step 2: You are confronted with a perplexing problem, test or temptation.

     Step 3: Your flesh wants to make a decision.

     Step 4: The Holy Spirit searches the files in your mind to find the most appropriate Scripture.

     Step 5: The Holy Spirit displays that Scripture on the computer screen in your mind.

     Step 6: With both choices in clear view, you decide if you want to please yourself or please God, and then you make the appropriate decision.

Let me see if I can make it clearer:

     Step 1: You memorize Scripture to help you specifically with your passion.

     Step 2: While minding your own business, you start thinking about sex and the video with

Girlfriend, the rap artist, doin' her thing, and one thought leads to another. The next thing you know, your passions are off to the races.

Step 3: Because you have memorized Scripture, the Holy Spirit comes in early during the temptation process and searches the files of your mind. These Scriptures come to mind, which will settle you down if you listen to them:

For the lips of a strange woman drop as an honeycomb, and her mouth is smoother than oil: But her end is bitter as wormwood, sharp as a two-edged sword. Her feet go down to death; her steps take hold on hell.

Proverbs 5:3-5

Hearken unto me now therefore, O ye children, and attend to the words of my mouth. Let not thine heart decline to her ways, go not astray in her paths. For she hath cast down many wounded: yea, many strong men have been slain by her. Her house is the way to hell, going down to the chambers of death.

Proverbs 7:24-27

Now concerning the things whereof ye wrote unto me: It is good for a man not to touch a woman. Nevertheless, to avoid fornication, let every man have his own wife, and let every woman have her own husband.

I Corinthians 7:1-2

3. Don't stay single forever.

Listen to this: **The only sex that God smiles upon is when you are married.**

A. The Bible says that it is better to marry than to burn with passion. Please note that some people have the gift of singleness, i.e. God has made them not to need sex. If that is the way you are, don't worry about marriage. If you don't have the gift, then you should plan to get married someday and have a wonderful sex life. I repeat, if you have the gift of singleness, don't worry about getting married.

B. Children need a mother and father in the home. You need to be a responsible man and accept the challenge to sacrificially love your wife and your children. Too many men are wimping out on their families. Don't take the easy way out. Ask God to help you grow into a nurturing, responsible man.

C. Never mess with another man's wife! NEVER! NEVER! NEVER! Go find Tyson, Holyfield, or Foreman and smack them in the face, but DON'T MESS WITH A MAN'S WIFE!!! When you get married, **don't fool around!** It is impossible to fool around and not suffer DEARLY in the end. Oh, yeah, it will be fun at first, but in the end, in the end, in the end! The Bible acknowledges that it will be fun at first:

Stolen waters are sweet, and bread eaten in secret is pleasant.

Proverbs 9:17

Can a man take fire in his bosom, and his clothes not be burned? Can one go upon hot coals, and his feet not be burned? So he that goeth in to his neighbor's wife; whosoever toucheth her shall not be innocent. But whoso committeth adultery with a woman lacketh understanding: he that doeth it destroyeth his own soul. A wound and dishonor shall he get; and his reproach shall not be wiped away. Jealousy is the rage of a man: therefore he will not spare in the day of vengeance. He will not regard any ransom; neither will he rest content, though thou givest many gifts.

Proverbs 6:27-29;32-35

There is no escaping the consequences of having sex with another man's wife. The Bible very accurately declares that the husband will be enraged when he finds out about it. No present or gift will cool his anger.

I want to warn you also to avoid the aggressive married woman who wants to find some action with a young man. Unfortunately, this is very common today.

For by means of a whorish woman a man is brought to a piece of bread: and the adultress will hunt for the precious life.

Proverbs 6:26

When it comes to avoiding the traps that women will set for you, it is important to remember these things:

1. Don't listen to her rap. Proverbs 6:24 says: "*To keep thee from the evil woman, from the flattery of the tongue of a strange woman.*" It is not wise to let a woman talk to you in a seductive manner. Most men don't handle that very well.

2. Don't think on her beauty in your mind. Proverbs 6:25a says: "*Lust not after her beauty in thine heart.*" You are vulnerable to what you think about. If you think on her beauty, it may cause you to weaken in her presence. You will unknowingly give her more credibility than she deserves.

3. Don't stare her in the face. Proverbs 6:25b says: "*neither let her take thee with her eyelids.*" A woman's eyes are powerful weapons against a young man. Some older men can look them in the eyes and let them cry, but most young men can't handle it.

Questions
for Introspection and Discussion (to make you think)

1. On a scale of 1 to 10 with 10 being the greatest, how good are you at controlling your passions?

Circle one: 1.   2.   3.   4.   5.   6.   7.   8.   9.   10.

2. Have you ever started watching a movie and turned it off or left when you decided that it was inappropriate material? Yes___ No___

3. What do you do when you have problems with your passion? Do you let it fly or do you challenge it? Fly___ Challenge___

4. Do you fantasize about being with a beautiful woman? Yes___ No___

5. Do you realize the importance of working to control not only your thoughts of passion but all thoughts? Yes___ No___

6. Do you realize that TV and the movies saturate us with sex not because it is good for us but because IT SELLS?! Yes___ No___

7. List five results or consequences of not controlling your passion.
   1._____
   2._____
   3._____
   4._____
   5._____

8. Can you see through the lie that TV presents when it shows passion with no consequences? Yes___ No___

Applicable Scriptures: Please have a boy read the Scripture, then use the questions to facilitate discussion. Conclude by quoting the Scripture from the Living Bible, which was written for teenagers. *Please remember that the reading of Scripture according to Isaiah 55:11 is the most important thing you will do with the boys. This section is where the Holy Spirit really works in their hearts, so don't skip it.*

(1) *Keep thy heart with all diligence for out of it are the issues of life.* Proverbs 4:23

[Question] **Can you control your passions?**

[Question] **Are you aware of the things you feel strongly about?**

[Question] **Have you analyzed why you feel the way you do about certain issues?**

The Living Bible translates Proverbs 4:23 like this: *Above all else, guard your affections. For they influence everything else in our life.*

(2) *The heart is deceitful above all things, and desperately wicked: who can know it?* Jeremiah 17:9

[Question] **Does your heart ever lie to you?**

[Question] **Do you feel that it is bogus to say that your heart is wicked?**

[Question] **Do you know who originated wickedness?**

The Living Bible translates Jeremiah 17:9 like this: *The heart is the most deceitful thing there is, and desperately wicked. No one can really know how bad it is!*

(3) *He that hath no rule over his own spirit is like a city that is broken down, and without walls.* Proverbs 25:28

[Question] **Are you known for uncontrollable outbursts of anger?**

[Question] **Do you realize that a person who can't control his anger is vulnerable?**

The Living Bible translates Proverbs 25:28 like this: *A man without self-control is as defenseless as a city with broken-down walls.*

(4) *Let not sin therefore reign in your mortal body, that ye should obey it in the lusts thereof.* Romans 6:12

[Question] **Some people are controlled by their sinful passions. Are you?**

[Question] **It is normal to be tempted by your passions, but it is dangerous to give in to each temptation. What do you feel are some of the dangers?**

[Question] **What sin do you feel is destroying our communities?**

The Living Bible translates Romans 6:12 like this: *Do not let sin control your puny body any longer; do not give in to its sinful desires.*

(5) *All things are lawful unto me, but all things are not expedient: all things are lawful for me, but I will not be brought under the power of any.* I Corinthians 6:12

[Question] **Your enemy satan wants to control you by making you passionate about the wrong things. Are you under the bondage of any drug or habit right now?**

The Living Bible translates I Corinthians 6:12 like this: *I can do anything I want to if Christ has not said no, but some of these things aren't good for me. Even if I am allowed to do them, I'll refuse to if I think they might get such a grip on me that I can't easily stop when I want to.*

(6) *For a whore is a deep ditch; and a strange woman is a narrow pit.* Proverbs 23:27

[Question] **A loose woman can destroy you very quickly. Even though they may look good, you must avoid them. How do you plan to do this?**

[Question] **Many men find themselves in ditches and pits because they don't think before getting involved with women, but just follow their passions. When you see a woman, what controls you, your mind or your passions?**

The Living Bible translates Proverbs 23:27 like this: *O my son, trust my advice—stay away from prostitutes. For a prostitute is a deep and narrow grave. Like a robber, she waits for her victims as one after another become unfaithful to their wives.*

Additional Scriptures Used In Chapter Fourteen As Found In The Living Bible

Honor your marriage and its vows, and be pure; for God will surely punish all those who are immoral or commit adultery.

Hebrews 13:4

But I say: Anyone who even looks at a woman with lust in his eye has already committed adultery with her in his heart.

Matthew 5:28

For the lips of a prostitute are as sweet as honey, and smooth flattery is her stock in trade.

Proverbs 5:3

Listen to me, young men, and not only listen but obey; don't let your desires get out of hand; don't let yourself think about her. Don't go near her; stay away from where she walks, lest she tempt you and seduce you.

Proverbs 7:24-27

NOW ABOUT THOSE questions you asked in your last letter: my answer is that if you do not marry, it is good. But usually it is best to be married, each man having his own wife, and each woman having her own husband, because otherwise you might fall back into sin.

I Corinthians 7:1-2

Mentor: Read this page before you meet with your boys.

15 How To Avoid The Lure Of Homosexuality

Definition of homo [Gr *homo- <homos*, SAME] *combining form* same, equal, like.

CONNECTING WITH AND LEARNING FROM YOUR RICH, PERSONAL, PAINFUL, PRODUCTIVE PAST. I know of specific occasions where I have been approached by a homosexual either overtly or covertly. Most men can recall an instance when they were looked at or approached by a homosexual. Share your experience with the young men and relate to them how you handled it.

CAUTION: Don't fall for the lie that to address homosexuality from the Biblical perspective makes you homophobic. It is not homophobic but Biblical! **Homosexuality is a significant contributor to the destruction of the Black family. The Black community should aggressively oppose this sinful and destructive lifestyle.**

CONCERN: In your discussions it should be made very clear that God loves the homosexual but hates homosexuality.

CHARGE: We want to charge the young men to prepare themselves and save themselves for their future wives. To engage in homosexual behavior is to give away your manhood. Aggressively oppose any advances from a man who wants to get intimate with you.

CURE: Agree with mother nature. Mother nature does not acknowledge same sex relationships. As long as nature rejects that lifestyle, wise men should reject it also.

ACTIVITY: Observe how the media seeks to gloss over the destructive nature of homosexuality by laughing at it or only showing it in acceptable settings.

15 How To Avoid The Lure Of Homosexuality

The increase in the trend of men having sex with men in the Black community is having a serious negative impact on the family. When a man decides to live this way, some of the results are:

- One less man to lead a household.
- One more negative example for our youth.
- One more potential AIDS victim.
- One more life that will be severely scarred by sin.

I feel very strongly about this issue and speak unreservedly about it. The homosexual lifestyle is one that young men should avoid at all costs. It is one of many paths to a miserable life. Well, let's look at how to avoid the lure of homosexuality. First of all, we need to guard against the internal lure and the external lure. There are those who will tell you that they were "born gay." This statement disagrees with what secular studies have said and with what God has said:

> *So God created man in his own image, in the image of God created he him; male and female created he them.*
>
> Genesis 1:27

So, according to God, no man is born gay. But it is true that all men are born with certain **bents, weaknesses, tendencies or areas of susceptibility** that could lead one to believe that he was born a certain way. For example, there are people who seem to have been born to steal. Look at why we say this:

- They are good at it.
- They seem to do it with no guilty feelings.
- They show no desire to change and it seems like they will never change.

All these things being true, I still don't believe that they were born thieves. The brother who is a compulsive womanizer feels that he was made that way. He gets married and cheats on his wife and feels that it is something that he was made to do. This brother has **a predisposition, a proclivity, a preference** toward that behavior, and he is not about to change.

What about the brother that has a tendency toward laziness? This brother feels that it is OK to sponge off of his woman. He feels that this is natural and he has no intention of changing. He has a **predisposition, a proclivity, a preference** toward that behavior. These people were not made that way, but they may have **private passions, predispositions, and preferences** that make it difficult for them to kick certain habits. These bents can be considered internal lures. Please note:

Just because you may have an unnatural attraction to men does not mean that you were born gay!

Just like any weakness in any area, you must decide that it is fundamentally wrong and not do it. I want you to know today that every successful adult male has had a weak area that he had to overcome or that he is still fighting to overcome. This weakness would destroy this man if he ever allowed himself to be overtaken by it. So, the internal lure of homosexuality needs to be dealt with. This internal lure could be the result of several things:

1. Sexual abuse at the hands of a man.
If you have been abused by a man, you need to talk about it with your pastor or CHRISTIAN counsellor. To keep it inside only allows the thief to work undetected. Talking will turn the light on and expose the negative trends that may be developing subconsciously.

2. Unprocessed hurts from the past.
When something bad happens to us, we need to process it (cry, yell, hurt, hate, but finally heal). If this is not done, these subconscious hurts from the past will control you and result in weird behavior.

3. Early exposure to pornography.
When little children are exposed to pornography, it affects them adversely and may lead them to pursue perverted sex.

4. Satanic suggestion.
Satan deals with us through suggestions. Have you ever had a thought go through your mind that you totally disagreed with, knew was wrong, and didn't want to have anything to do with—yet you kept thinking it? That is satan yelling in your ear. His suggestions are easy to identify because they are wrong, usually are perverted, involve intrigue and suspense, and usually hide the penalty from you. I find it very interesting that the Bible acknowledges that when a married man has an affair with another man's wife, it can be *temporarily* fun. The Bible also clearly states that in the end there will be devastation.

> *Stolen waters are sweet, and bread eaten in secret is pleasant.*
> Proverbs 9:17

> *But whoso committeth adultery with a woman lacketh understanding: he that doeth it destroyeth his own soul. A wound and dishonor shall he get; and his reproach shall not be wiped away. For jealousy is the rage of a man: therefore he will not spare in the day of vengeance. He will not regard any ransom; neither will he rest content, though thou givest many gifts.*
> Proverbs 6:32-35

So the thing to do is to test all of your bright ideas against the Word of God, and then you will be able to tell if it is a bright idea or a satanic suggestion.

The external lure of homosexuality has to do with the traps that are set in our society by circumstance and by design. A young man whose body has just matured to the point where he desires to have sex must be careful. The reason for this is that he has limited or no sexual experience to guide him during this period of heightened sexual pressure. During this period of life, there are some things that a young man should never do:

1. Never masturbate in a crowd.
Masturbation or self-release is something that you want to avoid doing. If you decide to masturbate, never do it with other guys. There are many reasons for this:
- Someone may decide to assist you, and at this point it becomes homosexuality.
- You should seek to avoid being nude around men when they are sexually aroused and they want to make you an object of their lust.
- The sex act is a period of intense emotional, physical, and spiritual excitement and should never be publicized.

2. Avoid company with groups of aggressive homosexual men.
One thing that the TV doesn't show is the aggressive, violent side of the "gay" world. In the right setting, homosexual men may forcefully restrain and sodomize (have abnormal sexual intercourse, e.g. anal intercourse with) another man. Male-on-male rape is not at all uncommon.

When I was in high school, I had a friend who played football. He told me that one of the most muscular men on the team would look at a smaller player and tell him: "I'm going to #@*& you." And he meant it too! It is most interesting that because of his lifestyle, this individual was killed before he was 21 years old. Who knows how many men he damaged before his death?

Another problem in the Black community is the man returning from prison who has been victimized. It is very unfortunate when this happens, because that man will never be the same and will need counselling and prayer to fully recover his manhood.

3. Guard against a subtle change in your mindset.
Because of our society's growing acceptance of same-sex intercourse, many people find it no longer offensive. In order to guard yourself, wrong must stay wrong and right must stay right. There is an old saying which goes like this: **"WRONG IS WRONG EVEN IF EVERYBODY DOES IT AND RIGHT IS RIGHT EVEN IF NOBODY DOES IT."** Homosexuality is one of many perils that young men must guard against. What makes it dangerous is that many seek to convince society that it is normal, natural, acceptable behavior.

One hundred years ago, lying, stealing, homosexuality, adultery, fornication and beastiality were wrong, and they are still wrong today. I will admit that in the United States of America you have the right to do all of these things, but you will suffer now, and God is sitting at the crossroads of time with additional consequences in the life to come. Many acts may be legal, but that does not make them moral. Today there are those who seek to remove homosexuality from the wrong list and proclaim that those old standards don't apply here.

Listen to the timeless truth of how the Bible describes homosexuality:

Abomination: Thou shalt not lie with mankind, as with womankind: it is abomination.
Leviticus 18:22

Against Nature: For this cause God gave them up unto vile affections: for even their women did change the natural use into that which is against nature:
Romans 1:27

Unseemly: And likewise also the men, leaving the natural use of the woman, burned in their lust one toward another; men with men working that which is unseemly, and receiving in themselves that recompense of their error which was meet.
Romans 1:27

The bottom line is that you should seek to avoid the lure of homosexuality. Anything that a man wants bad enough, he can justify. Anything that a man wants to avoid bad enough, God will help him avoid. Resolve to grow to **UNTAINTED MANHOOD** with God's help.

The Effeminate Black Male
Let me mention something that applies here. A young man should seek to deal with any glaring effeminate traits that he has picked up over the years. It is easy and natural for a young boy who has been raised by his mother to pick up many of her habits. Usually, most of the glaring feminine moves, looks, attitudes and words are dropped when the young man goes to school and socializes with the other boys. In other cases, the boy will hold on to these traits too long. When this happens, the effeminate youth attracts the attention of older homosexual men, who will seek to induct and introduce the young man into a life of homosexuality.

Homosexuality, AIDS, And The Black Community
AIDS is spreading in the Black community at an alarming rate. One of the reasons for this is the closet homosexual. I have known many men who have struggled with the lure of homosexuality. Some of these men had wives and children. I know of some men who had fiiine women, yet they struggled with a desire for men.

As I look back and analyze those men who struggled with this, I become aware that they tried to keep their women or families. Only a couple of these men went all-out for men. Black men have a tendency to keep their homosexuality in the closet. The result of this for the Black community and the Black woman in particular is that heterosexual AIDS infections in the Black community are extremely high.

The homosexual lifestyle is unhealthy for our nation, and as young men and mature men we should stand and reject the "gay" influence in our personal lives, churches, community and nation. History shows that nations which embraced the homosexual lifestyle were in their last stages of decline. I pray that you will resolve to agree with God on this issue and order your life accordingly.

138

Questions
for Introspection and Discussion (to make you think)

1. Name 5 successful men who you know are successfully dealing with their bents.

_____

_____

_____

2. What negative personal bent do you have that you are aware of that needs to be dealt with?_____

_____

3. Do you display feminine characteristics? Yes___ No___ If so, what do you plan to do about

them?_____

4. Do you know any homosexual young men? Yes___ No___ If so, would you feel comfortable talking to them and trying to help them see how they are making a mistake? Yes___ No___

5. Do you understand the danger that the homosexual lifestyle brings to the Black community? Yes___ No___

6. Do you believe that opposing homosexuality is being homophobic, or do you see it as common

sense?_____

_____

7. Do you understand that God loves the homosexual but hates homosexuality? Yes___ No___

Applicable Scriptures: Please have a boy read the Scripture, then use
the questions to facilitate discussion. Conclude by quoting the Scripture from the Living Bible, which was written for teenagers. *Please remember that the reading of Scripture according to Isaiah 55:11 is the most important thing you will do with the boys. This section is where the Holy Spirit really works in their hearts, so don't skip it.*

(1) *But evil men and seducers shall wax worse and worse, deceiving, and being deceived.*
II Timothy 3:13
[Question] **Do you feel that homosexuality is spreading in the Black community?**
[Question] **How do you plan to avoid getting caught up in homosexuality?**
[Question] **How many people do you know who are HIV-positive?**
The Living Bible translates II Timothy 3:13 like this: *In fact, evil men and false teachers will become worse and worse, deceiving many, they themselves having been deceived by satan.*

(2) *Thou shalt not lie with mankind, as with womankind: it is abomination.* Leviticus 18:22
[Question] **Homosexuals try to make the point that the Bible does not condemn the homosexual lifestyle. Does Leviticus 18:22 make it plain?**
The Living Bible translates Leviticus 18:22 like this: *Homosexuality is absolutely forbidden, for it is an enormous sin.*

(3) *For this cause God gave them up unto vile affections: for even their women did change the natural use into that which is against nature:* Romans 1:26
[Question] **What do you think vile affections mean?**
[Question] **What do you think is meant by the term "natural use"?**
[Question] **Do you feel that mother nature agrees or disagrees with the homosexual lifestyle?**
[Question] **Are you mature enough to love homosexuals while hating the homosexual lifestyle?**
The Living Bible translates Romans 1:26 like this: *That is why God let go of them and let them do all these evil things, so that even their women turned against God's natural plan for them and indulged in sex sin with each other.*

(4) *And likewise also the men, leaving the natural use of the woman, burned in their lust one toward another; men with men working that which is unseemly, and receiving in themselves that recompense of their error which was meet.* Romans 1:27
[Question] **What do you think is meant by the term "unseemly"?**
[Question] **Recompense in this Scripture means consequence. Did you know that there are many diseases and physical conditions associated with the homosexual lifestyle?**
[Question] **Do you have any family members who are closet homosexuals? Do you have any flaming homosexuals in your family?**
The Living Bible translates Romans 1:27 like this: *And the men, instead of having a normal sex relationship with women, burned with lust for each other, men doing shameful things with other men and, as a result, getting paid within their own souls with the penalty they so richly deserved.*

(5) *And Asa did that which was right in the eyes of the LORD, as did David his father. And he took away the sodomites out of the land, and removed all the idols that his fathers had made.*
I Kings 15:11-12

[Question] **The Bible says that Asa did what was right when he took away the homosexuals. (Sodomites are what homosexuals were called in ancient times.) How do you feel we can encourage more brothers to go straight and love some of these lonely sisters out there?**

[Question] **The Black community has the largest percentage of HIV-positive people. The latest statistics attribute the increase to the bi-sexual men in our communities. Sex in the Black community is becoming more dangerous every day. How do you plan to protect yourself?**

The Living Bible translates I Kings 15:11-12 like this: *He pleased the Lord like his ancestor King David. He executed the male prostitutes and removed all the idols his father had made.*

Additional Scriptures Used In Chapter Fifteen As Found In The Living Bible

So God made man like his Maker. Like God did God make man; man and maid did he make them.

Genesis 1:27

Stolen melons are the sweetest; stolen apples taste the best!

Proverbs 9:17

Make This Statement To The Boys:

Before we go on to the next chapter, tell me which Scripture made you mad, glad or made you think.

Note to the Mentor: As a result of this lesson, are there any prayer requests that should be added to your list and forwarded to your prayer partners?

16 The Woman, A Man's Greatest Test

Definition: A woman is the mature female human being, distinguished from a man.

CONNECTING WITH AND LEARNING FROM YOUR RICH, PERSONAL, PAINFUL, PRODUCTIVE PAST. How many times have you heard men say: Women! You can't live with them and you can't live without them! If you are married, you should have plenty of personal examples of how you have been tested by a woman. Be sure to use an illustration in which you used wisdom in dealing with your woman.

CAUTION: Young men must realize that a relationship with a woman includes conflicts on a regular basis.

CONCERN: You are not born with the ability to resolve these conflicts, but you must learn how to resolve conflicts if you are going to have a good relationship. The only way to live successfully with a woman is to learn how to argue and make up.

CHARGE: When you get married, don't refuse to see a counsellor when you have problems. It is usually the men who say: "I don't need to talk to no man!" and refuse to go to counseling. The truth of the matter is that from time to time even the counselor needs counseling because life can be rough some times. Resolve now that you will get counseling when you need it.

ACTIVITY: A discussion of male and female differences would be appropriate. Also a discussion of techniques to resolve arguments.

Text To Be Read With Boys

16 The Woman, A Man's Greatest Test

Son, if you really want to be a man, learn how to treat a woman. Dealing with a woman WISELY is one of the greatest tasks that any man will face in his whole life! The reason this is the case is because a woman is different from a man. Women have bigger brains and sharper senses, and they live longer. Not only this, but a woman carries her feelings as a chip on her shoulder. She is emotionally more transparent than a man. Men today are attempting to treat women and relate to them as they do other men. This is very unwise.

Love Equals Motivation

God made a woman to respond to love. The Bible tells the man to LOVE his wife. When a woman is loved, she is at her best. For years, men have discovered the woman's need for love and exploited that need. It is a terrible thing for a man to worm, work and wiggle his way into a woman's heart by telling her that he loves her and then using love or what she perceives as love to keep her while he is unfaithful. It is a terrible thing when a man uses love, which is so dear and intimate to a woman, for anything other than sincere purposes.

The fact that love is such a motivator for women is common knowledge to most men. The problem comes in the fact that we don't capitalize on it in a positive way. A man must learn to love a woman even when she is unloving (evil). When she is loved, she will be motivated to be all that she can be.

Her Body Equals Fluctuation

Listen very carefully. You don't know anything about a woman's body until you have lived with one for a while. Even then, you haven't seen anything until you watch her go through nine months of pregnancy and view the delivery of a baby.

Each woman goes through four seasons in a month: spring, summer, fall and winter. These seasons are related to her monthly cycle and correspond to chemical fluctuations (hormones) in her system. The fluctuations vary from woman to woman, but all women fluctuate to some degree. In most cases, there is a direct correlation between this chemical fluctuation and her moods, energy level and sex drive. If a man does not understand these fluctuations and where his woman is at any given time, he may have a hard time relating to her wisely. Back a few years ago, men were more in touch with nature and were more knowledgeable of the woman's monthly cycle.

Your Strength Equals Stabilization

A woman needs for a man to be consistent and stable. When a woman fluctuates, she needs stability on the part of her man. In most relationships, it takes the woman and the man a few years to understand this dynamic. Once this is understood, it makes for a better relationship, one in which there is understanding and support.

Likewise, ye husbands, dwell with them according to knowledge, giving honor unto the wife, as unto the weaker vessel, and as being heirs together of the grace of life; that your prayers be not hindered.

I Peter 3:7

Never be satisfied with the amount of knowledge you have about your woman. Seek additional wisdom and knowledge from God, your woman, and an older man.

Wisdom is the principal thing; therefore get wisdom: and with all thy getting get understanding.

Proverbs 4:7

Give instruction to a wise man, and he will be yet wiser: teach a just man, and he will increase in learning.

Proverbs 9:9

Three Things That All Wise Young Men Should Avoid

1. Avoid the married woman.
Any young man who messes with a married woman is very foolish. When you do this, God is against you, the husband is against you and society frowns on it.

Wherefore they are no more twain, but one flesh. What therefore God hath joined together, let not man put asunder.

Matthew 19:6

But whoso committeth adultery with a woman lacketh understanding: he that doeth it destroyeth his own soul. A wound and dishonor shall he get; and his reproach shall not be wiped away. For jealousy is the rage of a man: therefore he will not spare in the day of vengeance. He will not regard any ransom; neither will he rest content, though thou givest many gifts.

Proverbs 6:32-35

Unfortunately, there are older married women who will entice young men with money, cars and sex. It is in your best interest to stay away from it all.

My son, if sinners entice thee, consent thou not.

Proverbs 1:10

2. Avoid the foolish woman.
Many men will hook up with a foolish woman because there is very little challenge there. Many foolish women are easy to get over on, so brothers go that way because they don't have to work so hard.

A foolish woman is clamorous: she is simple, and knoweth nothing. For she sitteth at the door of her house, on a seat in the high places of the city, to call passengers who go right on their ways: Whoso is simple, let him turn in hither: and as for him that wanteth understanding, she saith to him, Stolen waters are sweet, and bread eaten in secret is pleasant. But he knoweth not that the dead are there; and that her guests are in the depths of hell.

Proverbs 9:13-18

The danger with foolish women is you can get stuck with any woman you date. **ANY WOMAN YOU DATE MAY BECOME YOUR MATE!** If you have sex with her, you become one flesh, and she will be in your bloodstream for at least 5 years. The best approach is to avoid this woman altogether.

3. Avoid the wicked woman.

There is nothing more dangerous than a wicked woman. As our society becomes more wicked, the women of our society will become more wicked. This Scripture applies to women and men:

But evil men and seducers shall wax worse and worse, deceiving, and being deceived.
II Timothy 3:13

A wicked woman will lay a trap for a young man. Generally, the young man is partially blinded by the woman's beauty and is not able to make good decisions. A wicked woman will use her sexual powers to seduce the man and render him helpless. As old and wise as I am, I still avoid wicked women like the plague.

For the commandment is a lamp; and the law is light; and reproofs of instruction are the way of life: to keep thee from the evil woman, from the flatter of the tongue of a strange woman. Lust not after her beauty in thine heart; neither let her take thee with her eyelids. For by means of a whorish woman a man is brought to a piece of bread: and the adulteress will hunt for the precious life.

Proverbs 6:23-26

God has given men and women to each other to build up and complete each other. If wisdom is not used and Godly advice followed, there can be great suffering.

Marriage is honorable in all, and the bed undefiled: but whoremongers and adulterers God will judge.   Hebrews 13:4

Questions
for Introspection and Discussion (to make you think)

1. Do you have a girlfriend? Yes___ No___

2. Does she fluctuate? Yes___ No___

3. Are you consistent when she fluctuates? Yes___ No___

4. Are you prepared to love a woman constantly? Yes___ No___

5. Have you ever been tempted by a foolish woman? Yes___ No___ If yes, what did you do?

_____

6. Have you ever been tempted by a wicked woman? Yes___ No___ If yes, what did you do?

_____

7. Have you ever been tempted by a married woman? Yes___ No___ If yes, what did you do?

_____

8. Do you know an older, spiritual man who can help you understand women? Yes___ No___

9. What one question would you like to have answered? _____

_____

Applicable Scriptures: Please have a boy read the Scripture, then use the questions to facilitate discussion. Conclude by quoting the Scripture from the Living Bible, which was written for teenagers. *Please remember that the reading of Scripture according to Isaiah 55:11 is the most important thing you will do with the boys. This section is where the Holy Spirit really works in their hearts, so don't skip it.*

(1) *The mouth of strange women is a deep pit: he that is abhorred of the Lord shall fall therein.* Proverbs 22:14

[Question] **Women have been used as traps to catch men for centuries. What is it about a womans rap that men find so irresistible?**

[Question] **Thinking men can hear the lies that strange women speak. The question that you need to answer is, are you able to think clearly when a fine, fast woman raps to you?**

The Living Bible translates Proverbs 22:14 like this: *A prostitute is a dangerous trap; those cursed of God are caught in it.*

(2) *Likewise, ye husbands, dwell with them according to knowledge, giving honor unto the wife, as unto the weaker vessel, and as being heirs together of the grace of life; that your prayers be not hindered.* I Peter 3:7

[Question] **God will slow down the prayer life of a man who does not treat his wife right. With this in mind, do you feel a man can mistreat his wife and get away with it?**

[Question] **How can a man honor his wife?**

[Question] **Women are physically weaker than men. How should a man respond to this?**

The Living Bible translates I Peter 3:7 like this: *You husbands must be careful of your wives being thoughtful of their needs and honoring them as the weaker sex. Remember that you and your wife are partners in receiving God's blessings, and if you don't treat her as you should, your prayers will not get ready answers.*

(3) *Wisdom is the principal thing; therefore get wisdom: and with all thy getting get understanding.* Proverbs 4:7

[Question] **The fact that you are involved in this mentoring ministry shows that you value wisdom. Are you internalizing the wisdom that we are discussing?**

[Question] **Name three sources of wisdom.**

[Question] **Once you get wisdom, you can understand the world in which we live. Do you feel that you understand the world?**

The Living Bible translates Proverbs 4:7 like this: *Determination to be wise is the first step toward becoming wise! And with your wisdom, develop common sense and good judgment.*

(4) *Give instruction to a wise man, and he will be yet wiser: teach a just man, and he will increase in learning.* Proverbs 9:9

[Question] **Are you a wise man? Are you hungry for more wisdom?**

[Question] **Are you a just man? Are you increasing in learning?**

[Question] **How do you plan to apply what you are learning?**

The Living Bible translates Proverbs 9:9 like this: *Teach a wise man, and he will be the wiser; teach a good man, and he will learn more.*

(5) *Wherefore they are no more twain, but one flesh. What therefore God hath joined together, let not man put asunder.* Matthew 19:6

[Question] **If God says a husband and wife are one flesh, why do you feel so many couples get divorces?**

[Question] **What God has put together should not be messed with. A marriage is a holy sacred thing. With this in mind, would you mess with another man's wife?**

[Question] **Are you determined to stay together once you get married?**

The Living Bible translates Matthew 19:6 like this: *God created man and woman, and that a man should leave his father and mother, and be forever united to his wife. The two shall become one—no longer two, but one! And no man may divorce what God has joined together."*

(6) *But whoso committeth adultery with a woman lacketh understanding: he that doeth it destroyeth his own soul. A wound and dishonor shall he get; and his reproach shall not be wiped away. For jealousy is the rage of a man: therefore he will not spare in the day of vengeance. He will not regard any ransom; neither will he rest content, though thou givest many gifts.* Proverbs 6:32-35

[Question] **How do you feel about a man who will have sex with another man's wife just for the hell of it?**

[Question] **A man who commits adultery does not understand God, nor does he understand life. What do you think the Scripture means when it says "he destroyeth his own soul"?**

[Question] **According to this Scripture, what will the woman's husband do when he finds out?**

The Living Bible translates Proverbs 6:32-35 like this: *But the man who commits adultery is an utter fool, for he destroys his own soul. Wounds and constant disgrace are his lot, for the woman's husband will be furious in his jealousy, and he will have no mercy on you in his day of vengeance. You won't be able to buy him off no matter what you offer.*

(7) *My son, if sinners entice thee, consent thou not.* Proverbs 1:10

[Question] **Are you strong enough to walk away from a tempting situation?**

[Question] **It is just a matter of time until you will be tempted with a sexual temptation that could hurt you deeply. How do you plan to avoid it?**

[Question] **Do you envy people who seem to have it together and can say no to sexual temptation?**

The Living Bible translates Proverbs 1:10 like this: *If young toughs tell you, "come and join us"—turn your back on them!*

(8) *For the commandment is a lamp; and the law is light; and reproofs of instruction are the way of life: To keep thee from the evil woman, from the flatter of the tongue of a strange woman. Lust not after her beauty in thine heart; neither let her take thee with her eyelids. for by means of a whorish woman a man is brought to a piece of bread: and the adulteress will hunt for the precious life.* Proverbs 6:23-26

[Question] **What does this Scripture say will keep you from the evil woman?**

[Question] **How does this Scripture say that you should protect your heart?**
The Living Bible translates Proverbs 6:23-26 like this: *For their advice is a beam of light directed into the dark corners of your mind to warn you of danger and to give you a good life. Their counsel will keep you far away from prostitutes with all their flatteries. Don't lust for their beauty. Don't let their coyness seduce you. For a prostitute will bring a man to poverty, and an adulteress may cost him his very life.*

Additional Scriptures Used In Chapter Sixteen As Found In The Living Bible

A prostitute is loud and brash, and never has enough of lust and shame. She sits at the door of her house or stands at the street corners of the city, whispering to men going by, and to those minding their own business. "Come home with me," she urges simpletons. "Stolen melons are the sweetest; stolen apples taste the best!" But they don't realize that her former guests are now citizens of hell.

Proverbs 9:13-18

In fact, evil men and false teachers will become worse and worse, deceiving man, they themselves having been deceived by Satan.

II Timothy 3:13

Honor your marriage and its vows, and be pure; for God will surely punish all those who are immoral or commit adultery.

Hebrews 13:4

Make This Statement To The Boys:

Before we go on to the next chapter, tell me which Scripture made you mad, glad or made you think.

Note to the Mentor: As a result of this lesson, are there any prayer requests that should be added to your list and forwarded to your prayer partners?

17 How To Overcome Controlling Sexual Thoughts About Women

Definition: Sexual means of or pertaining to sex.
Thoughts are the products of mental activity.

CONNECTING WITH AND LEARNING FROM YOUR RICH PERSONAL, PAINFUL, PRODUCTIVE PAST. We all can remember times when we struggled to concentrate in school, in church, at the mall or while driving. Share with the young men your own struggles and thoughts about women. Tell the truth about your struggles, and if you are weak in this area, ask God to help you. Be sure to tell the young men that each generation should do better than the previous generation.

CAUTION: There is a richness found in a pure thought life that few find, and few people realize the value of it. I want the young men to realize that the goal of a pure thought life is a noble goal and that doing it is obtainable.

CHARGE: Make it a goal in life as a man not to be controlled by sexual thoughts. To do so will save you much pain and grief.

ACTIVITY: In your discussions with and lectures from older men, discuss how that failing to control your thought life leads to actions which will later be called mistakes.

17 How To Overcome Controlling Sexual Thoughts About Women

When I was in junior high school, I had a paper route. I never will forget the Tuesday evening that I was collecting from my customers and something happened that really shook me up. As I passed a particular apartment building on the lower level, I saw something that caused my eighth-grade mind to go into a meltdown. There was a young lady who was dressing, and she could clearly be seen through the window without any unnecessary peeping.

As I stood there, stunned, I thought: "That's what they look like!" I had never seen a live, naked female except my little sister. I can remember going home in shock, avoiding my mother's eyes because I knew that she could look at me and know that I had seen a live, naked girl. I can remember the funny feeling I got every time I walked past that building. In time I got over it, but it was a real shock for me at that time in life.

My, how things have changed! Kids in junior high school now are exposed to more sexual stimuli than the previous generations were, and as a result, it is necessary to discuss the impact that the exposure will have on them. The newspapers carry the stories every day of younger and younger girls having babies and young boys boasting of their sexual powers. The result is a lackadaisical, ho-hum attitude about the dangers of sex and very few people taking seriously the damaging effect of the sexual stimuli that young people are exposed to.

As a result of all of the sexual exposure, it becomes difficult to look at a beautiful woman and not take her clothes off in your mind. This puts the man in prison. Any man or woman who cannot look at someone of the opposite sex without undressing them in their mind is in PRISON!

The mind must be free, and you will need to fight to keep it free. THE MIND IS THE MOST IMPORTANT SEX ORGAN. So, the question then becomes: "How can I think pure thoughts when I encounter that gorgeous creature of the opposite sex?" I would like to equip you with some thoughts that will help you gain the victory in this area of life.

1. Tell yourself that the gorgeous body that you are looking at also has a soul and spirit.
The spirit of this person hangs out with God, and He is always closer to her than you will ever get to be. When you think this, you remind yourself that the woman is an eternal creature who will exist in spirit form for an eternity. Any woman's relationship with a man is temporary, but her relationship with God is eternal.

What! Know ye not that your body is the temple of the Holy Ghost which is in you, which ye have of God, and ye are not your own? For ye are bought with a price: therefore glorify God in your body, and in your spirit, which are God's.
I Corinthians 6:19-20

2. Tell yourself that the woman that you are looking at has a family.
She may have a father, brother, and family members that love her as a daughter, sister, or cousin. It is always a family affair when you get involved with a woman because families generally protect their women and women love their families. The goal is to respect the woman in your mind as well as with your actions. God judges not only your actions but also your thoughts.

But I say unto you, That whosoever looketh on a woman to lust after her hath committed adultery with her already in his heart.
Matthew 5:28

[Treat] the elder women as mothers; the younger as sisters, with all purity.
I Timothy 5:2

3. Tell yourself that the woman that you are looking at has goals, dreams and a mind of her own.
It is amazing to talk to a woman sometimes and see where her head is. A man is thinking about her body, and she is thinking something totally different.

4. Consider the fact that although she is pretty, she may have medical problems.
The female body is an amazing thing with many complicated parts. A woman has many things to deal with that men don't know anything about. You will learn more about this when you marry and live with a woman.

5. Realize that the personality and real character of the woman may not match her pretty face.
I know of a young lady who was so pretty that when she walked into a room, every male head turned in her direction. She knew that she was pretty, and she enjoyed all of the attention that she received. What was unfortunate about her situation was that she allowed it to go to her head, and her personality was terrible.

I know many men who hooked up with beautiful women just for their beauty, and shortly after the beginning of their marriage or relationship, they found out that they were very miserable. Remember that a pretty face can hide an empty mind, or an ugly mind.

6. Determine to what degree you choose to be controlled by lustful thoughts and females in general.
I stopped in a convenience store to get some gas. As I went inside to pay, there was a woman standing at the counter with some beautiful legs and shorts on that were cut very high. Standing behind her in line were four men; I made the fifth. As I stood there, I noticed that there was much

tension in the air because all of the men standing behind her were nervous. All of them could see her legs, but none of them wanted to act like they were bothered by them. As the lady paid for her gas and left, all of the men's heads turned as they took a last peek at the legs that carried her to her car.

After she left, the men in the store heaved a sigh of relief. I said to the man in front of me: "She had some pretty legs, didn't she?" He looked at me, shook his head and said: **"SURE DID!"** What I find interesting about this situation was the manner in which the men handled being in the presence of these pretty legs. There was a tenseness in the air because of the presence of this woman and how the men allowed themselves to be impacted by her. When this happens to you, this is what you do: acknowledge to yourself or another man that the woman is pretty. When you do this, you release the pressure that is going on in your mind. This will help defuse many of the additional negative thoughts that would occur if the situation were not faced head-on. This also allows you to be at peace with yourself because you are not fighting the negative thoughts that occur when you have secret sexual fantasies in your mind.

Somehow in our culture it has become acceptable behavior for a man to be out of control in the presence of a pretty woman. TV and movies make it appear that men have no control over the matter. **This is not the case!** You can CHOOSE to what degree you want to allow a woman's beauty to manipulate you.

> *I made a covenant with mine eyes; why then should I think upon a maid?*
> Job 31:1

I challenge you to do like Job did: he made an agreement with his eyes. Many men need to do this today.

Questions
for Introspection and Discussion (to make you think)

1. What do you think when a pretty young woman sits next to you?_____

2. Do you challenge negative sexual thoughts about women, or do you let your mind run wild?_____

3. Do you have a pretty sister? Yes___ No___

4. Who do you talk to about women or what source provides you with your information about women?_____

5. Have you considered the fact that if the Lord lets you live, you will be older one day and sex will not be a priority in your life? Yes___ No___

Applicable Scriptures: Please have a boy read the Scripture, then use the questions to facilitate discussion. Conclude by quoting the Scripture from the Living Bible, which was written for teenagers. *Please remember that the reading of Scripture according to Isaiah 55:11 is the most important thing you will do with the boys. This section is where the Holy Spirit really works in their hearts, so don't skip it.*

(1) *Lust not after her beauty in thine heart; neither let her take thee with her eyelids. For by means of a whorish woman a man is brought to a piece of bread: and the adultress will hunt for the precious life.* Proverbs 6:25-26

[Question] **Lust can be defined as too much passion. How do you keep from lusting?**

[Question] **A woman's eyes are very powerful. Have you ever had a woman to put her eyes on you? If yes, how did it make you feel?**

[Question] **What can a whorish woman do to a man?**

The Living Bible translates Proverbs 6:25-26 like this: *Don't lust for their beauty. Don't let their coyness seduce you. For a prostitute will bring a man to poverty, and an adulteress may cost him his very life.*

(2) *But I say unto you, That whosoever looketh on a woman to lust after her hath committed adultery with her already in his heart.* Matthew 5:28

[Question] **Jesus is concerned with the purity of your mind. Do you pollute your mind with pornography?**

[Question] **According to Jesus, if you undress a woman with your eyes, what have you done?**

[Question] **How would you feel if a brother looked at your sister like this?**

The Living Bible translates Matthew 5:28 like this: *But I say: Anyone who even looks at a woman with lust in his eye has already committed adultery with her in his heart.*

(3) *And it came to pass in an eveningtide, that David arose from off his bed, and walked upon the roof of the king's house: and from the roof he saw a woman washing herself; and the woman was very beautiful to look upon.* II Samuel 11:2

[Question] **David had idle time. How can idle time be dangerous?**

[Question] **What is the danger in looking at pictures of naked women?**

[Question] **David's night of ecstasy with this beautiful woman that he was staring at cost him years of incredible pain and suffering. It can do the same for you. Do you feel it is worth it?**

The Living Bible translates II Samuel 11:2 like this: *One night he couldn't get to sleep and went for a stroll on the roof of the palace. As he looked out over the city, he noticed a woman of unusual beauty taking her evening bath.*

(4) *But every man is tempted, when he is drawn away of his own lust, and enticed.* James 1:14

[Question] **There is a lust inside of you that leads you to desire women. How do you feel that lust can be controlled?**

[Question] **There is a progression: The look, the lust and the leap. Do you feel it is wisdom or weakness to turn away after a quick look?**

The Living Bible translates James 1:14 like this: *Temptation is the pull of man's own evil thoughts and wishes.*

(5) *But if they cannot contain, let them marry: for it is better to marry than to burn.* I Corinthians 7:9

[Question] **Do you feel it is OK to live together for a while before you get married?**

[Question] **Do you feel it is possible to have a girlfriend and not have sex with her?**

[Question] **Do you feel it is OK not to have a lust problem?**

The Living Bible translates I Corinthians 7:9 like this: *But if you can't control yourselves, go ahead and marry. It is better to marry than to burn with lust.*

(6) *I beseech you therefore, brethren, by the mercies of God, that ye present your bodies a living sacrifice, holy, acceptable unto God, which is your reasonable service. And be not conformed to this world: but be ye transformed by the renewing of your mind, that ye may prove what is that good, and acceptable, and perfect, will of God.* Romans 12:1-2

[Question] **Your body is not really yours. Your next breath is a gift from God. Do you feel that God is unreasonable to ask you to keep your body clean and pure?**

[Question] **God says that we should transform ourselves by renewing our minds, which is done through Bible study. How often do you read your Bible?**

[Statement] **Reading the Bible will let you know exactly what God's will is.**

The Living Bible translates Romans 12:1-2 like this: *AND SO, DEAR brothers, I plead with you to give your bodies to God. Let them be a living sacrifice, holy—the kind he can accept. When you think of what he has done for you, is this too much to ask? Don't copy the behavior and customs of this world, but be a new and different person with a fresh newness in all you do and think.*

(7) *Now concerning the things whereof ye wrote unto me: It is good for a man not to touch a woman. Nevertheless, to avoid fornication, let every man have his own wife, and let every woman have her own husband.* I Corinthians 7:1-2

[Question] **It is a joy to be married and have sex without being guilty, to have sex knowing that God is looking down with approval. Are you looking forward to this?**

[Question] **Do you feel that you can kiss and hug a girl over and over and not want to have sex?**

[Question] **How do you feel about not touching a girl until you are married?**

The Living Bible translates I Corinthians 7:1-2 like this: *NOW ABOUT THOSE questions you asked in your last letter: my answer is that if you do not marry, it is good. But usually it is best to be married, each man having his own wife, and each woman having her own husband, because otherwise you might fall back into sin.*

(8) *Finally, brethren, whatsoever things are true, whatsoever things are honest, whatsoever things are just, whatsoever things are pure, whatsoever things are lovely, whatsoever things are of good report; if there be any virtue, and if there be any praise, think on these things.* Philippians 4:8

[Question] **Are you good at keeping your mind on things true, honest, just, pure, lovely, and things of good report?**

[Question] **Why do you feel the Apostle Paul asked us to think on these things?**

The Living Bible translates Philippians 4:8 like this: *And now, brothers, as I close this letter let me say this one more thing: Fix your thoughts on what is true and good and right. Think about things that are pure and lively, and dwell on the fine, good things in others. Think about all you can praise God for and be glad about.*

Additional Scriptures Used In Chapter Seventeen As Found

In The Living Bible

Haven't you yet learned that your body is the home of the Holy Spirit God gave you, and that he lives within you? Your own body does not belong to you. For God has bought you with a great price. So use every part of your body to give glory back to God, because he owns it.
I Corinthians 6:19-20

Treat the older women as mothers, and the girls as your sisters, thinking only pure thoughts about them.
I Timothy 5:2

I made a covenant with my eyes not to look with lust upon a girl.
Job 31:1

Make This Statement To The Boys:

Before we go on to the next chapter, tell me which Scripture made you mad, glad or made you think.

Note to the Mentor: As a result of this lesson, are there any prayer requests that should be added to your list and forwarded to your prayer partners?

Notes:

18 Who Is Your Judge?

Definition: A judge is one qualified to pass a critical judgment.

CONNECTING WITH AND LEARNING FROM YOUR RICH PERSONAL, PAINFUL, PRODUCTIVE PAST. If you had an older, wiser man in you life who helped you during critical times in your life, you are blessed. If you did not have that wisdom available, you know the pain and loss you experienced. Relate to the young men your experience (good or bad) to help them see the value of judges.

CAUTION: Not all men are qualified to give you advice or judge you! Seek your judges wisely and prayerfully.

CONCERN: Young men frequently follow the wisdom or judgments of stars instead of the wisdom and judgment of saints! Before you follow someone's advice, look at their life and see how their advice works for them. Look at others who took that advice years ago and see how they turned out.

CHARGE: Determine to develop the discipline of submitting to Godly judges.

ACTIVITY: Look at the lives of Black stars from the past. Ask the question: "How did they live and where are they now?"

Text To Be Read With Boys

18 Who Is Your Judge?

Every young man needs a judge. Usually a father fills this role. A very fortunate young man will have many men in his life who judge him from time to time. Isaiah 1:23 talks about the Jews who are about to be destroyed. Listen to what he says: ***"Thy princes are rebellious, and companions of thieves: every one loveth gifts, and followeth after rewards: they judge not the fatherless, neither doth the cause of the widow come unto them."***

Consequences of Not Having Judges

This Scripture speaks about the consequences of not having judges. When the men of a society stop caring for, correcting, and instructing the young of that society (even though the children are not biologically theirs), destruction is just up the road. So, I ask the young man a question: "Who are your judges?" And I ask the mature Black man: "What young man are you judging?" When we speak of a judge, we are speaking of a mature older person who can provide guidance and correction.

A youth without a man to respect and receive guidance and correction from will find life difficult. No matter how gifted and talented he may be, the road will be rough if a young man is too free. A Judge to call him out when he is wrong will provide guidance for a young man and help him live longer.

Who Are the Best Possible Judges?

A judge may be a coach, teacher, uncle, pastor, boss, counsellor or any man who genuinely cares for you and seeks your best good. Be sure to consider the role that God plays in his life. People who love God are far from perfect, but at least you know where they are trying to come from.

How to Get the Most from Your Judges

People enjoy the opportunity to reproduce themselves. A man receives gratification from a son who follows in his footsteps. Most mature men would be flattered for you to ask them to participate in the process of molding you into a man. So, you need to show an older man that you have these qualities:

- **Desire.** Express your desire to be tutored, discipled and taught by the older man.
- **Patience.** Once you've expressed that desire, don't rush him. Even mature men have their hands full keeping their own lives together. Be patient.
- **Submission.** Be prepared to submit and do some things you don't want to do or that don't make a lot of sense to you. Think about it: if it made sense to you, you wouldn't need the older, wiser man to tell you to do it!
- **Transparency.** Be transparent with the older man. Don't hide your feelings. He was young once and knows what it is like.

Zeal. Anything he asks you to do, do it well.

Seek you out a wise man. Apart from kinfolk, your pastor should be one of your main judges. The reason is that a good pastor loves you, and God will work through your pastor to instruct you. This method is safe, and I recommend it.

Where no counsel is, the people fall: but in the multitude of counsellors there is safety.
Proverbs 11:14

Questions
for Introspection and Discussion (to make you think)

1. How many good, mature men are you subject to? List them.

_____

_____

_____

2. Do they know you feel this way?_____

3. Do you have the discipline to do what they say?_____

4. Can you think of a time when an older, wiser man asked you to do something, you refused to do it, and you later found out that he was right? Discuss or think about it. Ask yourself questions and learn how to benefit from a similar situation when it happens in the future.

_____

_____

5. Have you ever been to court and submitted to a judge on the bench? Yes___ No___

How did it feel?_____

6. Do you see the advantage of getting a judge who will guide you in a manner that will keep you away from the judge on the bench? Yes___ No___

Applicable Scriptures: Please have a boy read the Scripture, then use

the questions to facilitate discussion. Conclude by quoting the Scripture from the Living Bible, which was written for teenagers. *Please remember that the reading of Scripture according to Isaiah 55:11 is the most important thing you will do with the boys. This section is where the Holy Spirit really works in their hearts, so don't skip it.*

(1) *A wise man will hear, and will increase learning; and a man of understanding shall attain unto wise counsels.* Proverbs 1:5

[Question] **Do you listen to older men when they share wisdom with you?**

[Question] **Are you a wise young man?**

[Question] **Who serves as wise counsel in your life?**

The Living Bible translates Proverbs 1:5 like this: *I want those already wise to become the wiser and become leaders by exploring the depths of meaning in these nuggets of truth.*

(2) *Turn you at my reproof: behold, I will pour out my spirit unto you, I will make known my words unto you.* Proverbs 1:23

[Question] **Have you turned from any of your bad habits since reading this book?**

[Question] **Do you have God's Spirit in you?**

[Question] **Do you ever sense God communicating with you?**

The Living Bible translates Proverbs 1:23 like this: *Come here and listen to me! I'll pour out the spirit of wisdom upon you, and make you wise.*

(3) *My son, despise not the chastening of the LORD; neither be weary of his correction: For whom the Lord loveth he correcteth; even as a father the son in whom he delighteth.* Proverbs 3:11-12

[Question] **Do you realize that the men who correct you love you?**

[Question] **Do you get an attitude when you are corrected?**

[Question] **Are you mature enough to see correction as a sign that people care for you?**

The Living Bible translates Proverbs 3:11-12 like this: *Young man, do not resent it when God chastens and corrects you, for his punishment is proof of his love. Just as a father punishes a son he delights in to make him better, so the Lord corrects you.*

(4) *Hear, O my son, and receive my sayings; and the years of thy life shall be many.* Proverbs 4:10

[Question] **Being disobedient to wisdom can get you killed. Do you know any young men who were killed as a result of disobedience?**

[Question] **Do you want to grow to a ripe old age?**

The Living Bible translates Proverbs 4:10 like this: *My son, listen to me and do as I say, and you will have a long, good life.*

(5) *Let this mind be in you, which was also in Christ Jesus:* Philippians 2:5

[Question] **Jesus Christ allowed His Father to judge Him. Do you allow your elders to judge (correct) you?**

The Living Bible translates Philippians 2:5 like this: *Your attitude should be the kind that was shown us by Jesus Christ, who, though he was God, did not demand and cling to his rights as God, but laid aside his mighty power and glory taking the disguise of a slave and becoming like men.*

Additional Scriptures Used In Chapter Eighteen As Found In The Living Bible

Your leaders are rebels, companions of thieves; all of them take bribes and won't defend the widows and orphans.

Isaiah 1:23

Without wise leadership, a nation is in trouble; but with good counselors there is safety.

Proverbs 11:14

Make This Statement To The Boys:

Before we go on to the next chapter, tell me which Scripture made you mad, glad or made you think.

Note to the Mentor: As a result of this lesson, are there any prayer requests that should be added to your list and forwarded to your prayer partners?

Notes:_____

Mentor: Read this page before you meet with your boys.

19 The Principle Of Authority

Definition: Authority is the power to judge, act or commend.

CONNECTING WITH AND LEARNING FROM YOUR RICH, PERSONAL, PAINFUL, PRODUCTIVE PAST. We all have had good and bad experiences with authority. Relate from your personal experience how you went from the first level of authority to higher levels of authority. In a job dispute you go from your immediate supervisor to the department chairman to the head of your division and on up to the president of the company and maybe on to the courts.

CAUTION: Don't allow yourself to concentrate on the personality of any one person in authority. It is not the personality of the person but the authority of their position that must be respected.

CONCERN: I am concerned about our seemingly negative attitude toward and response to authority. Because of the abuses of the past, we find it difficult to trust many authority figures.

CHARGE: Encourage the boys to approach the authority figures in their lives objectively (without any bias). Encourage the boys to put the authority figures at ease and work with them to resolve problems.

ACTIVITY - Speak to an executive or authority figure about their responsibility. Let them tell their side of the story.

19 The Principle Of Authority

When I was 18 years old, I had a younger brother who was 2 years old. He was the first toddler that I encountered as an adult. I found his development very interesting, especially his first words. His favorite first words were: "Don't tell me!" He was in his own world, doing his own thing, and when you sought to guide or interact with him, he would say: "Don't tell me!" At times he would even put his hands over his ears, look away and say: "DON'T TELL ME!"

At the time, I would think that the kid was trippin', and I would ignore him. I have since learned that what he was doing was quite natural because the Bible teaches that we are born in a state of rebellion. We are born rebelling against anybody who puts restraints on us. King David knew this when he said:

> *Behold, I was shapen in iniquity; and in sin did my mother conceive me.*
> Psalm 51:5

> *The wicked are estranged from the womb: they go astray as soon as they be born, speaking lies.*
> Psalm 58:3

There was a time in my life when I had a problem with the concept of being born a sinner. And then I had kids. Each child said "da da" first, because it was easy to say. The second word was "NO!"

Because of the theological truth that we are born in sin, it becomes necessary for us to be born again, which frees us from the slavery of sin. Once we are born again, we no longer need to be slaves to passion, greed, anger, violence, girls, or any other thing.

With this in mind, we look at the principle of authority. One of the most difficult things for a man or woman to do is to submit to authority. Part of the reason we reject authority is due to our nature. Another reason is because of our culture. We have already discussed our nature, so let's look at our culture.

We have a culture that is very prideful. The media appeals to our pride in its programming and commercials. People are encouraged to do things to get even and vindicate themselves when "dissed" or insulted. We see that pride is rampant in our society.

With all of the emphasis on pride, the principle of authority suffers. Regardless of what men think, God has said that we all need authority in our lives. One of the classic Scriptures on this subject is I Corinthians 11:3:

But I would have you know, that the head of every man is Christ; and the head of the woman is the man; and the head of Christ is God.

I Corinthians 11:3

It is clear from Scripture and from observation that a young man who learns that there are people in his life that can tell him what to do will go further than the young man who rebels against authority. Let's list examples of authority figures in our lives: parents, teachers, preachers, deans, principals, police, employers, mayors, governors, presidents and God, just to name a few.

Now, what most young Black men don't understand is that there is a progression of authority in their lives. When you come into conflict with one of them you, are in conflict with ALL of them! Let me explain. When you fall out with the teacher, she calls the dean. When you fall out with the dean, he calls the principal. When you fall out with the principal, he calls the police, who escort you off of campus, and it goes on and on and on.

So the wise thing is to realize that WHEN YOU DEAL WITH ONE AUTHORITY FIGURE, YOU DEAL WITH THEM ALL! A police officer told me that when a Black male puffs his chest and resists his authority, he simply calls for back up.

The wise brother will deal with all authority figures in such a manner that they will not send him to the next level.

A wise young man will seek to win the favor of those in authority in his life. This does not mean that you have to kiss their toes, but it does mean that you should be kind to them. In most cases, they will respond in kindness. If they are mean to you, be pleasant to them anyway and God will bless you in spite of their attitude.

If you are lazy, evil, wrong, trippin' or acting inappropriately, it is the job of the authority figures in your life to make you get yourself together. It amazes me how some people can be as wrong as two left feet and complain when someone corrects them.

Questions
for Introspection and Discussion (to make you think)

1. What authority figure do you have the biggest problem with?_____

2. When was the last time you were mistreated by an authority figure?_____
How did you respond?_____

3. Do you ever feel rebellious for no apparent reason?_____

4. Do you listen to music or rap that encourages rebellion?   Yes ___ No___

5. What concrete steps are you taking to help you deal with the authority in your life?_____
_____

6. Did you understand that when you reject authority on any level, it will eventually send you up to the next level? Yes___ No___

When thou goest with thine adversary to the magistrate, as thou art in the way, give diligence that thou mayest be delivered from him; lest he hale thee to the judge, and the judge deliver thee to the officer, and the officer cast thee into prison. I tell thee, thou shalt not depart thence, till thou hast paid the very last mite.
Luke 12:58

Applicable Scriptures: Please have a boy read the Scripture, then use the questions to facilitate discussion. Conclude by quoting the Scripture from the Living Bible, which was written for teenagers. *Please remember that the reading of Scripture according to Isaiah 55:11 is the most important thing you will do with the boys. This section is where the Holy Spirit really works in their hearts, so don't skip it.*

(1) *Let every soul be subject unto the higher powers. For there is no power but of God: the powers that be are ordained of God. Whosoever therefore resisteth the power, resisteth the ordinance of God: and they that resist shall receive to themselves damnation. For rulers are not a terror to good works, but to the evil. Wilt thou then not be afraid of the power? Do that which is good, and thou shalt have praise of the same.* Romans 13:1-3

[Question] **Do you really understand that God has placed individuals in positions of authority in your life?**

[Question] **Do you understand that to when you resist authority, you are ultimately resisting God?**

[Question] **Are you afraid of authority figures when you have done no wrong?**

The Living Bible translates Romans 13:1-3 like this: *OBEY THE GOVERNMENT, for God is the one who has put it there. There is no government anywhere that God has not placed in power. So those who refuse to obey the laws of the land are refusing to obey God, and punishment will follow. For the policeman does not frighten people who are doing right; but those doing evil will always fear him. So if you don't want to be afraid, keep the laws and you will get along well.*

(2) *It is an abomination to kings to commit wickedness: for the throne is established by righteousness.* Proverbs 16:12

[Question] **Leaders are given their positions to promote justice. Why do you feel we have so many bad leaders?**

[Question] **Do you think that all bad leaders will eventually answer to God?**

The Living Bible translates Proverbs 16:12 like this: *It is a horrible thing for a king to do evil. His right to rule depends upon his fairness.*

(3) *Hear counsel, and receive instruction, that thou mayest be wise in thy latter end.* Proverbs 19:20

[Question] **Do you realize that wisdom is cumulative? It adds up. Do you feel like you are getting wiser?**

[Question] **Do you want to be seen as a wise person when you get older?**

The Living Bible translates Proverbs 19:20 like this: *Get all the advice you can and be wise the rest of your life.*

(4) *The king's heart is in the hand of the LORD, as the rivers of water: he turneth it withersoever he will.* Proverbs 21:1

[Question] **Do you believe that God controls the President?**

[Question] **The amazing thing is that God controls people even when they don't realize it. Do you feel that He is controlling you?**

The Living Bible translates Proverbs 21:1 like this: *JUST AS WATER is turned into irrigation ditches, so the Lord directs the king's thoughts. He turns them wherever he wants to.*

(5) *He that hath no rule over his own spirit is like a city that is broken down, and without walls.* Proverbs 25:28

[Question] **Can you be calm when you are getting rebuked?**

[Question] **When you are challenged by authority, do you engage your mouth before you engage your mind?**

[Question] **Do you realize that you are supposed to control yourself and not be controlled by parents, teachers and others?**

[Question] **How do you rate your overall self-control?**

The Living Bible translates Proverbs 25:28 like this: *A man without self-control is as defenseless as a city with broken-down walls.*

Additional Scriptures Used In Chapter Nineteen As Found In The Living Bible

But I was born a sinner, yes, from the moment my mother conceived me.
Psalm 51:5

These men are born sinners, lying from their earliest words!
Psalm 58:3

But there is one matter I want to remind you about: that a wife is responsible to her husband, her husband is responsible to Christ, and Christ is responsible to God.
I Corinthians 11:3

Get all the advice you can and be wise the rest of your life.
Proverbs 19:20

A man without self-control is as defenseless as a city with broken-down walls.
Proverbs 25:26

Make This Statement To The Boys:

Before we go on to the next chapter, tell me which Scripture made you mad, glad or made you think.

Note to the Mentor: As a result of this lesson, are there any prayer requests that should be added to your list and forwarded to your prayer partners?

Mentor: Read this page before you meet with your boys.

20 Is It Really Necessary To Curse???

Definition: A curse is the expression of a wish that misfortune, evil etc., befall another.

CONNECTING WITH AND LEARNING FROM YOUR RICH, PERSONAL, PAINFUL, PRODUCTIVE PAST. To what degree have you used profanity in the past? (Did you notice how I said "in the past"?). Think of a situation in which profanity played a negative role in your life, coming from your mouth or from the mouth of another. Share with the young men the negative effects of that experience and how it is better now.

CAUTION: Blacks have their own profanity vocabulary. It is promoted by Black actors and comedians, rappers with limited vocabularies.

CONCERN: The incessant cussing of rappers. Can you listen to this day in and day out and not be impacted?

CHARGE: Be careful about what you say. God keeps a record of each word that comes out of your mouth.

> *But I say unto you, That every idle word that men shall speak, they shall give account thereof in the day of judgment.*
>
> Matthew 12:36

20 Is It Really Necessary To Curse???

I was in the mall the other day, and there was a basketball court set up for a promotion. People were invited to take some shots for prizes. I must say that I was embarrassed at some brothers there who were foul. In a crowded mall, they were talking like this: "Yo man, what the *&^% &6%^&<, *$#&, you doin? You can't make no *&%^, ^%$&, $#% shots!" Not only were they using profanity, they were also very loud.

When you curse in public, you only show that you:
* Have a limited vocabulary.
* Have not been properly trained (no home trainin').
* Don't respect those who are offended by profanity.
* Don't respect yourself and the other Black men who will be looked upon negatively because of your behavior.
* Are probably not a person that people will want to get to know.

Profanity impresses no one but you. For some strange reason, the person who curses believes that something positive is being accomplished through his negative behavior.

If you are prone to foul language, you need to consider several things:
* Your motivation for cursing.
* Your understanding of cursing.
* How you are perceived because of your cursing.
* What you can do to stop cursing.

Let's consider your motivation for cursing.
All behavior is motivated by something. If you are prone to profanity, there is a reason why you continue to do it. In most cases, it is because you grew up around it and found it to be the language spoken in your environment. If this is the case, you need to do what was stated in Chapter One, where we discussed dealing with your orientation. If you curse because you are pressured by those around you, then you need to get a grip. This type of response to peer pressure is an indication that you have a weak personality. If your motivation is that it makes you feel big or powerful, this is a misbelief because the opposite is true.

Let's look at your understanding of cursing.
I was in the presence of an elderly gentleman who was angry, and he was cursing. He was so old that he had one foot in the grave and the other on a banana peel. As a pastor, I went to him and gently reminded him that he shouldn't curse. He looked at me angrily and said: "I ain't cursing, only God can curse somebody." I thought about what he said, and he was right.

When you curse, what you are really doing is asking God to place His displeasure and condemnation on something or someone. When you say: "Damn it!" or "Damn you," you are actually asking God to condemn that person or thing to Hell! If God were listening to you, the people you cursed would be in big trouble. The fact of the matter is that when you curse, God does not listen to you—he laughs at you.

> *Why do the heathen rage, and the people imagine a vain thing? He that sitteth in the heavens shall laugh: the LORD shall have them in derision.*
> Psalm 2:1-4

Cursing really makes a mockery of God and the fact that people who reject Him will actually be damned because they refused the free gift of salvation. It is a dangerous thing to play with God by cursing.

Let's consider how you are perceived because of your cursing.
When you curse around other people who curse, you fit in. If fitting in is your major goal in life, then it will be necessary for you to curse for the rest of your life. Fitting in around those who curse is not what I consider to be a progressive attitude and approach to life. Cursing appeals to the wrong crowd. I suggest that you choose to appeal to the crowd that rejects this lifestyle and attitude.

Let's consider how to stop if you have started cursing.
1. Start with a realization that God is displeased by the behavior.

> *I call heaven and earth to record this day against you, that I have set before you life and death, blessing and cursing: therefore choose life, that both thou and thy seed may live:*
> Deuteronomy 30:19

God's design for us is a pure heart and clean lips. The fact that you are angry is not an issue with God.

2. Realize that you will hear all of your words again when you stand before God in judgment.

> *But I say unto you, that every idle word that men shall speak, they shall give account thereof in the day of judgment. For by thy words thou shalt be justified, and by thy words thou shalt be condemned.*
> Matthew 12:36-37

The Bible clearly teaches that not one word that comes out of your mouth will go unnoticed by God. The book of Revelation teaches that God has a book called the Book of Life which contains a list of those who will go to heaven. He has many additional books. These books contain the deeds of all mankind. It is for this reason that the Christian believes that evil words and deeds will not go unpunished.

And I saw the dead, small and great, stand before God; and the books were opened: and another book was opened, which is the book of life: and the dead were judged out of those things which were written in the books, according to their works.

Revelation 20:12

3. Ask God to give you a disdain for profanity.

Create in me a clean heart, O God; and renew a right spirit within me.

Psalm 51:10

I am amazed at the men I know personally whom God has touched and changed. God can clean your heart, which will result in a clean tongue.

A wholesome tongue is a tree of life: but perverseness therein is a breach in the spirit.

Proverbs 15:4

4. Tell some person that you hang with that you are trying to stop cursing.

Confess your faults one to another, and pray one for another, that ye may be healed. The effectual fervent prayer of a righteous man availeth much.

James 5:16

There is power in open confession before God and friends who want to help you overcome your weakness. Always strive to hang with people who will hold you accountable. This may require that you find some new friends who will agree with your new direction in life. It is OK and advisable to leave old friends who are not a good influence.

5. Work to replace curse words with new, powerful words that will express your feelings and emotions in place of the curse words.

The tongue of the wise useth knowledge aright: but the mouth of fools poureth out foolishness.

Proverbs 15:2

The Lord God hath given me the tongue of the learned, that I should know how to speak a word in season to him that is weary: he wakeneth morning by morning, he wakeneth mine ear to hear as the learned.

Isaiah 50:4

A desire to express disgust, anger or disappointment in the most emphatic way can be communicated through words other than curse words. To adequately express your emotions is another reason to enhance your vocabulary.

Questions
for Introspection and Discussion (to make you think)

1. Do you curse?   Yes____ No____

2. Do you come from a cursing environment? Yes____ No____

3. Give your reason for cursing or not cursing_____

_____

4. What is your perception of those who curse?_____

_____

5. Do you really believe that God is concerned about what comes out of your mouth? Yes____ No____

6. Do you believe that there will be a future judgment for your words and deeds? Yes____ No____

7. Are you committed to increasing your vocabulary? Yes____ No____

Applicable Scriptures: Please have a boy read the Scripture, then use the questions to facilitate discussion. Conclude by quoting the Scripture from the Living Bible, which was written for teenagers. *Please remember that the reading of Scripture according to Isaiah 55:11 is the most important thing you will do with the boys. This section is where the Holy Spirit really works in their hearts, so don't skip it.*

(1) *Thou art snared with the words of thy mouth, thou art taken with the words of thy mouth.* Proverbs 6:2

[Question] **What do you think about people who curse?**

[Question] **Your words are what people use to form an opinion about you. How can curse words affect their opinion?**

The Living Bible Translates Proverbs 6:2 like this: *You may have trapped yourself by your agreement.*

(2) *For my mouth shall speak truth; and wickedness is an abomination to my lips.* Proverbs 8:7

[Question] **What percentage of the time do you speak truth?**

[Question] **Would your lips fall off if you began to speak truth and kindness?**

[Question] **Do you dislike profanity or is it all right?**

The Living Bible Translates Proverbs 8:7 like this: *Everything I say is right and true, for I hate lies and every kind of deception.*

(3) *The lips of the righteous feed many: but fools die for want of wisdom.* Proverbs 10:21

[Question] **Why do fools die?**

[Question] **Righteous lips do what?**

[Question] **In this Scripture you have two choices. Which do you choose to be?**

The Living Bible Translates Proverbs 10:21 like this: *A godly man gives good advice, but a rebel is destroyed by lack of common sense.*

(4) *The lips of the righteous know what is acceptable: but the mouth of the wicked speaketh frowardness.* Proverbs 10:32

[Question] **To say the right thing at the right time is worth more than wealth. Do you speak with wisdom or do you just run your mouth?**

[Question] **The mouth can only speak what is in the heart. What is in your heart?**

[Question] **I ask this question again: Are you righteous (in right standing with God)?**

The Living Bible Translates Proverbs 10:32 like this: *The upright speak what is helpful; the wicked speak rebellion.*

(5) *Lying lips are abomination to the LORD: but they that deal truly are his delight.* Proverbs 12:22

[Question] **Why do you think God hates lying lips?**

[Question] **Why do you think God loves those who tell the truth?**

The Living Bible Translates Proverbs 12:22 like this: *God delights in those who keep their promises, and abhors those who don't.*

(6) *He that keepeth his mouth keepeth his life: but he that openeth wide his lips shall have destruction.* Proverbs 13:3

[Question] **Do you know when to talk and when to keep your mouth shut?**

[Question] **Have you ever seen someone run their mouth and get in trouble?**

The Living Bible Translates Proverbs 13:3 like this: *Self-control means controlling the tongue! A quick retort can ruin everything.*

(7) *Even a fool, when he holdeth his peace, is counted wise: and he that shutteth his lips is esteemed a man of understanding.* Proverbs 17:28

[Question] **Do you talk even when you don't know what to say.**

[Question] **Do you struggle to keep your mouth shut sometimes?**

The Living Bible Translates Proverbs 17:28 like this: *even a fool is thought to be wise when he is silent. It pays him to keep his mouth shut.*

Additional Scriptures Used In Chapter Twenty As Found In The Living Bible

WHAT FOOLS THE nations are to rage against the Lord! How strange that men should try to outwit God! But God in heaven merely laughs! He is amused by all their puny plans.
Psalm 2:1,4

I call heaven and earth to witness against you that today I have set before you life or death, blessing or curse. Oh, that you would choose life; that you and your children might live!
Deuteronomy 30:19

And I tell you this, that you must give account on Judgment Day for every idle word you speak. Your words now reflect your fate then: either you will be justified by them or you will be condemned.

Matthew 12:36-37

I saw the dead, great and small, standing before God; and The Books were opened, including the Book of Life. And the dead were judged according to the things written in The Books, each according to the deeds he had done.

Revelation 20:12

Create in me a new, clean heart, O God, filled with clean thoughts and right desires.
Psalm 51:10

Gentle words cause life and health; griping brings discouragement.
Proverbs 15:4

Notes:_____

_____

_____

_____

_____

_____

_____

_____

_____

_____

_____

_____

_____

_____

_____

_____

_____

_____

_____

21 How Grown Is Grown?

Definition: Grown means having completed its growth; fully developed; mature.

CONNECTING WITH AND LEARNING FROM YOUR RICH, PERSONAL, PAINFUL, PRODUCTIVE PAST. As adults we can all look back at periods when we thought that we were grown but found out that we were not. It may have involved a conflict with our parents. It may have been a situation where we bit off more than we could chew. Think back and share a situation with the young men.

CAUTION: To separate yourself from your parents is not a sign that you are grown. Many young people move out on their own and are forced into adult situations when they are not really grown.

CONCERN: You are only young once. Don't rush out of your parents' home. I suggest that you enjoy your youth as long as you can.

CHARGE: Be obedient to the wisdom of older, wiser loved ones who encourage you to mature in certain areas.

ACTIVITY: When interacting with older people, ask them: "At what point are you grown?"

21 How Grown Is Grown?

A strong point of contention for children and their parents is the subject of maturity. The reason there is tension in this area is because the child and the parent have different opinions about how mature the child is. See if this sounds familiar:

Parent:	"You can't stay out past 11:00!"
Child:	"Aw, Momma! I know how to watch myself!"
Parent:	"You are too young to date!"
Child:	"Other kids my age are already dating!"
Parent:	"Don't take the car on the interstate!"
Child:	"I can drive on the interstate as good as you can!"

These are a few examples of typical discussions that parents have with their young men. I often tell young men to be patient with their parents as they struggle to let them grow up. I also tell parents (especially mothers) to be careful not to hold on to their young men too tightly.

My sixteenth birthday was one of the greatest days of my life. I had been waiting for years to be able to get behind the wheel of a car legally. I didn't sleep much the night before. The next day, I was up early and on the bus to the driver's license place. After becoming a legal driver, I was made aware of the responsibilities that came with the license.

I was now sinking all of my money into a raggedy hoopty (car) that ran some of the time. I now received requests from friends and family to take them places. It became difficult to tell the difference between those who liked me and those who liked my car. After a while, the car was no big deal, just a means to get from point "A" to point "B." When considering the subject of maturity, there are some points you should keep in mind:

1. You are constantly reaching new levels of maturity.
Growth is one of the most exciting aspects of living. The maturing process is one in which you understand today what you couldn't understand yesterday. It is amazing that at certain ages it is impossible for the average brain to understand and process certain information. This is why in school you learn to spell, read, add, multiply, divide, or do decimals at the age when the mind is able to handle it. Just as this is true in school, it is true in life. There are certain things you cannot understand until you reach a level of maturity that comprehends these concepts. I think that this concept is easy to understand when you look back to the past and see how you have grown in your understanding of the world around you. When you do look back and examine the past, you will see

that you are reaching new levels of maturity.

2. Remember that no matter where you are on the maturity scale today, you will change.
Most people become more mature as time passes. With this in mind, you should realize that your points of reference and your values will change. Your understanding of what is important to you in high school will change when you get in college. Your understanding of what is important in college will change when you graduate and get married. Once you have children, everything changes again.

Most men look back and wish they had made some different decisions back in junior high school, like studying more, not wasting time, not experimenting with drugs, not taking some of the chances they took, or realizing that they should have listened to Mrs. Thompson, Dean Smith and Coach Russell. With this fact in mind, most men look back and wish they had made wiser, more mature decisions when they were young. It would be wise for young men to seek wisdom when making decisions while in junior high school, high school, college and beyond. You are going to change when it comes to the maturity used in making decisions.

One common regret that many men have later in life is in the area of education. Many men regret not studying more! Because of their current level of maturity, they see the benefit of studying and staying in school. Remember that no matter where you are on the maturity scale today, you will change.

3. You don't automatically get wiser with age.
Wisdom and understanding, which are the ingredients for growth, are missing from many young men today. The reason for this is that they are not getting wisdom. YOU WILL NEVER BE SAFELY GROWN UNTIL YOU GET WISDOM! Wisdom is something that you GET. It must be obtained and does not come naturally. It comes when young men rub shoulders with older, wiser men and with God.

Wisdom allows you to see the bigger picture. Men without wisdom only see the immediate situation. A man without wisdom will go to bed with a girl without considering the long-term consequences. A man without wisdom will walk out of school because he cannot overlook one incident that made him mad.

Wisdom is different from knowledge because wisdom tells you when to use your knowledge. A man who has knowledge without wisdom is an educated fool. One of the best sources of wisdom that I know about is the Book of Proverbs, which is found in the middle of your Bible. I meditate on one chapter of Proverbs a week, reading it each morning, and I have found it a great source of wisdom. Remember, you don't automatically get wiser with age.

You will never be safely grown until you get wisdom!

4. Avoid the person who claims to have the maturity thing all together.
The maturity process is like standing on the edge of a cliff. You must constantly work hard to balance yourself or you may have a big accident. The person who claims to have it all together is

either lying or not aware of the world around them. There is a danger in being impressed with others who seem to be so cool and handle their problems with ease. Any person who will be honest with you will admit that he needs more wisdom sometimes. There are days when I use all the wisdom that I have trying to deal with my problem for that day. Any person who will not admit to that fact is lying.

Sufficient unto the day is the evil thereof.
Matthew 6:34b

This is one of the ways that God matures us. He takes us to the outer, raw, frightening limits of our understanding with a problem. While in this condition and position, we see that we are inadequate. God then provides us with additional wisdom through His Spirit, His Word, His man or some part of His creation. When this process takes place, we are growing and becoming more mature. So, avoid the person who claims to have the maturity thing all together.

5. Consider your subsidization.

To be subsidized is to be supported financially. It is the responsibility of the parents to protect and provide for their children. As long as you live in your parents' house and are subsidized by them, you are not grown. You may be old, but you are not grown. One of the necessary lessons for maturity is what you learn when you provide for yourself. When you get out on your own, you get a perspective that you have never had before. Not only does this help you grow up, but it also enables your parent(s) to experience an empty home, which is part of their maturity process. My mother recently had the experience of the last child leaving. She now has the freedom to go and come as she pleases, take trips and enjoy life. This is a freedom that your parents deserve.

I challenge you to realize that no matter how grown you think you are, there is a lot of growing to do in each area of life. I also challenge you to be a sponge around those with wisdom, be willing to step up to new levels of maturity and accept new challenges. Finally, I challenge you to be gracious and kind with your wisdom. It was given to you, so never look down on those with less wisdom than you have.

Questions
for Introspection and Discussion (to make you think)

1. Do you consider yourself smart for your age? Yes____ No____

2. Do you consider yourself wise for your age? Yes____ No____

3. Can you accept a wise statement before you fully understand it? If an older, wise man shares wisdom with you, do you reject it if you have not experienced it? Yes____ No____

4. When was the last time you thought you were grown and found out (the hard way) that you were not grown? Explain._____

5. Using a scale of 1 to 10 with 10 being the highest, rate your maturity in these areas:
    Girls:
    1 2 3 4 5 6 7 8 9 10
    Staying away from drugs, gangs, and evil people:
    1 2 3 4 5 6 7 8 9 10
    Money:
    1 2 3 4 5 6 7 8 9 10
    Understanding and relating to adults:
    1 2 3 4 5 6 7 8 9 10
    Your education:
    1 2 3 4 5 6 7 8 9 10

6. Rate your maturity in these same areas two years ago:
    Girls:
    1 2 3 4 5 6 7 8 9 10
    Staying away from drugs, gangs, and evil people:
    1 2 3 4 5 6 7 8 9 10
    Money:
    1 2 3 4 5 6 7 8 9 10
    Understanding and relating to adults:
    1 2 3 4 5 6 7 8 9 10
    Your education:
    1 2 3 4 5 6 7 8 9 10

7. Name five specific things that you are doing to get more wisdom:
    1. _____
    2. _____
    3._____
    4._____
    5._____

8. As a result of this lesson, will you realize that maturity or being grown is not a magic number like 16,18, or 21, but a life-long process of acquiring wisdom and applying it in each decision we make?

Applicable Scriptures: Please have a boy read the Scripture, then use the questions to facilitate discussion. Conclude by quoting the Scripture from the Living Bible, which was written for teenagers. *Please remember that the reading of Scripture according to Isaiah 55:11 is the most important thing you will do with the boys. This section is where the Holy Spirit really works in their hearts, so don't skip it.*

(1) *My son, hear the instruction of thy father, and forsake not the law of thy mother: For they shall be an ornament of grace unto thy head, and chains about thy neck.* Proverbs 1:8-9

[Question] **How can instruction be like fine jewelry around your neck?**

[Question] **Your parents and elders will be older than you are as long as they live. What should your attitude toward them be?**

The Living Bible Translates Proverbs 1:8-9 like this: *Listen to you father and mother. What you learn from them will stand you in good stead; it will gain you many honors.*

(2) *Trust in the Lord with all thine heart; and lean not unto thine own understanding.* Proverbs 3:5

[Question] **Who knows what's best for your life, you or the Lord?**

[Question] **Who understands more about life, you or the adults in your life?**

The Living Bible translates Proverbs 3:5 like this: *trust the Lord completely; don't ever trust yourself.*

(3) *Better is a poor and wise child than an old and foolish king, who will no more be admonished.* Ecclesiastes 4:13

[Question] **If it is important for kings to be corrected, what do you think should happen to young people?**

[Question] **Would you rather be poor and wise or rich and stupid?**

[Question] **To tell the truth, in healthy relationships there always some admonishing going on. Are you prepared for this?**

The Living Bible Translates Ecclesiastes 4:13 like this: *It is better to be a poor but wise youth than to be an old and foolish king who refuses all advice.*

(4) *Wisdom strengtheneth the wise more than ten mighty men which are in the city.* Ecclesiastes 7:19

[Question] **Godly wisdom in more powerful than a gang of homies. Have you asked God for wisdom today?**

The Living Bible translates Ecclesiastes 7:19 like this: *A wise man is stronger than the mayors of ten big cities!*

(5) *If any of you lack wisdom, let him ask of God, that giveth to all men liberally, and upbraideth not; and it shall be given him.* James 1:5

[Question] **How does this Scripture say that God gives wisdom?**

[Question] **Do you feel that you lack wisdom or that you have all you need?**

[Question] **Would you be bold enough to stop right now and pray to God for wisdom?**

The Living Bible translates James 1:5 like this: *If you want to know what God wants you to do, ask him, and he will gladly tell you, for he is always ready to give a bountiful supply of wisdom to all who ask him; he will not resent it.*

(6) *Children, obey your parents in the Lord: for this is right.* Ephesians 6:1

[Question] **Do you obey your parents?**

[Question] **How old do you feel you should be when you no longer have to obey your parents?**

[Question] **Why does this Scripture say that you should obey the Lord?**

The Living Bible translates Ephesians 6:1 like this: *CHILDREN, OBEY YOUR parents; this is the right thing to do because God has placed them in authority over you.*

(7) *When I was a child, I spake as a child, I understood as a child, I thought as a child: but when I became a man, I put away childish things.* I Corinthians 13:11

[Question] **When you are young, it is OK to act immaturely. Once you grow up, what type of behavior should you have?**

[Question] **The problem we are having in our communities is that so many men want to "play" even into their 30's and 40's. Do you feel that you will "play" for many years or will you settle down and take responsibility like a man?**

The Living Bible translates I Corinthians 13:11 like this: *It's like this: when I was a child I spoke and thought and reasoned as a child does. But when I became a man my thoughts grew far beyond those of my childhood, and now I have put away the childish things.*

Make This Statement To The Boys:

Before we go on to the next chapter, tell me which Scripture made you made, glad or made you think.

Note to the Mentor: As a result of this lesson, are there any prayer requests that should be added to your list and forwarded to your prayer partners?

Notes:

Mentor: Read this page before you meet with your boys.

22 Understanding The White Man

Definition: White means having a light colored skin; some white people have notions of racial superiority.

CONNECTING WITH AND LEARNING FROM YOUR RICH, PERSONAL, PAINFUL, PRODUCTIVE PAST. One day my dad explained to me that the White man has always been in front of the Black man in America. The Black man has always had to study the White man to survive. Share your experience with White men from a Biblical perspective. I have known Godly White men and I have known white men who were the personification of evil.

CAUTION: Don't allow the conversation to degenerate into a White-people-bashing session.

CONCERN: The development of an attitude of fairness is the goal.

CHALLENGE: I challenge the young men to do what Martin Luther King Jr. espoused, which was to judge each man based on the content of his character and not on the color of their skin.

ACTIVITY: Have an open conversation with a White person about the misconceptions that each race has about the other.

22 Understanding The White Man

The real deal with the White man is that he is scared. He is scared about the economy, the fact that his kids may be on drugs and the possibility that his wife may divorce him. He is afraid that his life as he has known it for many years will change. Please note that there are two types of White men. The first type trusts in his own strength and ingenuity. We will call him the self-contained White man. The second type trusts God for his future. We will call him the Christ-contained White man.

The type of White man that we need to be concerned about is the one who trusts in himself and his money. Because of the browning of America, this man has to face a level of competition that he has never had to deal with before. The self-contained White man lives in the midst of a changing world that he can't control. Because of this, he is frustrated. The apostle Paul described this man like this:

> *Whose end is destruction, whose God is their belly, and whose glory is in their shame, who mind earthly things.*
>
> Philippians 3:19

When you add these conditions to the fact that the White race has suffered from a decline in Godly men just as the Black race has, you can see why it is so easy for unspiritual White men to blame others for their situation.

One thing that most men hate is change. We are all creatures of habit, and change threatens us. Resistance to the Civil Rights movement in the United States was fueled in part by a fear of change. We can see the struggle in our government over what should and shouldn't change. So, the real deal with the White man is that he does not want things to change much.

As I said earlier, White men are scared. The media perpetuates the fear. Each evening on the news they see Black men committing crimes against helpless victims. Consequently, when they meet a Black male who looks like those seen on TV, common sense tells them to beware.

For those Black men who have had the opportunity to develop good friendships with White men who are educationally and economically similar, they learn that the difference between Black and White men are cosmetic and cultural. Close interracial friends soon learn that they struggle with the same things. The major differences between Black and White are those which come as a result of economic and educational opportunities.

One of the greatest challenges that Black and White men face is the challenge of giving each other the opportunity to evaluate each other on the basis of the individual's character as opposed to the way one looks.

The problem is that it is not that simple. You cannot judge a book by its cover. I work with youth, and so I occasionally dress like a man much younger than I actually am. When I dress in jeans and tennis shoes, it is very common for me to be followed around in the mall by the security staff. Yes, that's right, the Reverend Doctor Harold Davis, who is on the pastoral staff of Canaan Missionary Baptist Church, is followed around in the mall when he dresses a certain way. The reason this happens is that people are scared and they will judge you based on how you look.

This is a terrible reality that Black and White people must realize. I am not as hard on White people as I used to be when they are suspicious of me based on how I look. I can remember being afraid of White people because of how they looked.

I am a member of a predominantly Black church with a few very faithful and loving White members. Not too long ago, a young White Christian brother and his friend cut off all of their hair and came to Bible study. They sat on the far side of the church. From where I sat, I had difficulty seeing who they were with all of their hair cut off.

As I looked at the two unknown White men with all of the skin showing on the top of their heads, I was initially uncomfortable. They reminded me of the racist, violent skinheads who were gaining popularity. After service, when I was able to get close enough to see who they were, I realized that I, just like White people, could jump to conclusions based on what could be seen.

Ignorance of individuals or ignorance of groups of individuals fosters fear. And then again, we all know that there are some people who are just ignorant and have decided to hate people that are different than they are. Listen to what King David prayed concerning these men:

> *Deliver me, O LORD, from the evil man: preserve me from the violent man; which imagine mischiefs in their heart continually are they gathered together for war. They have sharpened their tongues like a serpent; adders' poison is under their lips. Selah. Keep me, O LORD, from the hands of the wicked; preserve me from the violent man; who have purposed to overthrow my goings.*
>
> Psalms 140:1-4

I am convinced, based on the Bible and history, that those who hate without cause will be rewarded with evil on earth and also in the world to come. Freedom comes when a man frees his heart from malice or hate. Well, the current situation calls for a strategy that will guide our actions as we come into contact with White men. This strategy should include the following characteristics:
- You must be fair to the stranger.
- You must be able to have a clear conscience before God after each meeting or interaction with a White man.

1. Approach the individual from the position of strength.
Realize that God is with you because you are not prejudging the individual but extending to him

basic human and Christian kindness. Your response to his response will depend on your level of maturity.

2. If he responds with kindness equal to your level of kindness, you know that you are dealing with a reasonable person and you may proceed to get to know the man better.

3. If he responds with any degree of hostility, you may choose to move on to avoid endangering either man's delicate ego, which could result in words or weapons.
If you are in a situation where you must be around this person (school, work, army, etc.), you must first of all protect yourself by dotting your "i's" and crossing your "t's." From that point, you must decide which of the following options you wish to take.

Option A:
This is the best option, which involves letting Jesus use you as an instrument of HIS peace. By this I mean that Jesus wants to love this person through you and possibly win a White man to salvation through the efforts of a Black man. When this happens, a spontaneous party of praise breaks out in heaven which is so severe that it takes several minutes for the place to settle down. Interracial witnessing and winning of people to Christ is a tremendous example to those who are watching, and they are challenged to believe in God.

I have had the opportunity to witness to many White men and have had the privilege of winning some to Christ. I did this in some cases when they were not totally cordial, courteous or kind to me. I can tell you that the experience has made me a better, wiser, more mature man who has reaped personal benefits from option "A."

Option B:
This option involves you extending kindness to the man even though he is rude to you. God promises that when you do this it drives the man crazy!

> *Therefore if thine enemy hunger, feed him; if he thirst, give him drink: for in so doing thou shalt heap coals of fire on his head.*
>
> Romans 12:20

Remember, regardless of how he responds, you will be blessed by acting like Jesus would act.

Option C:
This option is the least desirable, which would involve extending no love to the man, just existing together while you must be there. This is the option that many Americans, Black and White, are taking, and it is unfortunate. If you are a Christian, a man who is secure in himself, God expects more. If you are not a Christian, I don't see any way possible to be kind to a racist White person, because the only way you can do this is to let Jesus love through you (remember Dr. King). This fair strategy will guide you as you meet the White man each day. When dealing with a White man, always try to determine if he is self-contained or Christ-contained. As a Black man, don't allow

yourself to fall into the narrow line of thinking which puts forth the idea that ALL White men are bad. History shows that good White men have stood side by side with Black men from the beginning of the civil rights movement even to today. In my own life, I can remember many Christ-contained White men assisting my father as he struggled to feed his large family.

When I stop and look at the world, I notice that White men are fighting White men in the old Soviet Republics, Koreans are fighting Koreans in Korea, and Africans are fighting Africans in Africa. When you study the conflicts in the world, it is plain to see that the source of conflict is not based on a man's color but on who contains the man. The source of all conflict among men is religious in nature. We know that in the end, man will be divided based on his religion.

So in order to understand the White man, resolve to get to know him well enough to see who contains him. If he is self-contained, greed will motivate him and his motto will be "Do unto others before they do unto you." If he is Christ-contained, his motto will be "Do unto others as you would have them do unto you." Pray that God will give you the discernment and wisdom to be sensitive to every man's heart and quick to discern who contains each man you meet.

Questions
for Introspection and Discussion (to make you think)

1. Tell the truth, shame the devil! Are you prejudiced? Yes___ No___

2. If you are, have you analyzed why you are?_____

3. Do you understand that prejudice and hatred in your heart only hurt you? Yes___ No___

4. What White man have you had problems with (because of the color of your skin), and how have you dealt with the situation?_____

5. What are you doing to combat the negative images that Black males have through the media?

_____

6. Which option do you most frequently use in dealing with White men?
Option A___ Option B___ Option C___

7. If you are not using Option "A," do you desire to grow to the point where you can use that option on a regular basis? Yes___ No___

8. All men are contained by someone. Who contains you?_____

Applicable Scriptures: Please have a boy read the Scripture, then use

the questions to facilitate discussion. Conclude by quoting the Scripture from the Living Bible, which was written for teenagers. *Please remember that the reading of Scripture according to Isaiah 55:11 is the most important thing you will do with the boys. This section is where the Holy Spirit really works in their hearts, so don't skip it.*

(1) *He that saith he is in the light, and hateth his brother, is in darkness even until now.*
I John 2:9
[Question] **Do you hate anybody?**
[Question] **Freedom from hate in your heart is true freedom. Can you say with good conscience that you are free?**
[Question] **Do you want to be delivered from hate in your heart? I dare you to stop right now and pray to Jesus asking Him to free you from hate in your heart.**
The Living Bible translates I John 2:9 like this: *Anyone who says he is walking in the light of Christ but dislikes his fellow man, is still in darkness.*

(2) *For there is no difference between the Jew and the Greek: for the same Lord over all is rich unto all that call upon him.* Romans 10:12
[Question] **Do you believe that God really sees everybody the same?**
[Question] **Who does this Scripture say that God is rich unto?**
The Living Bible translates Romans 10:12 like this: *Jew and Gentile are the same in this respect: they all have the same Lord who generously gives his riches to all those who ask him for them.*

(3) *There is neither Jew nor Greek, there is neither bond nor free, there is neither male nor female: for ye are all one in Christ Jesus.* Galatians 3:28
[Question] **There is no discrimination in God. Why do you feel that people discriminate?**
[Question] **Do you feel that we will ever be free from discrimination?**
The Living Bible translates Galatians 3:28 like this: *We are no longer Jews or Greeks or slaves or free men or even merely men or women, but we are all the same—we are Christians; we are on in Christ Jesus.*

(4) *Let all bitterness, and wrath, and anger, and clamor, and evil speaking, be put away from you, with all malice:* Ephesians 4:31
[Question] **It is God's desire that we not exhibit negative behavior toward others. Are you mature enough to be courteous around people that you do not care for?**
[Question] **You can decide that you are not going to be angry with people. It is called an act of your will. Are you willing not to be angry with White people?**
The Living Bible translates Ephesians 4:31 like this: *Stop being mean, bad-tempered and angry. Quarreling, harsh words, and dislike of others should have no place in your lives.*

(5) *Brethren, be not children in understanding: howbeit in malice be ye children, but in understanding be men.* I Corinthians 14:20

[Question] **Do you feel that you have a good understanding for a young man your age?**

[Question] **Do you hassle your parents when you don't understand why they won't give you something or let you go somewhere?**

[Question] **Have you ever noticed how little children are quick to forgive? Do you think that with God's help you can be that way?**

The Living Bible translates I Corinthians 14:20 like this: *Dear brothers, don't be childish in your understanding of these things. Be innocent babies when it comes to planning evil, but be men of intelligence in understanding matters of this kind.*

(6) *But evil men and seducers shall wax worse and worse, deceiving, and being deceived.* II Timothy 3:13

[Question] **Some teach that the world is getting better. What does this verse say about that?**

[Question] **With God's help we can get better. Have you asked Him to help you grow in grace and wisdom?**

The Living Bible translates II Timothy 3:13 like this: *In fact, evil men and false teachers will become worse and worse, deceiving many, they themselves having been deceived by satan.*

(7) *Owe no man any thing, but to love one another: for he that loveth another hath fulfilled the law.* Romans 13:8

[Question] **It is a fact that you should not be heavily in debt. Do you owe people money?**

[Question] **It is a fact that you owe other men and women love. Can you say that you love everybody?**

[Question] **It takes a real man to be a Christian and do what God says do. Do you feel that you could live a Christian life?**

The Living Bible translates Romans 13:8 like this: *Pay all your debts except the debt of love for others—never finish paying that! For if you love them, you will be obeying all of God's laws, fulfilling all his requirements.*

Make This Statement To The Boys:

Before we go on to the next chapter, tell me which Scripture made you mad, glad or made you think.

Note to the Mentor: As a result of this lesson, are there any prayer requests that should be added to your list and forwarded to your prayer partners?

23 Cops And Robbers

Definition: The Police are the governmental department (of a city, state, etc.) organized for keeping order, enforcing the law, and preventing, detecting, and prosecuting crimes.

CONNECTING WITH AND LEARNING FROM YOUR RICH, PERSONAL, PAINFUL, PRODUCTIVE PAST. I have had many encounters with Law Enforcement. Speeding tickets were the source of my negative encounters. I must say that in my experiences, the officers conducted themselves professionally. I also must state that I have personal friends who are police officers and I know them to be fair, considerate individuals. What about you? Share from your personal experience with the young men.

CAUTION: Keep the dialogue positive and present law officers in the best light.

CONCERN: There are bad cops out there and it is very unfortunate when you encounter one. For those who have encountered bad cops, don't allow that experience to spoil your view of all cops.

CHALLENGE: To see police officers as individuals with a job to do not as people who are out to get us.

ACTIVITY: Arrange a heart-to-heart talk with a black cop. Let him share how it hurts him to arrest young black men and how he would rather help them.

23 Cops and Robbers

One of the great challenges facing young Black men is the legal system, with the local police department in particular. Not long ago, I was going to a friend's house to pick up my son. As I neared his house, I noticed four police cars up the street. I went around the block to avoid the scene and passed one police car in the process. As I parked my car and got out, a policeman approached me and told me to stand still. The thought that first went through my mind was: "What does he want?" The second thought was: "I don't like being told what to do." The third thought was: "Be cool and remember Rodney King." As the officer approached me, I purposely maintained an attitude and posture of confidence (not arrogance).

The officer and I talked, and I was very pleasant with him and treated him with all of the respect that his uniform deserved. He informed me that there had been an altercation (fight) up the street and one of the men had on a red shirt (I had on a red shirt) and blue pants (I had on blue pants). After talking with me very briefly, the officer determined that I was not the person that he was looking for and APOLOGIZED and went his way.

One of the joys of getting older is you learn how to handle potentially dangerous situations. You develop a perspective that is broader than your own interests. You learn to see the other side of the picture. When it comes to law enforcement, the young Black male needs to be taught how to handle himself objectively around policemen. To help gain some objectivity, let's look from the perspective of the police department.

Police Are People And Police Are Human.
- If you hit them, they will hit you back.
- They make mistakes just like anybody else.
- There are good cops and bad cops.

I had a lady come to my office crying about the fact that she and her husband had an argument and somebody called the police. When the police arrived, the argument had been settled and the couple was fine. The officers talked with the couple to determine what had happened. One officer was satisfied and was ready to leave. The other officer insisted that he needed to remove the children from the home in the event of future violence. The officers were divided, but the older officer insisted on taking the children out of the home.

There is a reason why people act the way they act. It was later discovered that the older officer had had personal problems with his wife and children earlier in life, and his children had been removed for a time. Every time he was confronted with a situation where children were involved, he quickly removed the children from the situation regardless of how minor the violence was between parents.

There will be times when you are confronted by a policeman who may not make the best judgment. Remember that they are human and subject to the same passions that all humans are subject to.

Police Make Mistakes.
When we watch TV or movies and there is a good guy and a bad guy, we get to see both sides at the same time. The camera will shift from what the criminal is doing to the police on their way to the crime. In real life, this is not the case. The police usually don't know who committed a crime. They know it could be anybody, so they suspect everybody.

Blacks resent the fact that from the White perspective, many of us look the same. Well, to me Koreans and Japanese look the same. They resent that. I mean them no harm, but my knowledge of them is limited. In some parts of the country, the police are very limited and easily make mistakes identifying young Black men.

Police Are Hindered.
The laws of our land are written to protect us from the infringements of government. These laws trickle down to the local level and put restrictions on the local police department. A criminal:
- Must be caught according to certain guidelines.
- Must be arrested according to certain guidelines.
- Has many loopholes to use to get off of the hook.

The police are frustrated when they risk their lives to arrest a criminal and see him on the streets the next day continuing to do his thing. The police know where the crack houses are, but they cannot bust the crack houses without sufficient concrete evidence. This evidence is hard to get because witnesses don't want to testify against pushers.

Police Are Hesitant.
During their training period, the police are shown pictures of fellow officers who were killed in the line of duty. These pictures are shown to encourage them to be very careful when approaching criminals.

Let me paint a picture of a typically dangerous situation. A young executive at the local bank has been having trouble with his wife, and this has disturbed him deeply. He decides to go home and discuss the problem with her so that they can iron things out. When he goes home unannounced, he finds his wife and another man intimately involved. At that moment he snaps, and all of his pent-up frustration comes out. He goes into his den, grabs his .38 and begins to chase the man that has just run out of his house. The first man gets in his car and takes off. The second man follows in his BMW. Now, Officer Smith is sitting at the corner of 4th and Lexington during his morning shift. He notices the blue BMW going at a high rate of speed down Lexington, and he engages in pursuit. He has no idea what is wrong—he just knows to be cautious. After two blocks, the BMW pulls over. Officer Smith and other officers approach the car. Now, what do you think happens next? You don't know, but you do know that if you were Officer Smith, you would be hesitant because of the potential danger.

196

Police are also hesitant because whenever they have on a uniform, they are a walking target for a criminal or any deranged person who happens to have a gun.

Because I realize this, I am patient with police when they tell me to stand still while they check me out.

Police Are Hired.

I taught elementary school for a while, and it was a job I loved very much. I enjoyed the little children and wanted to impact their lives in a positive way. One day, a parent pointed out to me that as a taxpayer, he paid my salary. I had never thought of it that way. I now realize that teachers, policemen, politicians and all public employees are hired by the public. So if I hire them, why should I fear them? When I started viewing the policeman as a person that I pay who is there to help me and my city, my attitude about him changed.

Too many young people see themselves as detached and distant from the local police officer, but that is not how a good police officer views you. They have a responsibility to protect you from others and sometimes from yourself. I suggest that you seek to develop an attitude of cooperation with your local police department, because in most cases they only want to serve you.

Questions
for Introspection and Discussion (to make you think)

1. Do you know a policeman personally? Yes___ No___

2. Are you afraid of the police? Yes___ No___

3. Do you cooperate with them when they ask you questions, or do you freeze up?_____

4. How has TV influenced your attitude about cops?_____

5. If you view policemen negatively, would you be willing to sit down and talk to a policeman to get to know him better? Yes___ No___   If you would like to talk to a policeman, ask an adult to set up a meeting with one.

6. Would you consider being a policeman? Yes___ No___ Why or why not?_____
_____

7. What role do you feel that the police play in society? _____

8. We all know that there are some bad cops. Do you believe that there are some really good cops out there? Yes___ No___

Applicable Scriptures: Please have a boy read the Scripture, then use
the questions to facilitate discussion. Conclude by quoting the Scripture from the Living Bible, which was written for teenagers. *Please remember that the reading of Scripture according to Isaiah 55:11 is the most important thing you will do with the boys. This section is where the Holy Spirit really works in their hearts, so don't skip it.*

(1) *Let every soul be subject unto the higher powers. For there is no power but of God: the powers that be are ordained of God. Whosoever therefore resisteth the power, resisteth the ordinance of God: and they that resist shall receive to themselves damnation. For rulers are not a terror to good works, but to the evil. Wilt thou then not be afraid of the power? Do that which is good, and thou shalt have praise of the same.* Romans 13:1-3

[Question] **Are you subject to the higher powers?**

[Question] **Who is responsible for the powers or authorities that have been placed in your life?**

[Question] **Are you afraid of the powers of society?**

The Living Bible translates Romans 13:1-3 like this: *OBEY THE GOVERNMENT, for God is the one who has put it there. There is no government anywhere that God has not placed in power. So those who refuse to obey the laws of the land are refusing to obey God, and punishment will follow. For the policeman does not frighten people who are doing right; but those doing evil will always fear him. So if you don't want to be afraid, keep the laws and you will get along well.*

(2) *Put them in mind to be subject to principalities and powers, to obey magistrates, to be ready to every good work.* Titus 3:1

[Question] **Who reminds you to obey authorities?**

[Question] **What do you say to yourself when you see a cop?**

[Question] **Are you ready right now to do some honest work?**

The Living Bible translates Titus 3:1 like this: *REMIND YOUR PEOPLE to obey the government and its officers, and always to be obedient and ready for any honest work.*

(3) *Submit yourselves to every ordinance of man for the Lord's sake: whether it be to the king, as supreme; or unto governors, as unto them that are sent by him for the punishment of evildoers, and for the praise of them that do well. For so is the will of God, that with well-doing ye may put to silence the ignorance of foolish men.* I Peter 2:13-15

[Question] **Are there any laws that you feel are unfair?**

[Question] **How does the Lord want you to put foolish men to silence?**

The Living Bible translates I Peter 2:13-15 like this: *For the Lord's sake, obey every law of your government: those of the king as head of the state, and those of the king's officers, for he has sent them to punish all who do wrong, and to honor those who do right. It is God's will that your good lives should silence those who foolishly condemn the Gospel without knowing what it can do for them, having never experienced its power.*

(4) *A soft answer turneth away wrath: but grievous words stir up anger.* Proverbs 15:1

[Question] **Do you speak kindly to your authority figures?**

[Question] **How do you feel when people yell at you?**

[Question] **What do grievous or mean words do?**

The Living Bible translates Proverbs 15:1 like this: *A SOFT ANSWER turns away wrath, but harsh words cause quarrels.*

(5) *He that refuseth instruction despiseth his own soul: but he that heareth reproof getteth understanding.* Proverbs 15:32

[Question] **How do you feel you hurt yourself when you refuse instruction?**

[Question] **What is the benefit of listening to those who correct you?**

The Living Bible translates Proverbs 15:32 like this: *If you profit from constructive criticism you will be elected to the wise men's hall of fame. But to reject criticism is to harm yourself and your own best interests.*

Make This Statement To The Boys:

Before we go on to the next chapter, tell me which Scripture made you mad, glad or made you think.

Note to the Mentor: As a result of this lesson, are there any prayer requests that should be added to your list and forwarded to your prayer partners?

Notes:_____

24 Understanding The Certainty Of Change

(And Preparing For It)

Definition: Change is the act or process of substitution, alteration, or variation.

CONNECTING WITH AND LEARNING FROM YOUR RICH, PERSONAL, PAINFUL, PRODUCTIVE PAST. After high school and college, time flies. Once you have kids, they grow very rapidly and the aging process becomes more pronounced. Talk about how life's changes have slipped up on you and be candid about the changes that you were not ready for.

CAUTION: The goal is to be pro-active with life's changes and not reactive.

CONCERN: Encourage the young men not to cry over the opportunities they have already missed.

CHARGE: Take note of significant changes that you were not ready for and where necessary play catch-up. This may be the case especially with education. With the counsel of older men, attempt to anticipate upcoming changes and seek to be prepared for them.

ACTIVITY: In your conversations with older men, ask them what one change in their life was most challenging.

24 Understanding The Certainty Of Change

(And Preparing for It)

One of the problems of being young is that you have never been any older than you are. This is a problem for everyone, not just for young people. I am sure that you can remember anticipating a birthday or a time when you would graduate from one level to another: from elementary to junior high, from junior high to high school or from a learner's permit to a full-blown driver's license. In each case, when you got to the new level, you found out that it was not exactly what you thought it would be.

I would like to warn you that most of what will happen in your future will be different from what you expect it to be.

The reason it is different is that young men have limited life experience. In other words, they have not lived long enough to know experientially the results of certain behavior. Most men in their forties can from experience tell men in their twenties: "If I had only known then what I know now." They have experience now that they didn't have then. I want you to consider the benefits of counseling, talking to and listening to those who are older than you are. The life experience of older men can save you MANY headaches.

The young men of our generation are missing dialogue with the elders, which is one of the most stabilizing benefits that other generations have had.

In the African tradition, the Griot (elder in the village who had wisdom and knew history) passed it on to the younger generation. In the Biblical tradition, the first manuscripts with God's wisdom were delivered over 4,000 years ago. Men have sought wisdom through God's word and through the elders. There is no new wisdom and no new way to get it but through God and the elders. A man who counsels exclusively with his homeys and himself is a FOOL.

I want to discuss some areas in your life that you should be willing to expose to the wisdom of your elders and counsellors.

1. Because of your limited knowledge of the future and the certainty of change, your value system should be exposed to the wisdom of your counsellors.
Please note that every man has things that he values. Some things may be good and some may be bad. You need wisdom to determine what to add and subtract from your value system. Have you

evaluated your value system? Your value system needs to be based on transcendent values. These are values that transcend culture, race, and time. Transcendent, because they originated from God.

2. Because of your limited knowledge of the future and the certainty of change, what you learned in your orientation family should be exposed to the wisdom of your counsellors.
When young adults move out of their parents' home, they are challenged to deal with new discoveries they make on a daily basis. These discoveries involve the realization that in our homes we did some things that were rather backwards. You may be able to identify some of these things before you leave home. In any case, we are thrust out into a world not fully understanding how our orientation will fit into the larger society.

One of my daughters, at two years old, would bite people. Her mom and I would brush it off and grin because it was kinda cute. She only did it at home, so we did not work hard enough to break her of that bad habit. We were visiting some friends in Chicago who had a three-year-old girl. My two-year-old daughter walked up to the three-year-old, took a bite and grinned, waiting for the three-year-old to grin back and play like mom and dad. The three-year-old didn't grin, but she said to herself: "I know how to do that." The three-year-old then bit my daughter back! My daughter was traumatized because no one had ever bitten her back. Welcome to the real world.

I submit that your home shelters you from many elements of the real world. When you enter the larger world, you are exposed to different ways of doing things. When you discover a truth or way of doing things that is better than what you learned at home, you need to make this new behavior a new habit. Once you start growing up, you need to ask yourself these questions:
•   What is it that I need to know that my parents didn't teach me?
•   How am I learning to compensate for shortcomings?
•   Have I acknowledged that my parents taught me some things incorrectly?

A skill and discipline that each young man should develop is the art of REPARENTING ONE'S SELF. As you grow, you will discover that there are things you should have learned while you were elementary school age.

If you are mature enough to realize that you don't know something, then you are mature enough to see to it that you learn it.

If your parents neglected to teach you that:
  A. stealing is wrong,
  B. lying catches up with you,
  C. you reap what you sow,
  D. you should do your homework,
  E. fast girls ain't NO good for you,
  F. you ought to get out of that bed and do something constructive,
  G. not everybody is your friend, and
  H. your attitude will take you a long way.

You need to learn these things. If you were not taught these principles or many other basic truths, then as soon as you become aware of them, you need to teach yourself or reparent yourself.

3. Because of your limited knowledge of the future and the certainty of change, your socialization skills should be exposed to the wisdom of your counsellors.
My lovely wife is a singer of classical music. She has sung with some of the major symphony orchestras in this country. Occasionally, I accompany her to a concert. I am not extremely cultured and have very basic tastes.

Not too long ago, she was invited to a dinner at a *SERIOUS* country club. I went along as her husband. As we took our seats, I immediately knew that I was in trouble. On the table before me were a knife, two spoons and three forks. One fork was to eat my meat with, one was for the salad, and I had no idea what the other fork was for. Now, if you want to look foolish at the country club, all you have to do is to use the wrong fork at the wrong time. My wife was gracious enough to very discreetly point to the right fork at the right time and saved me from looking out-classed.

Many young people want to better themselves, but they have not accepted the fact that if you want to operate in bigger circles you must learn some new things. If you want to go places, you must be willing to learn about the acceptable social skills of the larger culture. The President of the United States has people who are specially trained to make sure that he conducts himself properly when he is around people from other cultures. I suggest that we seek to behave in a culturally appropriate way.

4. Because of your limited knowledge of the future and the certainty of change, your attitudes toward women should be exposed to the wisdom of your counsellors.
You must be careful about what you tell yourself regarding women. What you tell yourself regarding women will develop into your attitude about women.
     A. Never seek to use women for your own personal pleasure. If you use them, it only **guarantees** that you will be used by someone else. What is worse is that it may come back on your children later in life. The principle here is that you reap what you sow. Sow the wind and it will come back as a tornado.
     B. Seek a healthy, safe, Biblical attitude about women.

The elder women as mothers; the younger as sisters, with all purity.
I Timothy 5:2

This Scripture provides safe guidelines for young men when it comes to their approach to women.
     C. Remember that to have sex with a woman creates a bond that will never be completely broken. You will carry that memory for years to come. To have sex with a woman is to steal from her future husband.

5. Because of your limited knowledge of the future and the certainty of change, you should strive for personal excellence with the help of your counsellors.

A. Never compare yourself to other men. To do so is unfair because we are all unique when it comes to gifts and talents. Use standards as the yardstick for improvement and seek to be better than you used to be.

B. Become a life-long learner. If you blew it in high school, determine to go back and get it right. If you are blowing it now, decide to stop and get it together. There are many things that you are too immature to deal with as you pass through life. Don't allow yourself to be defeated by any subject or obstacle that you were unable to conquer. Allow yourself to mature, then go back and try it again. The bottom line is that when you stop learning, you are basically brain-dead. Resolve to become a life-long learner.

C. Associate with progressive people who are ahead of you. Think about this: The people that you hang with are the people that you will:

- Talk to.
- Listen to.
- Go places with.
- Spend money with.
- Party with.
- Go to church with.
- Become friends with.

What is important to them will become important to you. My point is that you are influenced by the folks you hang with. **There is no such thing as innocently hanging with people who don't share your goals.**

A drug addict who was living on the streets and eating out of a McDonald's dumpster sat in my office and told me: "YOU CAN'T HANG WITH THE COOLIE BOYS AND DON'T DO DOPE." So if you associate with people who are not only talking about doing something but are actually doing what they are talking about doing, your attempts to be successful will be aided by their presence. If, on the other hand, the people you hang with only *talk* about being progressive, then you should be careful because they could weaken your excitement about getting ahead. If they make statements like "Next year, I'm going to get back in school" and next year never comes, you should get a clue. You will be pulled up or down based upon who you hang with.

6. Because of your limited knowledge of the future and the certainty of change, you should develop a relationship with God with the help of your counsellors.
God is there where you are right now. You can ignore Him and choose to deal with Him at some future date. That does not diminish the fact that your moment-to-moment existence is in His hands.

A. God knows your purpose in this life. Many people search for the perfect career, but they should first search for God's purpose for their life. Many young people come to the University of Illinois and study for four years, get a college diploma and with their diploma in hand tell you: "I don't know what I want to do with my life." This is called four wasted years and a lot of wasted money. This can be avoided if we would only get our direction from God. Now, I am sure that someone is thinking: "I don't want to be a preacher." Well, you don't have to be a preacher to find your purpose and serve God. God may choose for you to serve Him by teaching school, coaching soccer, being a housewife, being an honest politician, fighting drugs in your neighborhood, etc. It is a very simple procedure to say to God: **"Jesus, please lead me to your purpose for my life and strengthen me in it, for your glory, Amen."**

      B. Only God can give you peace. Peace comes from knowing God. When you know God, you have faith in the fact that you are on a winning team which may occasionally lose a game but is guaranteed to make it through the playoffs and win the championship.

      C. Realize that God controls the future. The quality of your future wife, job, home, children and happiness are all directly related to your present relationship with God. God sees the future; we can only see today and speculate about the future.

Change is inevitable and uncertain, but we can be better prepared by consulting with those who have experienced life.

Questions
for Introspection and Discussion (to make you think)

1. Do you have plans for the future? Yes____ No____

2. How detailed are your plans for the future?_____

_____

3. Have your plans changed in the last five years? Yes____ No____

4. At your young age, have you locked yourself into a career? Yes____ No____

5. At your young age, have you locked yourself into a relationship? Yes____ No____

6. Have you noticed how time has changed someone you know, like your mother, father, brother or sister? Yes____ No____

7. How have you changed in the last year?_____

_____

8. Do you understand that you can't regress (go back) to the way that things used to be? Yes____ No____

9. Are you prepared to learn to deal with the future, one day at a time? Yes____ No____

Applicable Scriptures: Please have a boy read the Scripture, then use the questions to facilitate discussion. Conclude by quoting the Scripture from the Living Bible, which was written for teenagers. *Please remember that the reading of Scripture according to Isaiah 55:11 is the most important thing you will do with the boys. This section is where the Holy Spirit really works in their hearts, so don't skip it.*

(1) *Boast not thyself of tomorrow; for thou knowest not what a day may bring forth.* Proverbs 27:1

[Question] **Do you consider God when you speak of your plans for tomorrow?**

[Question] **Can you remember a day when something totally unpredictable happened?**

The Living Bible translates Proverbs 27:1 like this: *DON'T BRAG ABOUT your plans for tomorrow—wait and see what happens.*

(2) *Whereas ye know not what shall be on the morrow. For what is your life? It is even a vapour, that appeareth for a little time and then vanisheth away.* James 4:14

[Question] **Do you believe that the psychics that you call on the phone can predict the future?**

[Question] **Do you feel that life is long or short?**

The Living Bible translates James 4:14 like this: *How do you know what is going to happen tomorrow? For the length of your lives is as uncertain as the morning fog—now you see it; soon it is gone.*

(3) *For all flesh is as grass, and all the glory of man as the flower of the grass. The grass withereth, and the flower thereof falleth away:* I Peter 1:24

[Question] **How are grass and the human body similar?**

[Question] **Can you imagine what you will be like when you are 60 years old?**

[Question] **Think of the oldest person you know. Do you realize that they were once young and attractive?**

The Living Bible translates I Peter 1:24 like this: *Yes, our natural lives will fade as grass does when it becomes all brown and dry. All our greatness is like a flower that droops and falls;*

(4) *So teach us to number our days, that we may apply our hearts unto wisdom.* Psalm 90:12

[Question] **How many days do you feel that you have to live?**

[Question] **This Scripture says that if you count your days, you will do what?**

[Question] **When a person knows they are going to die soon, what do they usually do?**

The Living Bible translates Psalm 90:12 like this: *Teach us to number our days and recognize how few they are; help us to spend them as we should.*

(5) *Man that is born of a woman is of few days and full of trouble.* Job 14:1

[Question] **When old people look back on their lives, do you think they feel that life was long or short?**

[Question] **Do you ever feel like your life is full of trouble?**

The Living Bible translates Job 14:1 like this: *"HOW FRAIL IS man, how few his days, how full of trouble!*

Make This Statement To The Boys:

Before we go on to the next chapter, tell me which Scripture made you mad, glad or made you think.

Note to the Mentor: As a result of this lesson, are there any prayer requests that should be added to your list and forwarded to your prayer partners?

25 Is Jesus The Answer To Our Problems?

Definition: Jesus is the founder of the Christian religion.

CONNECTING WITH AND LEARNING FROM YOUR RICH, PERSONAL, PAINFUL, PRODUCTIVE PAST. All of us have acknowledged that Jesus Christ is the Son of God and able to save us from our sins or we have denied that fact. It is very difficult to live in America and not be confronted with some facts about Jesus Christ at some time or another. Share with the young men your personal experience with Jesus Christ and why you feel that He is the answer.

CAUTION: Be sure not to take the young men too fast. If they are totally unchurched, you may want to allow the Spirit of God some time to soften their hearts as you deal with this subject.

CONCERN: Don't be discouraged when the young men's enthusiasm for Jesus Christ is not what you feel that it should be. What you see on their faces and their responses now are not a clear barometer of how they will respond to your words. Remember that you may only plant a seed that will bloom later.

CHALLENGE: Challenge the young men to read historical data about Jesus Christ. Encourage them to compare Him to all of the other dead gods that compete for His sacred position.

ACTIVITY: Consider an actual theological study of the doctrines of Islam compared to the doctrines of Christianity.

25 Is Jesus The Answer To Our Problems?

Well, I know what ain't the answer!

> **Drugs** ain't the answer,
> Getting **pregnant** ain't the answer,
> **Dysfunctional** families ain't the answer,
> **Flunkin'** out of school ain't the answer,
> Black on Black **crime** ain't the answer,
> White on Black **crime** ain't the answer,
> Black on White **crime** ain't the answer,
> Talkin' 'bout what we **ain't** got ain't the answer,
> Talkin' 'bout what we **can't** do ain't the answer,
> **Knockin'** boots ain't the answer,
> Watchin' **TV** ain't the answer,
> Hangin' with folks who ain't goin' **nowhere** ain't the answer,
> **Violent** rap music ain't the answer,
> Sexually **abusive** rap music ain't the answer,
> **Givin'** in to peer pressure ain't the answer,
> **Cussin'** the teacher out ain't the answer,
> Misdirected **anger** ain't the answer,
> Passive-aggressive **behavior** ain't the answer,
> Having more than one woman to boost your **ego** ain't the answer,
> **Back-stabbing** ain't the answer,
> Mental **slavery** ain't the answer.

Every man is required to make a personal decision. He has to decide if Jesus was a lunatic, a liar or the LORD! Every man, in the private chambers of his heart, must make a decision that will determine his eternal destiny. Was Jesus a Pretender, a Phoney or the Potentate? Was He Demented and Dangerous, or was He Deity? Some say He was Effeminate, some say He was Enraged, and others say that He was Emmanuel.

Many decisions that we make greatly affect others. This decision must be made alone and will have an eternal effect on the decision-maker. Did Jesus really walk on the earth, witness to men and wash away our sins?

I believe that Jesus did all of those things. I have personally worked through my doubts and see the reality of Jesus Christ as a historical person. As I searched my heart, the world and the Bible, I found some truths that have led me to conclude that Jesus Christ is what He said He is in John 14:6: *"Jesus saith unto him, I am the way, the truth, and the life: no man cometh unto the Father, but by me."*

Let me share with you some of my reasons:

1. The Witness of Nature

It is very difficult to look at the ocean, mountains, forests, and stars in the sky and not wonder about God. Throughout civilization, men have looked at nature and thought about God. This is what is called "Natural Revelation." It refers to what man sees of God in nature. With only natural revelation and no written book, men have always sought for God and concluded that God was there somewhere.

> *The heavens declare the glory of God; and the firmament showeth his handiwork.*
> Psalm 19:1

> *I will praise thee; for I am fearfully and wonderfully made: marvelous are thy works; and that my soul knoweth right well.*
> Psalm 139:14

2. The Witness of History

The history of the world is full of the influence of Jesus Christ. Jesus Christ has a 2,000-year track record with the inhabitants of planet Earth. It was not until the 1700's, during the Age of Enlightenment, that men started questioning the validity of the Biblical claims to Christ's authority. Also, when the Bible speaks of historical accounts, it is always 100% accurate. Biblical history corresponds with secular history.

In the Bible, there are books of history which chronicle in detail the events of secular history. The Bible has accurately predicted the rise and fall of kings and kingdoms. The outcomes of wars have been predicted before they were ever fought. NO OTHER RELIGIOUS BOOK even comes close to the Bible when it comes to historical accuracy.

3. The Witness of Prophecy

Prophecy is the ability to predict something before it happens. When it comes to prophecy, there is **NO OTHER RELIGIOUS BOOK THAT EVEN COMES CLOSE TO BEING AS ACCURATE AS THE BIBLE! (Not even close!)** The Bible has made thousands of predictions that have come true to the letter, and there are more yet to be fulfilled.

> *The LORD of hosts hath sworn, saying, Surely as I have thought, so shall it come to pass; and as I have purposed, so shall it stand:*
> Isaiah 14:24

4. The Witness of Science

The Bible is not a science book, but whenever the Bible touches on the subject of science, it is 100% correct. For example: Men said that the world was flat. The Bible says in Ecclesiastes 1:6 that it is round. In the 1700's, men let the blood out of a sick person because they thought that would heal them. The person usually died before he got better. The Bible says in Leviticus 17:11 that the life of a person is in the blood. In recent years, much has been made of the fact that when two people have sex, they share blood. Not only do they share blood, but they share any diseases that may be present in their bodies. One person's body becomes part of the other person's body. According to I Corinthians 6:16, when two people have sex they become one flesh. The examples are numerous where science has affirmed the Biblical position.

5. The Witness of His Impact on Society

No man in history has impacted our society like Jesus has. Our nation and the laws of this nation were modeled on Biblical teachings. Marriage has found its standards in the Bible. Historian Philip Schaff said, "This Jesus of Nazareth, without money and arms, conquered more millions than Alexander, Caesar, Mohammed, and Napoleon; without science and learning, He shed more light on things human and divine than all philosophers and scholars combined; without the eloquence of schools, He spoke such words of life as were never spoken before or since, and produced effects which lie beyond the reach of orator or poet; without writing a single line, He set more pens in motion, and furnished themes for more sermons, orations, discussions, learned volumes, works of art, and songs of praise, than the whole army of great men of ancient and modern times."

6. The Witness of Changed Hearts

I feel that a changed heart is the greatest evidence that Jesus Christ is real and that He is the answer to our contemporary problems. I have lived long enough to see Jesus change the hearts of some men that I thought were too mean to be touched, even by God! Convicts, murderers, dope pushers, pimps—you name it, Jesus can touch them and they will change.

> *Therefore if any man be in Christ, he is a new creature: old things are passed away; behold, all things are become new.*
>
> II Corinthians 5:17

> *And Saul also went home to Gibeah; and there went with him a band of men, whose hearts God had touched.*
>
> I Samuel 10:26

Maybe you know someone who gave their life to Jesus and was changed so dramatically that everybody noticed. Believe me when I tell you that it happens every day as men give their lives to Christ. The process of giving your life to Christ is very simple. Listen to the message given in these popular Scriptures:

> *For God so loved the world that He gave His only begotten Son that whosoever believeth on Him should not perish but have everlasting life.*
>
> John 3:16

Behold, I stand at the door, and knock: if any man hear my voice, and open the door, I will come in to him, and will sup with him, and he with me.

Revelation 3:20

That if thou shalt confess with thy mouth the Lord Jesus, and shalt believe in thine heart that God hath raised him from the dead, thou shalt be saved. For with the heart man believeth unto righteousness; and with the mouth confession is made unto salvation.

Romans 10:9-10

Reading these Scriptures shows you that salvation is belief in Jesus Christ as Savior. Belief in your heart and confession with your mouth will get you saved. It is not based on a feeling but on the fact that Jesus is the door to the Father and heaven if we would only trust in Him.

A simple prayer like this will serve as a confession of faith: *Lord Jesus, I confess that I am a sinner and I need a Savior. Please forgive me of my sins, come live in my heart and receive me into your kingdom. In Jesus' name I pray, Amen.* From this point, you grow in grace and the knowledge of the Lord, but everybody starts at the same place, which is the confession of sins and the acknowledgment of Jesus as your Savior.

If you are confused about salvation or want to know more about it, seek out a pastor who will take the time to talk to you about it. If all else fails, contact me and I will help you locate a pastor or church in your area who will help you.

Questions
for Introspection and Discussion (to make you think)

1. Who do you believe that Jesus is?_____

2. What is the basis for your belief?_____

3. Has your belief ever been questioned? Yes___ No___

4. Have you ever doubted what you believe? Yes___ No___

5. Do you have questions about Jesus or salvation that no one has ever answered? Yes___ No___

6. If you have questions, what are they? _____

_____

7. Have you developed a relationship with someone who knows more about Jesus than you do? Yes___ No___

8. Do you have an open mind when they share Jesus with you? Yes___ No___

Applicable Scriptures: Please have a boy read the Scripture, then use the questions to facilitate discussion. Conclude by quoting the Scripture from the Living Bible, which was written for teenagers. *Please remember that the reading of the Scripture according to Isaiah 55:11 is the most important thing you will do with the boys. This section is where the Holy Spirit really works in their hearts, so don't skip it.*

(1) *For God so loved the world, that he gave his only begotten Son, that whosoever believeth in him should not perish, but have everlasting life.* John 3:16

[Question] **In the relationship between God and man, who loved first?**

[Question] **What was God's gift to the world?**

[Question] **What do you have to do to get everlasting life?**

[Question] **How long does everlasting life last?**

The Living Bible translates John 3:16 like this: *For God loved the world so much that he gave his only Son so that anyone who believes in him shall not perish but have eternal life.*

(2) *Let not your heart be troubled: ye believe in God, believe also in me. In my Father's house are many mansions: if it were not so, I would have told you. I go to prepare a place for you. And if I go and prepare a place for you, I will come again, and receive you unto myself; that where I am, there ye may be also. And whither I go ye know, and the way ye know. Thomas saith unto him, Lord, we know not whither thou goest; and how can we know the way? Jesus saith unto him, I am the way, the truth, and the life: no man cometh unto the Father, but by me.* John 14:1-6

[Question] **If you believe in God, should you worry all of the time?**

[Question] **Jesus promised to come again and do what?**

[Question] **Complete this sentence: "Jesus saith unto him,—**

The Living Bible translates John 14:1-6 like this: *"LET NOT YOUR heart be troubled. You are trusting God, now trust in me. There are many homes up there where my Father lives, and I am going to prepare them for your coming. When everything is ready, then I will come and get you, so that you can always be with me where I am. If this weren't so, I would tell you plainly. And you know where I am going and how to get there."*

(3) *Neither is their salvation in any other: for there is none other name under heaven given among men, whereby we must be saved.* Acts 4:12

[Question] **According to Acts 4:12, can salvation be found in Mohammed, Buddha, or self-realization?**

[Question] **All names have some power. What Name has ALL power?**

The Living Bible translates Acts 4:12 like this: *There is salvation in no one else! Under all heaven there is no other name for men to call upon to save them.*

(4) *For I delivered unto you first of all that which I also received, how that Christ died for our sins according to the Scriptures; and that he was buried, and that he rose again the third day according to the Scriptures: And that he was seen of Cephas, then of the twelve: After that, he was seen of above five hundred brethren at once; of whom the greater part remain unto this present, but some*

216

are fallen asleep. I Corinthians 15:3-6

[Question] **In I Corinthians 15:3-6 there are at least 5 things mentioned that Christ did. Name them.**

[Question] **How many people are reported to have seen Christ at once after He was risen from the dead?**

[Question] **Put the main points of this Scripture in your own words.**

The Living Bible translates I Corinthians 15:3-6 like this: *I passed on to you right from the first what had been told to me, that Christ died for our sins just as the Scriptures said he would, and that he was buried, and that three days afterwards he arose from the grave just as the prophets foretold. He was seen by Peter and later by the rest of "the Twelve." After that he was seen by more than five hundred Christian brothers at one time, most of whom are still alive, though some have died by now.*

Additional Scriptures Used In Chapter Twenty Five As Found In The Living Bible

THE HEAVENS ARE telling the glory of God; they are a marvelous display of his craftsmanship.

Psalm 19:1

Thank you for making me so wonderfully complex! It is amazing to think about. Your workmanship is marvelous--and how well I know it.

Psalm 139:14

He has taken an oath to do it! For this is his purpose and plan. Isaiah 14:24

When someone becomes a Christian he becomes a brand new person inside. He is not the same any more. A new life has begun!

II Corinthians 5:17

When Saul returned to his home at Gibe-ah, a band of men whose hearts the Lord had touched became his constant companions.

I Samuel 10:26

Look! I have been standing at the door and I am constantly knocking. If anyone hears me calling him and opens the door, I will come in and fellowship with him and he with me.

Revelation 3:20

For if you tell others with your own mouth that Jesus Christ is your Lord, and believe in your own heart that God has raised him from the dead, you will be saved. For it is by believing in his heart that a man becomes right with God; and with his mouth he tells others of his faith, confirming his salvation.

Romans 10:9-10

26 Never Forget The Shoulders That You Stand On

Definition: To support something means to carry or bear the weight of it to keep it from falling, slipping or sinking; hold it up.

CONNECTING WITH AND LEARNING FROM YOUR RICH, PERSONAL, PAINFUL, PRODUCTIVE PAST. I can point to specific men and state the specific contributions that those men made to my life. In other cases I can state that the men have contributed to my life but it is more difficult to state specifically how. Share with the young men some men who stand tall in your life, men upon whose shoulders you stand.

CAUTION: Don't allow the young men to feel that they have never been helped by anyone. It is impossible to live in this life and not receive kindness in some form from someone. It may be necessary to go back a few generations or out of the family altogether, but there is someone somewhere who has helped every young man. You may want to run through the list of Black heroes.

CONCERN: It is a concern when young men feel like they are not connected to this society. Work hard to show them that a hand has fed them while they were small to get them to this point.

CHALLENGE: The goal is for each man to provide strong shoulders for the next generation coming along.

ACTIVITY: Point to your own shoulders and state that it is your desire for the young men that you mentor to receive strength from your shoulders.

26 Never Forget The Shoulders That You Stand On

I have been impacted by many men, but I stand primarily on the shoulders of two men. The first man was John Thomas Davis (1904-1993), my father. The second man upon whose shoulders I stand is Rev. B.J. Tatum, my pastor and mentor. I praise God for these men and others who have influenced my life. I am what I am because of their influence.

Every culture acknowledges the aged. In many African tribes, it is the elders who make decisions, arrange marriages, decide when to go to war and so forth. I am not suggesting that we go to those extremes, but I am suggesting that the wisdom and strength that young men receive from older men is invaluable.

The shoulders of an older man serve as a foundation that enables young men to rise to higher heights. The strong shoulders at home give young men courage outside the home. It is the fact that there is a strong man who will fend for you that makes a difference. James Brown (The Godfather of Soul) says: "I'm a man, I'm a son of a man. If I don't get you, then Papa can."

I was fortunate to have a father until I was grown. As a grown man with children, there was still a strength I found from the fact that my father was only a few miles or a phone call away. Since he has passed, I have felt a sense of abandonment, confusion, and instability. Now that the physical shoulders are gone, I must stand on the strength that I received while they were here and the memories I have of having them.

Remembering the shoulders of our forefathers gives us a sense of connectedness to our past, which gives us strength to face the trials of today. When I think of my father's struggles in racist America and how he survived, I am encouraged to stand and face the battles that face my contemporary generation. I live in a different age than my father did, yet my struggles are the same, and different. In spite of the differences between my father's decade and mine, the differences in specific details of the battles are small. The fact remains that it will take the same qualities of manhood to win in the present and future that it took to win in the past.

I can unequivocally say that the shoulders upon which I stand are the shoulders of undaunted manhood. I must say that my father never ran in the face of adversity. He was challenged to the outer limits of his strength, but he never ran. I will never forget this fact.

I feel that every young man needs to look in his past and find the strong shoulders in his family tree. Maybe your father's shoulders were not strong. If that is the case, then you should go back another generation to the shoulders of your grandfather. Don't be discouraged by the soft shoulders in your family tree—just keep looking until you find the strong ones and learn from them.

There is also a need to look outside of the family to find strong shoulders to stand on. As a Black man, I have my heroes. There have always been local Black men who were models in the community who served as heroes. I saw some of these men in church, as teachers in school or as entrepreneurs in the Black neighborhood. When we look to the national level, we see the Black men who are making substantial contributions to society. As a young man, I revered Rev. Martin Luther King, Jr. as an example of real manhood. There were so many Blacks who were becoming firsts in prominent positions in our nation. I was very proud of these men. It was their shoulders that enabled me to go to the integrated school, go to the bank to get a loan, live where I could afford to live and stay in any motel in the country.

It is a terrible, terrible, terrible fact that many young Black men are forgetting that they are where they are because of the toil and sacrifice of others. Because of the sacrifice of my father, I was the first one in our family to get a college degree. I realize that I did not do it by myself; I reached that height only by standing on another Black man's shoulders. It is a fact that the young man who feels that he has made it and is making it alone is not aware of his roots, nor does he have a general understanding of Black history.

I would like to make a few suggestions for you at this time regarding the shoulders that you stand on.

1. Seek to become fully aware of whose shoulders you stand on.
It is a mistake to take your support for granted. Many Black males who have fathers take them for granted and assume that they will always be there. To do this causes you to miss many opportunities for growth that may soon be gone. Take time to examine the strength you have received from men who are family members and those who are non-family members. Take time to examine their influence again for a new and fresh stream of energy, strength, and encouragement.

2. Honor those individuals openly.
At this point in my life, I speak freely about my father and others who are deceased. I also speak highly of the men who are living from whom I have derived strength and direction. My Pastor, Rev. B.J. Tatum, has been a model for me of what it is to be a minister, husband and father. I have known him for fifteen years. During my early Christian years, he was in front of me, providing support and stability for my faltering feet and a source of protection from the dangers around me. Now that I am older and have experienced healthy growth as a result of his protection, preparation and prompting, we walk side by side, fulfilling the ministry that God has given to our church. I appreciate his strong shoulders, and I thank him publicly and privately.

3. Accept their challenge to surpass their accomplishments.
The fact that a man provides shoulders for you is proof that he wants you to get ahead in life. You should see his effort as a challenge to exceed him even if he doesn't verbalize that fact. We should seek to surpass the accomplishments of our forefathers because we build upon their foundation.

4. Determine to be strong shoulders and not soft shoulders.

The fact of the matter is that if you are a man, there will be many people who will need to derive strength from your strong shoulders. When you are a teenager, there are small children who look up to you and want to be like you. When you become a man, children and women of all ages will look up to you for strength to help them face their struggles. Whether or not you become strong shoulders for those around you is a choice that you will consciously make. I encourage you to accept the challenge set by the high standards of our forefathers upon whose strong shoulders we stand.

Questions
for Introspection and Discussion (to make you think)

1. Have you considered the fact that you stand on the shoulders of other Black men in history? Yes___ No___

2. Have you considered their impact on your life? Yes___ No____

3. Give the names of the men upon whose strong shoulders you stand._____
_____
_____

4. Have you thanked them lately? Yes___ No___

5. Have you decided to become strong shoulders for those younger than you who are coming along? Yes___ No___

6. What actions are you taking to assure that you will be strong for others?_____

Applicable Scriptures: Please have a boy read the Scripture, then use the questions to facilitate discussion. Conclude by quoting the Scripture from the Living Bible, which was written for teenagers. *Please remember that the reading of the Scripture according to Isaiah 55:11 is the most important thing you will do with the boys. This section is where the Holy Spirit really works in their hearts, so don't skip it.*

(1) *The just man walketh in his integrity: his children are blessed after him.* Proverbs 20:7

[Question] **What do you think it means to walk in integrity?**

[Question] **According to this Scripture, why should a man walk in integrity?**

[Question] **What do you think it means to be blessed?**

The Living Bible translates Proverbs 20:7 like this: *It is a wonderful heritage to have an honest father.*

(2) *Praise ye the LORD. Blessed is the man that feareth the LORD, that delighteth greatly in his commandments. His seed shall be mighty upon the earth: the generation of the upright shall be blessed. Wealth and riches shall be in his house: and his righteousness endureth for ever.* Psalm 112:1-3

[Question] **According to this Scripture, the man who "fears" or greatly respects the Lord is what?**

[Question] **Do you delight in the commandments or laws of God?**

[Question] **Do you see the laws of God as something that keeps you from having fun or something designed to protect you?**

The Living Bible translates Psalm 112:1-3 like this: *PRAISE THE LORD! For all who fear God and trust in him are blessed beyond expression. Yes, happy is the man who delights in doing his commands. His children shall be honored everywhere, for good men's sons have a special heritage. He himself shall be wealthy, and his good deeds will never be forgotten.*

(3) *Thou shalt not bow down thyself to them, nor serve them: for I the LORD thy God am a jealous God, visiting the iniquity of the fathers upon the children unto the third and fourth generation of them that hate me; And showing mercy unto thousands of them that love me, and keep my commandments.* Exodus 20:5-6

[Question] **What or who do you worship other than God?**

[Question] **What do you think it means that God is jealous?**

[Question] **What does God show to people who love Him?**

The Living Bible translates Exodus 20:5-6 like this: *You must never bow to an image or worship it in any way; for I, the Lord your God, am very possessive. I will not share your affection with any other god! And when I punish people for their sins, the punishment continues upon the children, grandchildren, and great-grandchildren of those who hate me; but I lavish my love upon thousands of those who love me and obey my commandments.*

(4) *No man can enter into a strong man's house, and spoil his goods, except he will first bind the strong man; and then he will spoil his house.* Mark 3:27

[Question] **Who was the strong person who protected you while you were little?**

[Question] **Who do you plan to be strong for in the future?**

The Living Bible translates Mark 3:27 like this: *satan must be bound before his demons are cast out, just as a strong man must be tied up before his house can be ransacked and his property robbed.*

(5) *A good man leaveth an inheritance to his children's children: and the wealth of the sinner is laid up for the just.* Proverbs 13:22

[Question] **Has anyone left you an inheritance?**

[Question] **Have you been left the inheritance of a good name, a strong mind and body?**

[Question] **What do you plan to do with what you have been left?**

The Living Bible translates Proverbs 13:22 like this: *When a good man dies, he leaves an inheritance to his grandchildren; but when a sinner dies, his wealth is stored up for the godly.*

(6) *Thou shalt rise up before the hoary head, and honor the face of the old man, and fear thy God: I am the LORD.* Leviticus 19:32

[Question] **Do you respect older people?**

[Question] **Do you use courteous manners around older people?**

[Question] **Do you give up your seat when an older person is standing?**

[Question] **Do you do this for all older people and not just your relatives?**

The Living Bible translates Leviticus 19:32 like this: *You shall give due honor and respect to the elderly, in the fear of God. I am Jehovah.*

Make This Statement To The Boys:

Before we go on to the next chapter, tell me which Scripture made you mad, glad or made you think.

Note to the Mentor: As a result of this lesson, are there any prayer requests that should be added to your list and forwarded to your prayer partners?

27 Your Father Should Teach You How To Die

Definition: Death is the act or fact of dying; permanent ending of all life in a person, animal, or plant.

CONNECTING WITH AND LEARNING FROM YOUR RICH, PERSONAL, PAINFUL, PRODUCTIVE PAST. Death is one thing that all families and individuals must deal with. Some face it and accept it as a unavoidable reality, and others fight it all of the way. Share with the young men your experiences with losing loved ones and also your mindset as it relates to your own personal, imminent death.

CAUTION: It is important to remember while you teach this lesson that Jesus Christ conquered death when He rose from the grave. As a result of His resurrection, we are no longer afraid of death.

CONCERN: I am concerned that as you conclude this lesson and depart from the young men that they leave with a sense of hope instead of hopelessness. Again point to Jesus as the solution.

CHARGE: I challenge you and the young men today to take care of your most important business. The destiny of your eternal soul is the most important issue facing you today. If you have settled your account with Jesus, then rejoice and be glad.

ACTIVITY: As you share with the elders, let an old mother tell you about what the Lord has done for her. Also, a visit to the local funeral home is always an eyeopener.

27 Your Father Should Teach You How To Die

Death is something that our society tries not to think about. We try to leave our thoughts about death in funeral parlors and hospital emergency rooms. Society does not ban the violence that leads to death, but it bans the idea of dealing with death. A wise father will address the issue of death with his son. It is important to come to grips with this concept early in life because it will have a great impact on the quality of life a young man will live.

I clearly remember the great concern I had each December as the calendar came closer and closer to the 25th. My parents had done a good job of impressing me with the fact that I'd better watch out, I'd better not pout, I'd better not cry, I'm telling you why, because Santa Claus is coming to town. I confess that Santa Claus impacted my behavior. As a grown man, I am glad that I was also instructed regarding God. I was taught that there was a destination in life—there is a goal to be obtained and a crown to wear. I was clearly impacted by the fact that heaven was to be my ultimate goal.

When a father teaches a son that the ultimate goal in life is heaven, many problems have been prevented or curtailed before they happen. There are other benefits also:
1. Guidelines for behavior are set (the Ten Commandments).
2. The idea of metaphysical realities (spirit world) is implanted.
3. The child understands that there are forces more powerful than himself.
4. A father providing a spiritual example gives religion a strong image which is more acceptable to a young man.
5. When a father strives for heaven, it becomes a family affair.
6. The goal of heaven will provide peace for a man at the time of death.

My father's death was and is a form of comfort and assurance to me. My father loved the Lord and lived within the parameters of Godliness. When his hour came to leave this existence and start another, it came peacefully. The hour was a time of contradiction in which there was the pain involved when bodily systems shut down in death, yet at the same time there was a peace as this turbulent existence ended and the new, eternal existence with God started.

There has been much written about out-of-body experiences and those who have approached the gates of heaven and returned. I submit that those experiences are as different from heaven as sitting in an airport lobby is from taking a flight on a 747.

There is a difference between the death of a Godly man and the death of a Godless man. I have personally observed and know of many cases where men who lived Godless lives faced their hour of death. It is not a pleasant sight to watch a Godless person die. In some cases they heave and pant, their eyes roll around in their head, and they attempt to fight something. The Godly people that I have observed leaving this world, left peacefully.

If I had no other proof for the existence of God and heaven other than how men die, that would be enough.

A personal relationship with Jesus gives you peace when you come to that helpless hour, and with assurance you can rest in HIM. One of the greatest faith builders is the death of a loved one who believed in God and trusted Him calmly in their last hour. Let me make some suggestions for the young man who knows little about this subject:

1. Realize that one of the key points of Christianity is that Jesus conquered death.
All other religious leaders are dead and still in the grave. So, death for the Christian is not the ultimate thing to fear. We fear what we don't know, and I know enough about death not to fear it.

2. A funeral is more representative of life than a party is.
If you really want to see life's greatest challenge, go to a funeral and you will see what each man ultimately faces.

3. You can overcome your fear of death and dead people.
There was a time in my life where the thought of death scared me to death.

4. When you are afraid of death, it paralyzes your effectiveness.
Just think what would have happened if Martin Luther King, Jr., Malcolm X, or Abraham Lincoln had been afraid of death? Their impact on society would have been diminished, and we all would have suffered. You should adopt the attitude of facing the fear and proceeding to accomplish your goal even in the face of death.

5. As soon as possible, get some life insurance.
They call it life insurance, but it is really death insurance. It is very sad when someone dies and there is not enough money to bury them. Don't leave your loved ones with this responsibility. The price of a decent funeral varies in different parts of the country, but you should have no less than $5,000.00 in insurance to cover burial expenses.

Questions
for Introspection and Discussion (to make you think)

1. Tell the truth, shame the devil! Are you ready for death? Yes___ No___

2. Are you afraid to die? Yes___ No___

3. If you were to die today, what would be the most significant contribution that you would leave

behind or for what would be remembered?_____

4. Have you trusted Jesus Christ to handle your entrance into heaven? Yes___ No___

If not, who have you trusted?_____

5. Whose death has been most significant to you?_____

_____

6. How did that death change you?_____

_____

7. Do you understand that the death of Jesus was the most important death in history because it satisfied God's anger with all men? Yes___ No___

Applicable Scriptures: Please have a boy read the Scripture, then use the questions to facilitate discussion. Conclude by quoting the Scripture from the Living Bible, which was written for teenagers. *Please remember that the reading of the Scripture according to Isaiah 55:11 is the most important thing you will do with the boys. This section is where the Holy Spirit really works in their hearts, so don't skip it.*

(1) *And I say unto you my friend, Be not afraid of them that kill the body, and after that have no more that they can do.* Luke 12:4

[Question] **Which is more important to you, the body or the soul?**

[Question] **Do you understand that the real you is not the body that you live in?**

[Question] **Is killing somebody the worst thing that can happen to them?**

The Living Bible translates Luke 12:4 like this: *Dear friends, don't be afraid of these who want to murder you. They can only kill the body; they have no power over your souls.*

(2) *Precious in the sight of the LORD is the death of his saints.* Psalm 116:15

[Question] **How does God feel when one of His children dies?**

[Question] **Do you think that God attends funerals?**

[Question] **Are you one of God's saints?**

The Living Bible translates Psalm 116:15 like this: *His loved ones are very precious to him and he does not lightly let them die.*

(3) *But we see Jesus, who was made a little lower than the angels for the suffering of death, crowned with glory and honor; that he by the grace of God should taste death for every man.* Hebrews 2:9

[Question] **Who did Jesus taste death for?**

[Question] **Right now, Jesus is exalted and glorified. While He was on earth, He was made a little lower than who?**

The Living Bible translates Hebrews 2:9 like this: *But we do see Jesus—who for a while was a little lower than the angels—crowned now by God with glory and honor because he suffered death for us.*

(4) *It is better to go to the house of mourning, than to go to the house of feasting: for that is the end of all men; and the living will lay it to his heart.* Ecclesiastes 7:2

[Question] **What do you think a house of mourning is?**

[Question] **When was the last time you went to a funeral?**

[Question] **Why do you think this Scripture teaches that it is better to go to a funeral than it is to go to a party?**

The Living Bible translates Ecclesiastes 7:2 like this: *It is better to spend your time at funerals than at festivals. For you are going to die and it is a good thing to think about it while there is still time.*

(5) *Yea, though I walk through the valley of the shadow of death, I will fear no evil: for thou art with me; thy rod and thy staff they comfort me.* Psalm 23:4

[Question] **Do you ever fear evil?**

[Question] **Are you able to remember that God is with you during your trying times?**

The Living Bible translates Psalm 23:4 like this: *Even when walking through the dark valley of death I will not be afraid, for you are close beside me, guarding, guiding all the way.*

(6) *What man is he that liveth, and shall not see death? Shall he deliver his soul from the hand of the grave? Selah.* Psalm 89:48

[Question] **Do you realize that every man that you know of will die?**

[Question] **What is the difference between a rich man's death and a poor man's death?**

[Question] **What would you do today if you knew you were going to die tomorrow?**

The Living Bible translates Psalm 89:48 like this: *No man can live forever. All will die. Who can rescue his life from the power of the grave?*

(7) *O death, where is thy sting? O grave, where is thy victory?* I Corinthians 15:55

[Question] **Jesus Christ conquered death by rising from the dead. Everyone who puts their trust in Him will rise from the dead also. Have you put your trust in Him?**

[Question] **If you have ever been to a funeral, you know that when they close the casket there is a sense of finality to it. Do you believe that Jesus is going to raise all of the dead Christians to be with Him?**

The Living Bible translates I Corinthians 15:55 like this: *O death, where then your victory? Where then your sting? For sin—the sting that causes death—will all be gone; and the law, which reveals our sins, will no longer be our judge.*

Make This Statement To The Boys:

Before we go on to the next chapter, tell me which Scripture made you made, glad or made you think.

Note to the Mentor: As a result of this lesson, are there any prayer requests that should be added to your list and forwarded to your prayer partners?

Mentor: Read this page before you meet with your boys.

28 THE FINAL CHAPTER

The purpose at this point is for the young men to come clean with God, the mentor and himself. It will be very therapeutic for the young men to write down their feelings. The idea is that thoughts disentangle themselves as they come across the lips and through the fingertips. The young men may want to have a private session with you to discuss those things that are very private. This will be the perfect opportunity for the mentor to help the young men zero in on those problems that plague them the most.

Consider engaging others in this final session. By now, you know the boys pretty well and you may want to network with other adults to provide additional support. The question is often asked: "What do I do after we finish the book?" I advise that you continue to study with the boys. One of our main goals is to promote reading, to develop a love for books, and for the boys to begin their personal libraries. At the conclusion of your time with the boys, each boy should own at least two books: A Bible and *Talks My Father Never Had With Me.* At this point, you may want to introduce the boys to additional books that promote self-development. Feel free to contact our office for a book list.

28 THE FINAL CHAPTER

To conclude our time together, I want you to think very deeply and try to discover what significant needs you have that were NOT addressed in this book. What needs are there in your life that have an unhealthy amount of control over you? Have you been able to find help for this need from parent(s), teachers, preachers, or friends?

Remember, this book was not designed to address all possible problems, and I am sure that there is a personal situation that you would like to have addressed. I want to encourage you to consider your situation a personal challenge that with the help of God you can overcome. Please continue to read books by Christian authors in that area where you need strength. I want to tell you from personal experience that with a concerted effort on your part and God's help, you can overcome ANY obstacle.

Once you have determined the area in which you need to grow, your assignment is to do research on the topic by talking to older men about it and finding books written on it. After you have done that, share your findings with a mature man and get his response. Remember that the only problems that control you are the ones that you don't face up to.

Applicable Scriptures:

Please have a boy read the Scripture, then use the questions to facilitate discussion. Conclude by quoting the Scripture from the Living Bible, which was written for teenagers. *Please remember that the reading of the Scripture according to Isaiah 55:11 is the most important thing you will do with the boys. This section is where the Holy Spirit really works in their hearts, so don't skip it.*

(1) *I can do all things through Christ which strengtheneth me.* Philippians 4:13

[Question] **Do you believe that Christ is waiting and willing to help you with your problems?**

[Question] **How do you feel about your own ability? Do you believe that you can do anything?**

The Living Bible translates Philippians 4:13 like this: *For I can do everything God asks me to with the help of Christ who gives me the strength and power.*

(2) *Wisdom is the principal thing; therefore get wisdom: and with all thy getting get understanding.* Proverbs 4:7

[Question] **Are you seeking wisdom? If so, where are you seeking it?**

[Question] **The wisest person is one who understands himself. Do you feel that you understand yourself?**

The Living Bible translates Proverbs 4:7 like this: *Determination to be wise is the first step toward becoming wise! And with your wisdom, develop common sense and good judgment.*

ADDENDUM A:

MENTOR FORMS

Call Or Write For A Personalized Packet Of The Forms
And Letters Included In This Section

Study Packets:
Please remember that the *"Talks"* curriculum can be used as a correspondence course
for young men who are incarcerated or in another city. The study packets are
available from the publisher.

KJAC PUBLISHING
P.O. BOX 111
CHAMPAIGN, IL. 61824
1-800-268-5861

MENTOR APPLICATION FOR *TALKS* MENTORING CURRICULUM

Name_____Social Security Number_____/_____/_____

Home Address_____

_____

Work address_____

Work phone_____Home phone_____E-mail Address _____

Your Age _____Marital Status_____Number of Children_____

Church that you attend and Pastor's name_____

_____

Have you ever been convicted of a felony? Yes___ No___

Are you a homosexual? Yes___ No___

Preferred age of students: Elementary____ Middle School____ High School____

Preferred day and time to mentor:_____

How soon can you begin mentoring? _____

Do you promise to read and discuss each Scripture with the boys? Yes___ No___

Do you commit to finishing the book with the young men? Yes____No_____

Please list three character references with telephone numbers:

_____

_____

_____

How did you find out about the *Talks* mentoring curriculum? _____

_____

STUDENT APPLICATION FOR THE *TALKS* MENTORING MINISTRY

Student's Name _____

Address_____

Phone_____Birthday ____/____/____ Medical problems?_____

Mother'sName_____

Address_____

Father'sName_____

Address_____

Phone_____ Student's age_____ Grade_____

School_____

Home Room Teacher_____

What church are you a member of?_____

Are you involved in gangs? Heavy involvement_____ Medium involvement_____
Light involvement_____ No involvement_____

Briefly describe yourself_____

Hobby_____

Favorite Sport_____ Are you good at it? good___ average___ poor____

Best Friend's Name_____

Address_____

Comments:_____

_____

_____

Mentor Report Form
To Be Filled Out Weekly And Turned In To The Coordinator

Name_____

Meeting date ___/___/____

Those Present_____

_____

Those Absent_____

Contact made to those absent ___/___/___ Phone calls_____

Cards_____ Letters_____

Victory Reports_____

_____

_____

_____

Concerns or Questions resulting from this week's meeting?_____

_____

_____

_____

Specific confidential prayer requests to be sent to prayer partners_____

_____

_____

Monthly Report

Mentor_____

Report for the Month of _____ Year_____

Write the student's names and list the attendance record for the month.

1. _____ present_____ absent_____

2. _____ present_____ absent_____

3. _____ present_____ absent_____

4. _____ present_____ absent_____

Have you contacted those who have been absent?_____

Concerns that need to be discussed with the Pastor_____

_____

Victory Reports_____

_____

_____

_____

_____

Specific Confidential Prayer Requests_____

_____

_____

_____

Prayer List

Name_____

Date ____/____/____ Prayer Request_____

_____Date Answered____/____/____

Date ____/____/____ Prayer Request_____

_____Date Answered____/____/____

Date ____/____/____ Prayer Request_____

_____Date Answered____/____/____

Date ____/____/____ Prayer Request_____

_____Date Answered____/____/____

Date ____/____/____ Prayer Request_____

_____Date Answered____/____/____

Date ____/____/____ Prayer Request_____

_____Date Answered____/____/____

Date ____/____/____ Prayer Request_____

_____Date Answered____/____/____

Date ____/____/____ Prayer Request_____

_____Date Answered____/____/____

Date ____/____/____ Prayer Request_____

_____Date Answered____/____/____

Sample
The Mentoring Ministry
Participation Permission Slip

_____*Parent's name*_____, referred to as PARENT, is the parent and

lawful guardian of _____*Student's name*_____a minor, and agrees:

*Mentor's name*_____is organizing a series of meetings with ___*Your church name*_____

for the purpose of facilitating the maturing process of _____*Student's name*_____.

This interaction will commence on ____/____/____ and will end approximately 28 weeks later on

____/____/____.

____*Student's name*_____has the permission of PARENT to participate in this program

and all activities thereof. _____*Mentor's name,*_____ and the other employees and adult agents of

___*Your church name*___ are herewith given the following authority on the dates stated above: To

consent to any medical treatment that may be required by in the place and with the same authority

as PARENT. Further, in consideration of the services performed by the members, employees,

servants and agents of ___*Your church name,*___and the other employees and agents of are herewith

released from liability for all actions taken in good faith during the program.

Dated: _____

_____
Parent

Sample
The Mentoring Ministry
Trip Permission Slip

_____ _Parent's name_ _____, referred to as PARENT, is the parent and

lawful guardian of _____ _Student's name_ _____ a minor, and

agrees: _____ _Your church name_ _____is organizing a trip on

___/___/___ through ____/____/____.

_____ _Student's name_ _____has the permission to participate in this trip and

all activities thereof. _____ _Your church name_ _____ the members, other employees and

adult agents of _____ _Your church name_ _____are herewith given the following authority

on the date(s) stated above: To consent to any medical treatment that may be required by

_____ _Student's name_ _____in the place and with the same authority as PARENT.   Further,

in consideration of the services performed by _____ _Your church name_ _____and the members,

servants and agents of are herewith released from liability for all actions taken in good faith during

the trip.

Dated: _____

_____

_____

Parent(s) signature

Sample Letter To Parents

Dear Parent:

Your son _____ has been identified as a young man who would greatly benefit from the mentoring program at our church. Our church has developed a program that is specifically designed to give young men something that they cannot receive anywhere else. I would like to meet with you and your son to share more about this ministry. If you are unable to meet, please sign your name below indicating your approval of your son's participation. Upon receiving your letter we will send you additional information about the ministry.

Please sign your name indicating your approval for your child to participate in our mentoring ministry.

I_____approve of
(print name)

_____participating in the mentoring program
(Student)

sponsored by _____
(Church)

Sincerely,

_____
signature

"It takes a whole village to raise a child."
African Proverb!

Sample
Follow-up Letter To Parent(s)

Dear:

My name is _____ and I have been chosen to mentor your son in the mentoring ministry sponsored by my church. Your son has been enrolled in this ministry, which involves a curriculum that is designed to help him mature in a balanced and healthy way. The following chapter titles represents a partial list of subjects that I will discuss with your son and the other two young men.

1. The Importance Of Understanding Your Orientation
2. Ask Yourself The Question:"Have I Been Properly   Nurtured?"
3. Brothers And Sisters (Siblings)
4. Living In The Projects: A Housing Development
   (Or Living In The Trap Of A Poor Hood)
5. Blocks (Our Fears and Anxieties That Stop Us In Life)
6. What Kind Of Gang Are You In?
7. How Does Your Size Affect You? (Endomorph - Ectomorph - Mesomorph)
8. Drugs (The Contemporary Slavemaster)
9. My First Job
10. Your Concept Of The Work Ethic
11. I Was Treated Unfairly Today (Prejudice)
12. Proper Attitudes About Money

The program calls for one subject (chapter) to be covered each week or longer if necessary. With this partial copy of the table of contents you will be informed of the subject matter for the first few weeks. It is also a good idea for you to read the chapter as your son reads it so you can discuss it with your child. We strongly encourage you to discuss the subjects with your son. If you have any comments, questions or concerns, feel free to contact the church.

Sincerely

_____
Mentor

Sample Letter to Schools

Pastor: This letter will go to local Principals informing them of our program. If you choose to participate, your name will be listed below.

MENTORING PROGRAM
Sponsored By Participating Black Churches In Our City

Dear Principal:

We, the local Black churches, are very concerned about the plight of the young Black men in our area. As a result of our concern, we are spearheading a program that will provide guidance for a portion of the youth in our community. Many of the youth in your school are members of the Black churches of our city. With this in mind, we would like to introduce you to our structured program, which offers interaction between a mature adult and a developing youth. This program involves weekly sessions which follow a specific curriculum. The age range for the boys is Elementary through High School. We are searching our rolls in an attempt to reach all of our young men, but we are also aware of the fact that we have members who have had extended absences. If you know of a child who is a member of a local church and does not have a positive Black male role model, the Black churches of our city want to provide them. If you would like more information about this program, please contact one of the following participating churches for more information.

Participating Churches Listed Here:

Sample Letter To Teacher(s)

Dear Mr./Ms._____ My name is _____
and I am writing to inform you that _____ is involved in our Churches'
Mentoring Ministry. He is being instructed on issues vital to his education and success in life.
Please inform me of events and activities that he is involved in at school. I would like to attend in
support of him. The more notice that you can give me the better. I can be contacted at
_____ .

Please consider me a partner with you in helping _____ take full
advantage of the time he spends in your class. If you have any questions or concerns, please feel free
to contact me by calling my church.

Sincerely ,

_____
Mentor

Sample Letter To Pastors

Dear Leader:

I am excited to share with you a program that God has given me that will empower the Black Church to take the lead in redeeming our young Black men. I firmly believe that if the young Black men are going to be saved, the Black Church must take the lead in doing so. It is time to change our thrust from **"We Shall Overcome"** to **"We Must Save Our Youth!"**

The idea is to involve the men of your church in a mentoring program where each man will mentor a minimum of three young Black men per year. The curriculum is complete and very simple to use. Step-by-step guidelines are given in the Mentor's Guide which accompanies the text, <u>Talks My Father Never Had With Me.</u> I am asking for a time commitment of 90 minutes a week from your men. If you have 5 men mentoring, that translates into 15 young Black men that are receiving help. If you could get 15 men to mentor, it would translate into 45 young men receiving wise instruction.

I sincerely believe that Jesus IS the answer for the world today. We are the ones who know Him and it is incumbent upon us to creatively provide Biblical solutions to our complex social situation. May God bless and anoint you as you undertake this viable ministry.

Sincerely,

Rev. Harold Davis, M.M., D.Min.

Prayer Partner Form
MENTORING MINISTRY

Dear Pastor:

I would like to participate in the mentoring program by committing myself to faithfully pray for a child by name each day. Please send me the specific and general prayer requests for a child and I will pray for that child. I also agree to keep specific prayer requests confidential.

Name_____

Address_____

_____

Phone_____

Prayer Partner Form
MENTORING MINISTRY

Dear Pastor:

I would like to participate in the mentoring program by committing myself to faithfully pray for a child by name each day. Please send me the specific and general prayer requests for a child and I will pray for that child. I also agree to keep specific prayer requests confidential.

Name_____

Address_____

_____

Phone_____

Student's Contract

(To Be Completed And Given To The Mentor)

I _____

make this contract with my mentor

_____

to participate in the program with good intentions.

I will read the chapters and participate in the weekly sessions.

I will genuinely and respectfully consider what my mentor shares with me but will also feel free to express my opinions.

I will not share other people's private information outside of our cell group.

I also understand that my mentor has a busy schedule just like mine and there may be times when it will be necessary to reschedule. I will be understanding when this happens.

I will view this interaction as an opportunity to gain Godly wisdom which will benefit me for years to come.

How much better is wisdom than gold, and understanding than silver!
KING SOLOMON

_____
Student's Signature

_____
Mentor's Signature

_____
Witness

_____
Date

Mentor's Contract

(To Be Completed And Given To The Student)

I_____

make this contract with my student

_____

to participate in this program with good intentions.

I will read the chapters and participate in the weekly sessions.

I will genuinely and respectfully consider what my student shares with me but will also feel free to express my opinions.

I will not share other people's private information outside of our cell group.

I also understand that my student has a busy schedule just like mine and there may be times when it will be necessary to reschedule. I will be understanding when this happens.

I will view this interaction as an opportunity to share Godly wisdom which will benefit my student for years to come.

How much better is wisdom than gold, and understanding than silver!
KING SOLOMON

_____
Mentor's Signature

_____
Student's Signature

_____
Witness

_____
Date

Certificate of Completion

This certifies that

_____

has completed_____weeks of instruction with his mentor.

All the chapters of the book and related assignments were successfully completed.

Let it be resolved that your instructor has high expectations of you and trusts that you will become the leader that you are destined to be.

We believe that if you apply the principles we have studied, you will be an asset to any community in which you choose to live and we further believe that those who interact with you will find you to be a fair and just person.

Inasmuch as wisdom contributes to a successful life, you are strongly encouraged to maintain a close relationship with wise men who can guide you as you face the challenges of life.

Remember what we have shared and put the wisdom that you have learned into practice.

Sincerely

_____
Mentor

_____
Administrator

_____
Witness

Signed this_____day of _____

Notes:_____

Notes:_____

_____

_____

_____

_____

_____

_____

_____

_____

_____

_____

_____

_____

_____

_____

_____

_____

_____

Notes:

Notes:

Notes:_____

_____

_____

_____

_____

_____

_____

_____

_____

_____

_____

_____

_____

_____

_____

_____

_____

_____

Notes:_____

_____

_____

_____

_____

_____

_____

_____

_____

_____

_____

_____

_____

_____

_____

_____

_____

_____

Notes:_____

_____

_____

_____

_____

_____

_____

_____

_____

_____

_____

_____

_____

_____

_____

_____

_____

_____